Specificity and the Macroeconomics of Restructuring

Yrjö Jahnsson Series

Aspects of the Theory of Risk-Bearing, Kenneth J. Arrow, 1963

Monetary-Fiscal Analysis and General Equilibrium, Assar Lindbeck, 1967

An Essay on the Theory of Economic Prediction, L. R. Klein, 1968

The Two-Sector Model of General Equilibrium, Harry G. Johnson, 1970

The Crisis in Keynesian Economics, John Hicks, 1973

The Theory of Unemployment Reconsidered, Edmund Malinvaud, 1976

Asset Accumulation and Economic Activity, James Tobin, 1978

Growth, Shortage and Efficiency, János Kornai, 1980

Labour Management, Contracts and Capital Markets, Jacques H. Drèze, 1983

Models of Business Cycles, Robert E. Lucas, 1985

"Rational Behaviour," Amartya Sen, 1987 (unpublished)

Three Lectures on Poverty in Europe, Anthony B. Atkinson, 1990

"Models of the Firm," Bengt Holmström, 1992 (unpublished)

"Economic Theory and the East Asia Miracle," Paul R. Krugman, 1996 (unpublished)

The New Systems Competition, Hans-Werner Sinn, 1999

"The Timing of Transactions," Alvin Roth, 2002 (unpublished)

Specificity and the Macroeconomics of Restructuring, Ricardo Caballero, 2007

Specificity and the Macroeconomics of Restructuring

Ricardo J. Caballero

The MIT Press
Cambridge, Massachusetts
London, England

MIT Press books may be purchased at special quantity discounts for business or sales promotional use. For information, please e-mail special_sales@mitpress.mit .edu or write to Special Sales Department, The MIT Press, 55 Hayward Street, Cambridge, MA 02142.

This book was set in Sabon on 3B2 by Asco Typesetters, Hong Kong, and was printed and bound in the United States of America.

Library of Congress Cataloging-in-Publication Data

Caballero, Ricardo J.
Specificity and the macroeconomics of restructuring / Ricardo J. Caballero.
    p. cm.—(The Yrjö Jahnsson Lectures)
Includes bibliographical references and index.
ISBN 978-0-262-03362-6 (hardcover : alk. paper)
1. Technological innovations—Economic aspects—Mathematical models.
2. Creative destruction—Mathematical models. 3. Asset specificity—
Mathematical models. 4. Resource allocation—Mathematical models. I. Title.
HC79.T4C33 2007
339—dc22   2006033365

10 9 8 7 6 5 4 3 2 1

A mis Margaritas

Contents

Series Foreword

The Yrjö Jahnsson Foundation was established in 1954 by Mrs. Hilma Jahnsson, in accordance with the wishes of her deceased husband, Professor Yrjö Jahnsson. Yrjö Jahnsson was not only an academic but also a versatile entrepreneur. The Jahnssons' wealth accumulated in the 1920s and 1930s through successful real estate investments.

The Yrjö Jahnsson Foundation is now one of the largest grant-awarding foundations in Finland. The purpose of the Foundation is to develop and support Finnish research in economics and medical science. In economics the Foundation is the single most important source of private research funding. The Foundation also organizes scientific seminars and workshops.

In 1963 the board of the Foundation launched a special series of Yrjö Jahnsson Lectures in economics, to be organized in Helsinki every two or three years. The aim of the Lectures is to offer an internationally renowned economist a forum to synthesize and develop novel research ideas, and to offer the Finnish economics community firsthand access to the latest scholarly developments.

Professor Ricardo Caballero, the seventeenth Yrjö Jahnsson Lecturer, is one of the most influential thinkers in contemporary macroeconomics. In this book, expanded from the lectures delivered in Helsinki in August 2005, Ricardo Caballero analyzes how microeconomic restructuring and factor reallocation, by which new technologies replace the old, shape macroeconomic performance. He yields valuable and highly original insights into the institutional underpinnings of wage formation, unemployment, business cycles, and investment behavior. The book also provides a coherent and unified framework for policy analysis. The Foundation is confident that the profession will find this book indispensable as a text and as a reference. The Foundation is proud to have Ricardo Caballero join the distinguished list of Yrjö Jahnsson Lecturers.

The Yrjö Jahnsson Foundation

Arto Alho   Hannu Vartiainen
Managing Director   Research Director

Preface

This book is an extended version of my Yrjö Jahnsson Lectures, delivered in Helsinki during the summer of 2005. I am indebted to the Yrjö Jahnsson Foundation for honoring me with its prestigious lecture and for giving me the always necessary impetus to embark upon a project of this nature. I am especially thankful to Hannu Vartiainen for his kindness and attention to detail during my visit to Helsinki. Much of what is in the book is, directly and indirectly, the result of my joint work with Mohamad Hammour, to whom I am most grateful for many years of collaboration. This book would not have been possible without the help of an outstanding group of research assistants: Suman Basu, Francisco Gallego, Andrew Hertzberg, and Catarina Reis all exceeded the call of duty. I am also grateful to Olivier Blanchard, Steve Davis, Francesco Giavazzi, Arvind Krishnamurthy, Robert Shimer, Robert Townsend, Ivan Werning, and two anonymous reviewers for comments, and to John Arditi, Emily Gallagher, Lianna Kong, and Kathy Caruso for editorial assistance. I owe The MIT Press and Elizabeth Murry, in particular, a special gratitude for their effort in making the book more readable. Finally, I acknowledge financial support from the National Science Foundation.

Specificity and the Macroeconomics of Restructuring

I
Introduction

1

Introduction

Nothing endures but change. There is nothing permanent except change. All is flux, nothing stays still.—Heraclitus, ca. 500 BCE

1.1 Restructuring and Institutions

The core mechanism that drives economic growth in modern market economies is the massive ongoing microeconomic restructuring and factor reallocation by which new technologies replace the old. This process of Schumpeterian "creative destruction" permeates major aspects of macroeconomic performance—not only long-run growth, but also business cycles, structural adjustment, and the functioning of factor markets.

At the microeconomic level, restructuring is characterized by countless decisions to create and destroy production arrangements. These decisions are often complex, involving multiple parties as well as strategic and technological considerations. The efficiency of these decisions depends not only on managerial talent but also on the existence of sound institutions that provide a proper transactional framework. Failure along this institutional dimension can have severe macroeconomic consequences.

This book provides a unified framework to analyze and understand a wide variety of macroeconomic phenomena stemming from the limitations of the institutions aimed at alleviating microeconomic transactional problems. Some of these limitations are unavoidable, as they derive from the sheer complexity of these transactions. Others are man-made, originating from a wide variety of sources, which range from ill-conceived economic ideas to the achievement of higher human goals, such as the inalienability of human capital. In moderate amounts, these institutional limitations give rise to business-cycle patterns such as those observed in the most developed and flexible economies. They can help explain perennial macroeconomic issues such as the cyclical behavior of unemployment, investment, and wages. In higher doses, by limiting the economy's ability to harness new technological opportunities and adapt to a changing environment, institutional failure can result in dysfunctional factor markets, resource misallocation, economic stagnation, and exposure to deep crises.

Many of the major macroeconomic developments of recent decades fit naturally into this perspective. For example, in the early stages of transition, many post-communist Eastern European economies saw their potential for restructuring and catching-up stifled by an under-developed legal and institutional environment. In Western Europe, the heavy weight of labor market regulation has caused persistently high unemployment and sclerosis. The emerging markets crises of the 1990s exposed the fragility of economic systems that suffer from a lack of transparency and lax corporate governance standards. The United States' prolonged expansion in the 1990s, and its dramatic acceleration away from the rest of the world's advanced economies, reflected the virtues of an unshackled process of creative destruction. Japan's stagnation during the same period highlighted the dire macroeconomic consequences of a weak banking system that stifled creative destruction through its reluctance to liquidate zombie firms.

1.2 Specificity: A Common Thread

There is a logical unity in the analysis of institutions that affect the transactional environment (positively or negatively) and microeconomic restructuring. Essentially, macroeconomic models need to be made more "structural" in a precise sense. Although the basic modelling instinct is to assume that decisions are fully flexible, much of what happens in reality involves a degree of irreversibility. What one needs to introduce is the notion of *specificity*. Specificity means that factors of production are not fungible. More precisely, a factor is specific with respect to a given production arrangement—its current production relationship with other factors using a given technology—when its value would diminish if used outside this arrangement. Specificity introduces structure into the collection of production arrangements in the economy.

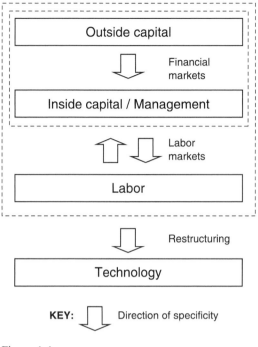

Figure 1.1
Specificity relationships
Source: Caballero and Hammour (2000).

Figure 1.1 depicts an example of a context within which different types of specificity arise in factor markets. Starting with the upper box, consider an entrepreneur who needs to find external financing for a project. Given the entrepreneur's informational advantage, special expertise, and effective control over the project, external capital becomes partly specific with respect to the entrepreneur once it is committed to the project. External financiers would lose some of their investment's value if they part with the entrepreneur. This gives rise to specificity in the *financing* relationship.

Moving down the figure, next the entrepreneur needs to hire labor. The resources he or she invests in searching for workers, training them, and building organizational capital are embodied in labor—both individually and as a group. Regulations may increase the specificity of capital with respect to labor. The right to strike or legal protection against dismissal, for example, effectively reduces the value of using capital outside its current labor relationship. This set of factors gives rise to specificity in the *employment* relationship.

Finally, moving to the bottom of the figure, the entrepreneur dedicates the project's resources to producing a certain range of goods using a certain process, and therefore builds specificity with respect to a certain *technology*—understood in its broadest sense.

The project, therefore, gives rise to two different types of specificity: "relationship specificity," which characterizes financial and labor market relationships; and "technological specificity," which characterizes production choices. Relationship specificity forms the underpinning of what *institutional arrangements* are about, as these arrangements determine the degree to which one party's specificity is exposed to the other party's opportunistic behavior. Technological specificity forms the underpinning of what *restructuring* is about, as outdated production units must be replaced by new ones.

The economy's continuous adaptation to new conditions consists of a large number of microeconomic decisions to initiate and terminate projects. In practice, each of these projects is infinitely more complex in terms of relationships and technology than that illustrated in figure 1.1. High specificity is the norm rather than the exception, and with it comes opportunism and inefficiencies that can only partially be resolved by contracts. It is this complex and dynamic world that constitutes the background for the macroeconomic analysis that follows.

1.3   Macroeconomic Implications and Outline

This chapter is followed by a summary of empirical work, contained in chapter 2, regarding the magnitude, main characteristics, and aggregate importance of the process of creative destruction in the United States and other developed and developing economies. The evidence points to a massive and persistent process of ongoing restructuring which takes place mostly within (rather than across) narrowly defined sectors. This process is important throughout all regions of the world; it is a key factor behind productivity growth; and it is hampered by institutional obstacles to adjustment in labor, financial, and goods markets. At the cyclical level, liquidations are countercyclical but, contrary to conventional wisdom, restructuring and reallocation appear to be procyclical.

Box 1.1
An empirical measure of relationship-specificity in investment across industries

Nunn (2005) constructs a measure of relationship-specificity for intermediate inputs transactions in the United States using the 1997 U.S. input-output tables. Table B1.1 presents the twenty six-digit industries for which the relationship-specificity index is the highest and the lowest. The index should be read as the proportion of intermediate inputs that are specific to the industry. The numbers are large. For example, in important industries such as automobile and light truck manufacturing almost 100 percent of transactions are relationship-specific. Nunn finds that countries with worse contract enforcement shy away from industries that rely heavily on relationship-specific investments.

Table B1.1
An empirical measure of relationship-specificity

20 least relationship-specific industries		20 most relationship-specific industries	
Measure	Industry	Measure	Industry
0.023	Poultry processing	0.979	Automobile and light truck manuf.
0.024	Flour milling	0.974	Heavy duty truck manuf.
0.034	Petroleum refineries	0.956	Electronic computer manuf.
0.035	Wet corn milling	0.895	Other computer peripheral equip. manuf.
0.050	Nitrogenous fertilizer manuf.	0.894	Audio and video equipment manuf.
0.053	Aluminum sheet, plate, and foil manuf.	0.890	Aircraft manuf.
0.056	Fiber, yarn, and thread mills	0.889	Broadcast and wireless comm. equip.
0.057	Primary aluminum production	0.885	Search, detection, and navig. instr.
0.096	Rice milling	0.875	Telephone apparatus manuf.
0.101	Coffee and tea manuf.	0.875	Aircraft engine and engine parts manuf.
0.112	Prim. nonferrous metal, ex. copper	0.857	Electricity and signal testing instr.
0.132	Tobacco stemming and redrying	0.854	Musical instrument manuf.
0.144	Other oilseed processing	0.850	Breweries
0.150	Noncellulosic organic fiber manuf.	0.839	Book publishers
0.150	Plastics packaging materials	0.832	Packaging machinery manuf.
0.153	Nonwoven fabric mills	0.825	Other engine equipment manuf.
0.157	Phosphatic fertilizer manuf.		
0.161	Resilient floor covering manuf.		

Box 1.1
(continued)

Table B1.1
(continued)

20 least relationship-specific industries		20 most relationship-specific industries	
Measure	Industry	Measure	Industry
0.167	Carpet and rug mills	0.819	Other electronic component manuf.
0.167	Synthetic dye and pigment manuf.	0.818	Air and gas compressor manuf.
		0.801	Electromedical apparatus manuf.
		0.801	Analytical laboratory instr. manuf.

Source: Nunn (2005).

After the two chapters that comprise part I, the rest of the book develops an analytical framework to shed light on these patterns and related phenomena. It also provides many contextual applications. The latter include an analysis of trade liberalizations, the transitional dynamics driving Western Europe's unemployment problem during recent decades, and the impact of financial frictions on cyclical restructuring and the cost of recessions in the United States. The book includes numerous boxes which summarize related work and provide real-world examples to illustrate the conceptual analysis. Examples of such boxes, to give a few, include discussions of Japan's experience during the postbubble era; the evidence that excessive labor market regulation has a negative impact on the speed of economic restructuring; the cyclical nature of merger waves; and summaries of the Danish model of active employment policies, the German Agenda 2010, and the institutional buildup in French labor markets over the postwar period.

The core of the book is organized into three main parts (in addition to the introduction and conclusion of the book). Part II, comprised of chapters 3 and 4, covers the basics and contains the key arguments behind the view presented in this book. Chapter 3 focuses on *relationship specificity* and its aggregate consequences; chapter 4 on *technological specificity*. Chapter 3 develops a simple static model to illustrate the main macroeconomic implications of opportunistic microeconomic behavior in the presence of relationship specificity and incomplete contracts. (*Opportunism* refers to the bargaining advantage that a member of a relationship acquires when the partner's investment in the relationship is specific.) These implications include involuntary unemployment, depressed creation, productivity sclerosis, excessive destruction during cyclical contractions, and bottlenecks during expansions.

Chapter 4 develops a dynamic version of the efficient (complete-contracts) counterpart of the static model in chapter 3, where the reason for ongoing restructuring is technological specificity. As time goes by, old units become outdated, and factor reallocation toward new and more productive units is required. This model can account for the average level of gross flows and, by adding a search friction or an unrealistically flat labor supply, it can also be used to generate significant unemployment fluctuations over the business cycle. However such a model fails to explain the decoupled nature of job flows over the business cycle— destruction rises during recessions while creation falls. Counterfactually, an efficient model of restructuring has a strong incentive to synchronize creation and destruction flows, as the main reason for the latter is to facilitate creation when the opportunity cost of reallocation is low (i.e., during recessions). Moreover, if for some reason creation cannot rise, then the incentive for destruction is also depressed. This tight link between the creation and destruction margins often implies, again counterfactually, that the Beveridge curve would be upward-sloping even if employment fluctuations are entirely driven by aggregate shocks (rather than by sectoral reallocation shocks).

This tendency toward synchronization, as exhibited by the efficient model, serves as a motivation for part III on inefficient restructuring, composed of chapters 5–7. I combine the insights of part II to discuss dynamic models which account for the facts of cyclical restructuring more naturally. Chapter 5 retains the dynamic structure of the model in chapter 4, but adds opportunism (incomplete contracts). In the first step, the model simply breaks the Hosios-Diamond condition for efficient search by changing the relative bargaining strength of the parties. Yet, this inefficient search model still has a strong tendency to synchronize the gross flows, although now the intensity of restructuring during the business cycle is inefficient. This result brings us to the second step, which introduces opportunism on specific investments, as treated in chapter 3. This single modification yields a substantial improvement in the model's ability to fit the facts. Not only does the nature of unemployment change from being an efficient reallocation mechanism to become an inefficient rationing outcome, but gross flows are decoupled: destruction rises and creation falls during cyclical downturns. This decoupling rotates the Beveridge curve, which is now downward-sloping as in the data. Moreover, if there is a reason to smooth creation, this exacerbates rather than dampens destruction's response to aggregate shocks.

Ultimately, these inefficient cyclical responses result from a form of wage rigidity. This rigidity, however, can be "overt" or "covert." If covert, the wage itself may appear highly flexible—even as flexible as in the efficient economy—in terms of its equilibrium response to aggregate shocks: the rigidity in this case is hidden in the large quantity fluctuations that come with such a wage response. Another feature displayed by this economy is sclerosis: an inefficiently slow pace of restructuring that depresses productivity. Absent structural reforms that remedy the source of opportunism at its roots, the two margins of inefficiency— unemployment and productivity—require a policy package with incentives fostering creation and production that vary in intensity over the business cycle.

Chapter 6 takes the degree of inefficiency one step further by adding an opportunism problem to the relationship between entrepreneurs and financiers. This extension exacerbates the problems stemming from the labor market opportunism discussed in chapter 5 and, most important, by further depressing the pace of restructuring in an already sclerotic economy, it adds an important cost of recessions. This yields a view on the connection between restructuring and recessions which is quite different from prevailing views. On the one hand, there is the (mostly partial equilibrium) labor literature that argues that because a significant share of separations are privately inefficient, an increase in restructuring during recessions is costly. On the other hand, there is the liquidationist Schumpeterian view that increased restructuring during recessions is necessary to cleanse the economy of excesses created during the preceding boom. As argued earlier and contrary to conventional wisdom, however, most of the evidence points not to a rise but to a fall in restructuring during recessions. The model presented in this chapter attributes this drop to the contraction in available funding that occurs during recessions.

Part III concludes with chapter 7, which applies the results from previous chapters to the problem of a transition economy opening up to the rest of the world. In this case opportunism manifests itself at the aggregate level through a sharp rise in destruction in the contracting sectors, an action which is not matched by an equal rise in creation in the expanding sectors. While in practice this outcome is often associated with a policy recommendation toward gradualism, such a response is at best a marginally beneficial policy if decoupled flows stem from opportunism. The reason is that gradualism exacerbates sclerosis by further depressing an already suboptimal level of creation in the expanding sectors. An optimal policy package, aside from directly addressing the source of opportunism, is to combine aggressive creation incentives in the expanding sectors with moderate and temporary production support in the contracting sectors.

Part IV, which completes the core section of the book, looks at the endogenous response of political institutions and technology to opportunistic exploitation of relationship specificity. Chapter 8 begins by observing that in the political arena, each factor of production has an incentive to build institutions that increase the other factors' net specificity. However, the incentive to do so is limited by the aggregate costs associated with opportunism as emphasized in the previous chapters. This is because it is the appropriating factor that suffers directly from segmentation, and it also shares the costs of unemployment and sclerosis. The political process' balancing act takes place slowly, but it has the potential to limit the extent of long-run inefficiencies if players are sufficiently forward-looking.

The more interesting endogenous response, however, involves technology. In addition to its normal productive efficiency role, technology selection now affects net specificity and hence influences equilibrium opportunism. The model shows how in equilibrium, technology selection is mostly determined by the appropriated factor of production. In turn this can lead to a phenomenon of excess substitution, whereby an initial institutional push by (say) labor can end up with lower employment *and* wages, once technology adapts to the new conditions.

Chapter 9 uses these insights to explain the dynamics of labor markets and technology in France—which is taken to be representative of the large continental European economies—in response to labor's institutional push in the late 1960s. It turns out that a dynamic model along the lines of the one developed in chapter 5, but enriched with a putty-clay structure and an endogenous technological menu, offers a parsimonious account for the highly nonlinear path of labor market variables in France since the late 1960s. The initial rise in unemployment and wages following the institutional push by labor corresponds to the system's short-run response to an increase in capital's net specificity, since much of the investment and technology selection is sunk. This classical response, however, became more complex in the 1980s when unemployment kept rising but wages began to fall rapidly, eventually bringing the labor share below prepush levels. This turn of events is the natural outcome of the model in response to an institutional push, once the passage of time depreciates old capital and facilitates technological substitution. Indeed, a noticeable fact throughout much of continental Europe during this episode was the sharp rise in capital-output ratios.

Part V concludes the book, and chapter 10 offers a brief summary of the view presented in this book and highlights its broad applicability to macroeconomic phenomena at all frequencies.

References and Suggested Readings

Aghion, Philippe, and Peter Howitt. 1997. *Endogenous Growth Theory*. Cambridge, Mass.: The MIT Press.

Bertola, Giuseppe, and Ricardo J. Caballero. 1994. "Cross-Sectional Efficiency and Labor Hoarding in a Matching Model of Unemployment." *Review of Economic Studies* 61(3): 435–456.

Blanchard, Olivier J., and Peter A. Diamond. 1990. "The Cyclical Behavior of the Gross Flows of U.S. Workers." *Brookings Papers on Economic Activity*, no. 2: 85–143.

Caballero, Ricardo J., and Mohamad L. Hammour. 2000. "Institutions, Restructuring, and Macroeconomic Performance." Invited lecture, XII World Congress of the International Economic Association, Buenos Aires, Argentina.

Davis, Steven J., John C. Haltiwanger, and Scott Schuh. 1998. *Job Creation and Destruction*. Cambridge, Mass.: The MIT Press.

Diamond, Peter A. 1982. "Wage Determination and Efficiency in Search Equilibrium." *Review of Economic Studies* 49(2): 217–227.

Hall, Robert E. 2006. "Job Loss, Job Finding, and Unemployment in the U.S. Economy over the Past Fifty Years." In Mark Gertler and Kenneth Rogoff, eds., *NBER Macroeconomics Annual 2005*, vol. 20, 101–137. Cambridge, Mass.: The MIT Press.

Johansen, Leif. 1959. "Substitution versus Fixed Production Coefficients in the Theory of Economic Growth: A Synthesis." *Econometrica* 27(2): 157–176.

Laertius, Diogenes. 1938. *Lives of Eminent Philosophers*. Cambridge, Mass.: Harvard University Press.

Ljungqvist, Lars, and Thomas Sargent. [2000] 2004. *Recursive Macroeconomic Theory*. Cambridge, Mass.: The MIT Press.

Mortensen, Dale T. 1990. "The Matching Process as a Noncooperative Bargaining Game." In John McCall, ed., *The Economics of Information and Uncertainty*, 233–254. Chicago, Ill.: University of Chicago Press.

Mortensen, Dale T., and Christopher A. Pissarides. 1994. "Job Creation and Job Destruction in the Theory of Unemployment." *Review of Economic Studies* 61(3): 397–415.

Moscarini, Giuseppe. 2001. "Excess Worker Reallocation." *Review of Economic Studies* 68(3): 593–612.

Nunn, Nathan. 2005. "Relationship-Specificity, Incomplete Contracts, and the Pattern of Trade." Mimeo., University of British Columbia.

Pissarides, Christopher. 2000. *Equilibrium Unemployment Theory*, 2nd ed. Cambridge, Mass.: The MIT Press.

Shimer, Robert. 2005a. "The Cyclical Behavior of Equilibrium Unemployment and Vacancies." *American Economic Review* 95(1): 25–49.

Shimer, Robert. 2005b. "The Cyclicality of Hires, Separations, and Job-to-Job Transitions." *Review* (Federal Reserve Bank of St. Louis) 87(4): 493–507.

Solow, Robert M. 1960. "Investment and Technical Progress." In Kenneth J. Arrow, Amuel Karlin, and Patrick Suppes, eds., *Mathematical Methods in the Social Sciences*, 89–104. Stanford, Calif.: Stanford University Press.

2

The Empirics of Aggregate Restructuring

The process of creative destruction is a major phenomenon at the core of economic growth and business cycles in market economies. This idea goes back at least to Joseph Schumpeter (1942), who considered it "the essential fact about capitalism" (83). In this chapter I review recent empirical work characterizing the process of creative destruction and the obstacles to its functioning. These facts set the stage for the theoretical framework and analysis conveyed in the rest of the book.

2.1 Restructuring and Gross Flows

Underlying any notion of restructuring is the assumption that choices of technology, output mix, and organizational modes are *embodied* in capital and skills. This means that adjusting the production structure requires that existing investments be scrapped and replaced by new ones. If, on the contrary, capital were perfectly malleable and skills fully generic, adjustment would be costless and instantaneous. At a conceptual level, it is the embodiment of technology combined with incessant opportunities to upgrade the production structure that place ongoing restructuring at the core of the growth process, irrespective of whether the economy is a technological leader or laggard.

Restructuring is closely related to factor reallocation. If investments need to be scrapped, it is because they are working with factors of production that must be freed up in order to combine with new forms of investment. In other words, restructuring generates a reallocation of factors in which technology is not embodied. This link has been exploited empirically to develop measures of reallocation that can be used as an index of restructuring. The most successful measures developed so

Box 2.1
Creative destruction over the past century

Table B2.1, taken from Cox and Alm (1992), illustrates how successive innovations make some jobs obsolete and, at the same time, create new jobs.

Table B2.1
Creative destruction over the past century

Unemployment is a common, though typically only temporary, result of technological progress. As entrepreneurs invent new products, old jobs often give way to new ones.

New product	Labor needed	Old product	Labor released
Automobile	Assemblers	Horse/carriage	Blacksmiths
	Designers	Train	Wainwrights
	Road builders	Boats	Drowers
	Petrochemists		Teamsters
	Mechanics		RR workers
	Truck drivers		Canalmen
Airplane	Pilots	Train	RR workers
	Mechanics	Ocean liner	Sawyers
	Flight attendants		Mechanics
	Travel agents		Ship hands
			Boilermen
Plastics	Petrochemists	Steel	Miners
		Aluminum	Founders
		Barrels/tubs	Metalworkers
		Pottery/glass	Coopers
			Pallers
			Colliers
Television	Electronic engineer	Newspaper	Reporters
	Actors	Theater	Actors
	Reporters	Movies	
	Electricians	Radio	
Computer	Programmers	Adding machine	Assemblers
	Computer engineers	Slide rule	Millwrights
	Electrical engineers	Filing cabinets	Clerks
	Software designers	Paper	Tinsmiths
			Lumberjacks
Fax machine	Programmers	Express mail	Mail sorters
	Electricians	Teletype	Truck drivers
	Software designers		Typists

Box 2.1
(continued)

Table B2.1
(continued)

New product	Labor needed	Old product	Labor released
Telephone	Electronic engineers	Mail	Postal workers
	Operators	Telegraph	Telegraph operators
	Optical engineers	Overnight coach	Coach drivers
	Cellular technicians		
Polio vaccine	Chemists	Iron lung	Manufacturers
	Lab technicians		Attendants
	Pharmacists		

Source: Cox and Alm (1992).

far are based on labor reallocation, although there have been attempts to look at other factors (see, e.g., Doms and Dunne 1998; Ramey and Shapiro 1998; and Eisfeldt and Rampini 2006 for capital).

The literature on gross job flows has constructed measures of aggregate gross job creation and destruction based on microeconomic data at the level of business units—namely, plants or firms (Davis, Haltiwanger, and Schuh 1998, henceforth DHS). Gross job creation over a given period is defined as employment gains summed over all business units that expand or start up during the period; gross destruction corresponds to employment losses summed over all units that contract or shut down during this time frame. Although job flows constitute a useful indicator of restructuring, the link between the two is loose. It is quite possible that plant equipment and organization may be entirely upgraded in a given location without a change in the number of jobs; conversely, it is possible that jobs may migrate from one location to another (e.g., for tax reasons) to perform exactly the same activity.

2.2   International Evidence on Gross Flows

Following the work of DHS for the United States, many authors have constructed more or less comparable measures of job flows for a variety of countries. These studies reach a consensus regarding two empirical

Box 2.2
Job flows from the LRD

Davis, Haltiwanger, and Schuh's (1998) seminal work opened up an entire area of research. They coherently organized and characterized the jobs data for U.S. manufacturing plants covering the period from 1972 to 1988 (the dataset has been subsequently updated in Faberman [2004] and Davis, Faberman, and Haltiwanger [2005]). The data include both quarterly and annual data taken from the Longitudinal Research Database (LRD), which is managed by the Center for Economic Studies (at the U.S. Bureau of the Census). The LRD takes information from the quinquennial Census of Manufactures and the Annual Survey of Manufactures, and incorporates information on between 10 and 20 percent of plants and roughly two-thirds of employment in the manufacturing sector.

The main statistics defined by the authors have been broadly adopted. These are as follows:

• *Job creation*   The sum of employment changes for firms that increase the workforce between years $t - 1$ and t, divided by average total employment in $t - 1$ and t.

• *Job destruction*   The negative of the sum of employment changes for firms that decrease the workforce between years $t - 1$ and t, divided by the average total employment in $t - 1$ and t.

• *Job reallocation*   Job creation plus job destruction. Or equivalently, the sum of the absolute value of firms' employment changes, divided by the average total employment in years $t - 1$ and t.

• *Net employment rate or net creation*   Job creation minus job destruction. Or, equivalently, the sum of employment changes for all firms between years $t - 1$ and t, divided by the average total employment in $t - 1$ and t.

• *Excess reallocation*   Job reallocation minus the absolute value of the net employment rate.

regularities which are relevant in characterizing the role of creative destruction in the growth process:

1. Gross job creation and destruction flows are large, ongoing, and persistent.
2. Most job flows take place within rather than between narrowly defined sectors of the economy.

Supporting the first conclusion, table 2.1 summarizes the average annual job flows measured for different economies. Regardless of the degree of development, in most market economies at least one in ten jobs turns over in a year. Job creation and destruction flows are simultaneous and ongoing. For example, in U.S. manufacturing—a sector that exhibits limited restructuring when compared with services (see, e.g., Davis, Faberman, and Haltiwanger 2005)—over the 1973–1993 period the lowest rate of job destruction in any year was 6.1 percent during the 1973 expansion; and the lowest rate of creation was 6.2 percent during the 1975 recession. These flows are not only large but also persistent. This is shown in table 2.2, which documents the percentage of newly created jobs that remain filled over different time horizons and of newly destroyed jobs that do not reappear over the same horizons. Overall, job flows data indicate extensive ongoing restructuring activity.

Supporting the second conclusion, table 2.3 shows the limited fraction of excess reallocation accounted for by employment shifts between narrowly defined sectors in various economies. Davis, Haltiwanger, and Schuh (1998) define excess job reallocation as the sum of job creation and destruction minus the absolute value of net employment change (intuitively, this is the sum of flows beyond that which is required to accommodate net employment changes). The fraction of excess job reallocation accounted for by worker reallocation *between* sectors never exceeds one-fifth, and is typically well below this level. More recently, Haltiwanger et al. (2004) present evidence that this fraction is below 25 percent even in a sample of Latin American economies during the 1990s (considering variation across two-digit industries). Since these economies were experiencing significant reforms and transformations typically associated with between-sector reallocation, the preponderance of *within*-sector reallocation is all the more striking.

There are two major factors behind within-sector reallocation: adjustment and experimentation. Several job characteristics that are important determinants of employment adjustment are not captured by output-based sectoral classifications. The job may be associated with capital or skills of an outdated vintage (see, e.g., Caballero and Hammour 1994), or may have suffered a highly idiosyncratic disruption. In addition, it appears that a large component of job flows is due to experimentation in the face of uncertain market prospects, technologies, cost structures, or managerial ability (see, e.g., Jovanovic 1982). This idea is supported by evidence from American manufacturing and elsewhere that newer

Table 2.1
International comparison of average annual gross job flow rates

Country	Period	Coverage	Employer unit	Job creation	Job destruction	Source
		Advanced economies				
Canada	1974–1992	Manufacturing	Plant	10.9	11.1	DH (1999a)
Canada	1983–1991	All employees	Firm	14.5	11.9	DH (1999a)
Denmark	1981–1991	Manufacturing	Plant	12.0	11.5	DH (1999a)
Denmark	1983–1989	Private sector	Plant	16.0	13.8	DH (1999a)
Finland	1986–1991	All employees	Plant	10.4	12.0	DH (1999a)
France	1985–1991	Manufacturing	Firm	10.2	11.0	DH (1999a)
France	1984–1992	Private sector	Plant	13.9	13.2	DH (1999a)
France	1990s	Manufacturing	Firm	19.5	17.5	WB (2004)
Germany	1983–1990	All employees	Plant	9.0	7.5	DH (1999a)
Israel	1970–1994	Manufacturing	Firm	10.0	8.0	IDB (2003)
Italy	1984–1993	Private sector	Firm	11.9	11.1	DH (1999a)
Netherlands	1979–1993	Manufacturing	Firm	7.3	8.3	DH (1999a)
New Zealand	1987–1992	Private sector	Plant	15.7	19.8	DH (1999a)
Norway	1976–1986	Manufacturing	Plant	7.1	8.4	DH (1999a)
Sweden	1985–1992	All employees	Plant	14.5	14.6	DH (1999a)
United Kingdom	1985–1991	All employees	Firm	8.7	6.6	DH (1999a)
United Kingdom	1981–1991	Manufacturing	Plant	10.0	13.5	IDB (2003)
USA	1973–1993	Manufacturing	Plant	8.8	10.2	DH (1999a)
USA	1979–1983	Manufacturing	Plant	10.2	11.5	DH (1999a)
USA	1979–1983	Private sector	Plant	11.4	9.9	DH (1999a)
Taiwan	1986–1991	Manufacturing	Firm	12.1	12.0	AB (2001)
Average				*11.6*	*11.6*	
Median				*10.9*	*11.5*	

Developing and emerging economies

Country	Period	Sector	Unit			Source
Argentina	1990s	Manufacturing	Plant	12.5	9.0	WB (2004)
Brazil	1991–2000	All employees	Plant	16.0	15.0	IDB (2003)
Chile	1979–1986	Manufacturing	Plant	13.0	12.2	DH (1999a)
Chile	1980–1999	Manufacturing	Plant	13.0	13.0	IDB (2003)
Colombia	1977–1991	Manufacturing	Plant	12.5	13.9	DH (1999a)
Colombia	1981–1999	Manufacturing	Plant	9.5	10.5	IDB (2003)
Estonia	1992–1994	All employees	Firm	9.7	12.9	DH (1999a)
Estonia	1990s	Manufacturing	Plant	12.5	11.0	WB (2004)
Hungary	1990s	Manufacturing	Plant	12.0	11.5	WB (2004)
Latvia	1990s	Manufacturing	Plant	15.0	9.0	WB (2004)
Mexico	1994–2000	All employees	Plant	19.5	13.5	IDB (2003)
Morocco	1984–1999	Manufacturing	Firm	18.6	12.1	DH (1999a)
Average				*13.7*	*12.0*	
Median				*12.8*	*12.2*	

Sources/Notes: DH = Davis and Haltiwanger; WB = World Bank; IDB = Inter-American Development Bank; AB = Aw and Batra.

Table 2.2
Average persistence rates for annual job flows (%)

		One-year horizon		Two-year horizon	
Country	Period	Job creation	Job destruction	Job creation	Job destruction
Denmark	1980–1991	71.0	71.0	58.0	58.0
France	1985–1990	73.4	82.1	51.5	68.2
Netherlands	1979–1983	77.9	92.5	58.8	87.3
Norway	1977–1986	72.7	84.2	65.1	79.8
USA	1973–1986	70.2	82.3	54.4	73.6

Source: Davis and Haltiwanger (1999a).

plants exhibit higher excess reallocation rates, even after controlling for a variety of plant characteristics (Davis and Haltiwanger 1999a; Bartelsman, Haltiwanger, and Scarpetta 2004). On the other hand, this evidence may reflect the role of financial frictions in restructuring, a theme I return to later in the book.

2.3   Gross Flows and Productivity

Given the magnitude of these gross flows, which take place mostly within narrowly defined sectors, the presumption is strong that these are an integral part of the process by which an economy upgrades its technology. Foster, Haltiwanger, and Krizan (2001) provide persuasive empirical support for this presumption.

Let us briefly review their methodology before reporting their main conclusion and that of related work. Consider the following index of industry-level productivity:

$$P_{it} = \sum_{e \in I} s_{et} p_{et}. \tag{2.1}$$

where P_{it} is an index of industry i productivity, s_{et} is the output share of plant e in industry i, and p_{et} is an index of plant-level productivity, all at time t. The change in the industry index can be decomposed into a *within-plant* and a *reallocation* (or *between-plant*) component:

$$\Delta P_{it} = \sum_{e \in I} s_{et-1} \Delta p_{et} + \sum_{e \in I} \Delta s_{et} p_{et}. \tag{2.2}$$

Table 2.3
Fraction of excess job reallocation accounted for by employment

Country	Period	Classification scheme	Employer unit	Number of sectors	Average workers per sector ('000)	% change between sectors
Advanced economies						
Finland	1986–1991	2-digit ISIC	Plant	27	49	6
France	1985–1991	Detailed	Firm	600	37	17
Germany	1983–1990	2-digit ISIC	Plant	24	1171	3
Italy	1986–1991	2-digit ISIC/Private sector	Firm	28	322	2
Netherlands	1979–1993	2-digit ISIC	Firm	18	10	20
New Zealand	1987–1992	2-digit ISIC	Plant	28	28	1
Norway	1976–1986	5-digit ISIC manufacturing	Plant	142	2	6
Sweden	1985–1991	2-digit ISIC	Plant	28	112	3
USA	1972–1988	4-digit SIC manufacturing	Plant	448/456	39	13
Developing and emerging economies						
Chile	1979–1986	4-digit manufacturing	Plant	69	4	12
Colombia	1977–1991	4-digit manufacturing	Plant	73	6	13
Morocco	1984–1989	4-digit manufacturing	Plant	61	4	17

Source: Davis and Haltiwanger (1999a).

The first term (within-plant) captures the increase in industry productivity due to plants' productivity improvements, keeping their share constant. The second term (between-plant) captures the increase in industry productivity due to the reallocation of shares across plants of different productivity levels (keeping productivity at time *t* constant). Foster, Haltiwanger, and Krizan (2001) find that reallocation accounts, on average, for 52 percent of decade-long productivity gains in the United States' manufacturing sector between 1977 and 1987. Moreover, in further decompositions they document that entry and exit account for half of this contribution: exiting plants have lower productivity than continuing plants. New plants, on the other hand, experience a learning and selection period, through which they gradually catch up with incumbents.

Other studies of American manufacturing based on somewhat different methodologies (Baily, Hulten, and Campbell 1992; Bartelsman and Dhrymes 1994) concur with the conclusion that reallocation accounts for a major component of industry-level productivity growth. Bartelsman, Haltiwanger, and Scarpetta (2004) provide further evidence along these lines for a sample of twenty-four countries and two-digit industries over the 1990s. Figures 2.1 and 2.2 present their results, which were

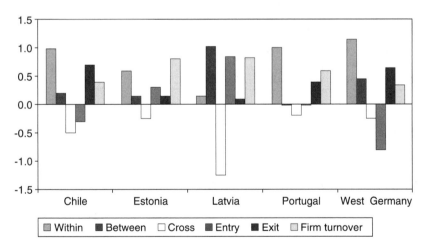

Figure 2.1
Firm-level labor productivity decomposition for total economy (five-year differencing [%], real gross output)
Source: Bartelsman, Haltiwanger, and Scarpetta (2004).
Note: Chile: 1985–1999. Estonia: 2000–2001. Latvia: 2001–2002. Portugal: 1991–1994. West Germany: 2000–2002.

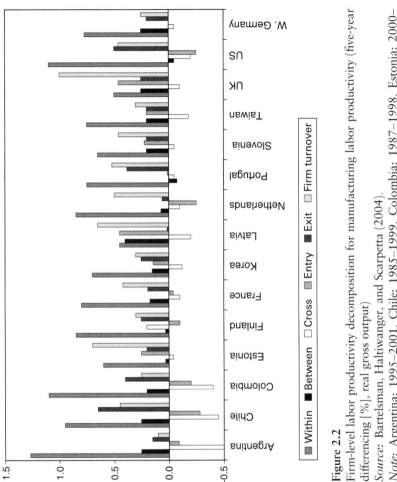

Figure 2.2
Firm-level labor productivity decomposition for manufacturing labor productivity (five-year differencing [%], real gross output)

Source: Bartelsman, Haltiwanger, and Scarpetta (2004).

Note: Argentina: 1995–2001. Chile: 1985–1999. Colombia: 1987–1998. Estonia: 2000–2001. Finland: 2000–2002. France: 1990–1995. West Germany: 2000–2002. Korea: 1988 and 1993. Latvia: 2001–2002. Netherlands: 1992–2001. Portugal: 1991–1994. Slovenia: 1997–2001. Taiwan: 1988, 1991, and 1996. UK: 2000–2001. US: 1992 and 1997.

obtained using the decomposition of labor productivity shown in equation (2.2). Both figures indicate that, for a five-year horizon, the within component plays a key role in productivity growth. Moreover, they find that the contribution of entry and exit explains between 20 and 50 percent of total productivity growth in the countries in their sample, which is surprisingly large given the relatively short horizon they consider and the gradual nature of the contribution of the reallocation process to productivity growth.

2.4   Gross Flows and Restructuring over the Business Cycle

2.4.1   The Rise of Liquidations during Recessions
Sharp liquidations constitute the most noted impact of contractions on restructuring. Figure 2.3 shows the path of quarterly job destruction and creation in American manufacturing between 1972 and 2004 (Faberman 2004, Davis, Faberman and Haltiwanger 2005, henceforth DFH). Destruction is not only significantly more volatile than creation,

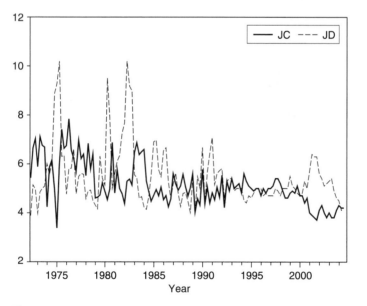

Figure 2.3
Job creation (JC) and job destruction (JD) in the U.S. manufacturing sector (%)
Sources: Faberman (2004); Davis, Faberman, and Haltiwanger (2005).

but it also exhibits sharp rises during recessions that are not matched by abrupt rises in creation.

This asymmetry between destruction and creation during recessions is especially pronounced in the 1970s and the 1980s, and it is most apparent once the series are detrended using the Hodrick-Prescott filter. Figure 2.4 shows that the detrended component of destruction is strongly negatively correlated with the detrended component of GDP, while the detrended component of creation exhibits no correlation with the detrended component of GDP. Moreover, the high correlation between detrended GDP and detrended destruction is significantly higher during contractions (periods during which detrended GDP is negative).

Liquidations rise sharply during severe contractions in other countries as well. The cases of Argentina, Brazil, Chile, Colombia, Finland, and Mexico during their correspondingly severe contractions illustrate this point. Job destruction exceeded 22 percent of manufacturing employment in Chile during the debt crisis of the early 1980s; it exceeded 19 percent of business employment in Finland during its early 1990s financial crisis; it reached 19 percent in Mexico during the "Tequila" crisis, 20 percent in Brazil during the Russian/LTCM crisis, 17 percent in the late 1990s Colombian recession, and 16 percent during the Argentinian collapse in the early 2000s.

2.4.2 Depressed Restructuring during Recessions

There is an extensive literature that extrapolates from the spikes in liquidations described above (and related evidence) to argue that recessions are times of increased *reallocation*. However, this extrapolation is *not* warranted in a modern market economy with its inherent heterogeneity.

Evidence from Gross Job Flows   As is apparent from much of the available evidence on job flows, the rise in liquidations during recessions is *not* accompanied by a contemporaneous increase in creation. Therefore, implicit in the increased-reallocation view is the idea that increased destruction is followed by a surge in creation during the recovery phase of the cyclical downturn. This presumption is the only possible outcome in a representative firm economy, as the representative firm must replace each job it destroys during a recession by creating a new job during the

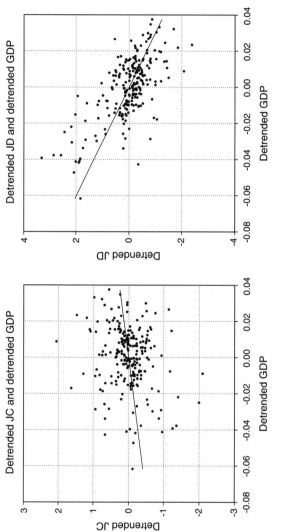

Figure 2.4
Cyclical correlation: Job creation, job destruction, and GDP
Source: Author's calculations using data from Faberman (2004); Davis, Faberman, and Haltiwanger (2005); Bureau of Economic Analysis.

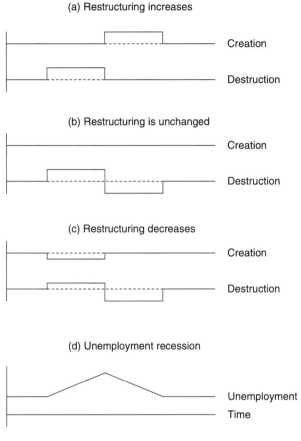

Figure 2.5
Recessions and cumulative restructuring
Source: Caballero and Hammour (2000).

ensuing recovery if the economy is to return to its natural rate of unemployment. This is illustrated in panel (a) of figure 2.5. In this case the recession-recovery episode produces the pattern of unemployment shown in panel (d).

However, once one considers a heterogeneous productive structure that experiences ongoing creative destruction, other scenarios are possible. For example, the peak in destruction during the recession may be followed by a trough in destruction of equal size during the recovery, adding up to a zero cumulative effect. More generally, as illustrated in panels (a)–(c), the cumulative effect of a recession on overall restructuring may be positive, zero, or even negative, depending not only on how the economy contracts, but also on how it *recovers*. Thus, to ascertain the relationship between recessions and economic restructuring one must examine the effect of a recession on aggregate destruction not only at impact, but *cumulatively* throughout the recession-recovery episode.

In Caballero and Hammour (2005) we explored this issue using quarterly gross job flows and employment data for American manufacturing during the 1972–1993 period. We denoted employment, creation, and destruction series in deviation from their mean by $\hat{N}_t$, $\hat{H}_t$, and $\hat{D}_t$, respectively. Up to inconsequential approximation errors, these series are related by the identity

$$\Delta \hat{N}_t = \hat{H}_t - \hat{D}_t. \tag{2.3}$$

Next, we assumed that employment fluctuations are driven by two types of shocks, an "aggregate" and a "reallocation" shock, and used a semistructural vector autoregression (VAR) approach to identify them. The stationarity of manufacturing employment during the above period implies, by equation (2.3), that the integral of $\hat{H} - \hat{D}$ must be stationary as well. For the latter to be consistent with finding a significant business-cycle effect on restructuring, which implies that the integrals of $\hat{H}$ and $\hat{D}$ have unit roots, these integrals must be cointegrated with cointegrating vector $(1, -1)$. Using this low-frequency restriction efficiently requires running a VAR with the cointegrating vector (equal to $\hat{N}$) and one of the integrals first-differenced (e.g., $\hat{D}$). We wrote our semistructural VAR as

$$\begin{bmatrix} \hat{N}_t \\ \hat{D}_t \end{bmatrix} = A(L) \begin{bmatrix} \varepsilon_t^a \\ \varepsilon_t^r \end{bmatrix},$$

where $A(L) = A_0 + A_1 L + A_2 L + \cdots$, and $(\varepsilon_t^a, \varepsilon_t^r)$ represent i.i.d. innovations that correspond to aggregate and reallocation shocks, respectively.

Aside from normalizations, achieving identification requires two additional restrictions. For this purpose, we assumed that the two innovations are independent of each other and that, at impact, a recessionary shock raises destruction and lowers creation. Based on Davis and Haltiwanger (1999b), we set the relative size of the absolute response of destruction compared to creation to 1.6, which is roughly the value that maximizes the contribution of aggregate shocks to net employment fluctuations with their estimates. We experimented with values of the relative response of destruction to creation in the range $[1, 2]$ without a significant change in our main conclusions.

Since we were particularly concerned with medium- and low-frequency statistics, we used a fairly nonparsimonious representation of the reduced-form VAR and allowed for five lags. The first and second columns of figure 2.6 represent impulse-response functions corresponding to recessionary two-standard-deviation aggregate and reallocation shocks, respectively, for (minus) employment, gross flows, and cumulative gross flows. Starting with the less central results, the second column depicts responses to reallocation shocks which, not surprisingly, raise reallocation. These are consistent with Davis and Haltiwanger (2001), who studied the response of job flows to oil shocks, which have a significant reallocation component (thus some recessions do indeed increase reallocation, when the shock itself has a large reallocation component).

The first column contains our main result: panels (a) and (b) portray the estimated impulse-response function of (minus) employment and job flows, respectively, to a negative aggregate shock. Employment naturally falls and, consistent with the findings documented by DHS, job destruction rises sharply at impact and job creation declines to a lesser extent. Less known in the literature is what comes next. Along the recovery path, job destruction *declines and falls below average for a significant amount of time*, more than offsetting its initial peak. On the other hand, job creation recovers, but it does not exceed its average level by any significant extent to offset the initial decline. The implication of this pattern for restructuring is most clearly seen in panel (c), which reports the negative cumulative responses of job creation and destruction (we also ran forty thousand bootstraps to test and reject at 2.5 percent significance the null hypothesis of no fall in restructuring following a recession). In summary, these patterns indicate that the restructuring process is *depressed* by an aggregate recessionary shock.

An important *caveat* is that data limitations did not allow us to analyze sectors outside of manufacturing. In particular, some workers who are laid off from manufacturing jobs may find temporary employment in other sectors. This may be interpreted as the aggregate economy exhibiting less depressed reallocation than manufacturing. However, the appearance of those temporary jobs—which involve negligible investment—probably does not represent true restructuring (see, e.g., Barlevy

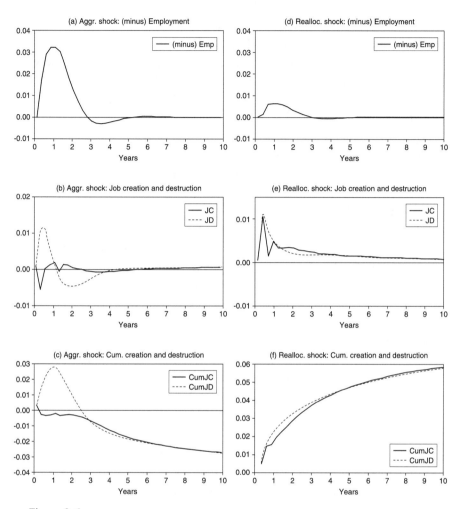

Figure 2.6
Impulse response functions of employment and job flows
Source: Caballero and Hammour (2005).

2002 for evidence on the lower-than-average quality of the jobs generated during recessions). On the other hand, since a significant portion of layoffs in American manufacturing is temporary, the effect is to bias our results against the depressed restructuring finding because the resulting temporary reallocation does not correspond to true restructuring either.

There are two points worth noting before concluding this section. First, the *procyclical* nature of reallocation is not exclusive to jobs. In Caballero and Hammour (2000), we documented a similar pattern for mergers and acquisitions. Eisfeldt and Rampini (2006) applied similar procedures to study the evolution of capital stocks in the American manufacturing sector with broadly consistent findings. In particular, they measure capital reallocation using data on flows of capital across firms and find that capital reallocation is also significantly procyclical. They relate this pattern to the existence of financial frictions.

Second, not all recessions are equal from the viewpoint of restructuring. In particular, one of the distinctive features of the American recession in 2001 and its subsequent recovery was the limited rise in job destruction at the onset of the recession. Nevertheless, it is a robust feature of the business cycle that the economy experiences a sharp contraction in restructuring during the recovery. Panel (a) in figure 2.7 illustrates this pattern for the private sector, and the remaining panels decompose these flows into services (panel [b]) and manufacturing (panel [c]). While manufacturing destruction still exhibits a significant rise at the onset of the recession, no similar pattern is observed in services, and the dominant feature throughout is depressed restructuring during the recovery. In a sense, the current recession-recovery episode has simply been consistent with a hidden fact present in previous recessions: contrary to conventional wisdom, restructuring *falls* rather than rises during recessions. Whether this is good, innocuous, or bad, depends on the specific reasons behind depressed restructuring and the degree of efficiency of the ongoing restructuring process. I will return to this issue once we have developed the models to address it.

Evidence from Corporate Restructuring   In Caballero and Hammour (2000), we approached the question of the pace of restructuring over the business cycle from the perspective of *corporate assets*. Studying the

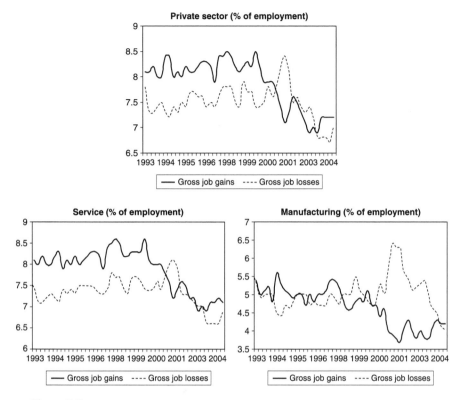

Figure 2.7
Job flows and the 2001 recession in the United States
Source: Job Openings and Labor Turnover Survey, Bureau of Labor Statistics, U.S. Department of Labor.

aggregate patterns of merger and acquisition (M&A) activity and its institutional underpinnings, we reached a conclusion that amounts to a rejection of the liquidationist perspective. Essentially, a liquidationist perspective in this context would consider fire sales during sharp liquidity contractions as the occasion for intense restructuring of corporate assets. While fire sales indeed take place, they do not seem to be the main source of corporate asset restructuring in the United States. The evidence points, on the contrary, to briskly expansionary periods characterized by high stock market valuations and abundant liquidity as the occasion for intense M&A activity. It also points to the importance of financial factors and their institutional underpinnings as core ingredients

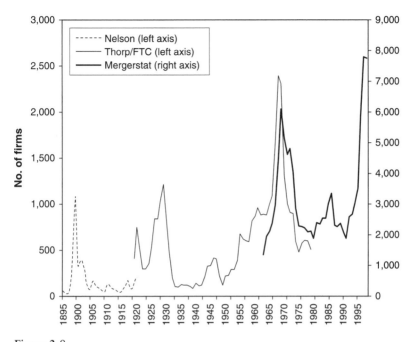

Figure 2.8
U.S. merger waves: 1885–1998
Source: Caballero and Hammour (2000).

in this restructuring phenomenon, an issue I return to later on in this chapter and in chapter 6.

Figure 2.8 presents data on the number of mergers and acquisitions in the United States over the past century. The figure shows an extreme concentration of M&A activity over time into essentially four merger waves.

The first merger wave took place at the beginning of the twentieth century. It consisted, to a large extent, of the simultaneous horizontal consolidation of several enterprises that took advantage of scale economies and often created a near monopoly in their industry. The second merger wave took place during the Roaring Twenties and affected nearly one-fifth of manufacturing assets. The frenzy ended abruptly with the great crash in October 1929. The third was the conglomerate merger wave of the late 1960s, the "go-go years" of the stock market, and consisted mostly of corporate diversification across industries. Advances in management science were supposed to allow conglomerates to effectively run a multitude of businesses spanning a variety of industries. Retrospectively, much of the earnings-per-share growth demonstrated at the time by leading conglomerates was financially driven. Finally, the late 1990s present the fourth merger wave, which in scale rivals all the previous ones. Enterprise restructuring is driven by trends toward globalization, corporate refocusing, and consolidation in the new information technology (IT) industries. Overall, mergers have played a key role in the evolution of industrial structure in response to technological and organizational revolutions.

The one robust determinant of the aggregate volume of M&A activity, as documented in most studies, is the valuation of the stock market (Golbe and White 1987). As an example, in the United States the positive correlation between M&A volume and the price-earnings (P/E) ratio of the Standard and Poor's 500 index is illustrated in panel (a) of figure 2.9 for the period 1963–1998. Moreover, panel (b) of figure 2.9 suggests that the share of all-cash transactions is lower and the share of stock transactions is higher when the market's valuation rises.

Thus, the evidence suggests that when market valuations rise, sellers become more liquid and are more willing to sell control. Generally speaking, illiquidity arises when a financially constrained asset owner faces a transaction cost. Transaction costs in the market for corporate control are mostly information-based. Financial constraints are central to the notion of illiquidity, because in the absence of such constraints the owner would be able to contractually transfer the asset's future cash flow without incurring the transaction cost. When a seller is illiquid, an increase in the price of his or her asset does two things: (1) it increases the willingness to incur the transaction cost, and (2) it relaxes the financial constraint. The latter effect enters as a pecuniary externality that helps explain the highly concentrated nature of merger waves. The fact that the share of stock transactions rises with market valuations confirms that the seller's side is at work, because buyers who pay with their stock are, in fact, also a sort of seller.

The previous interpretation of merger waves highlights another dimension of aggregate restructuring in which institutions, specifically in this example financial market institutions, play a central role. This reinforces the reverse-liquidationist view developed above based on labor market evidence. Great waves of asset restructuring have come during good

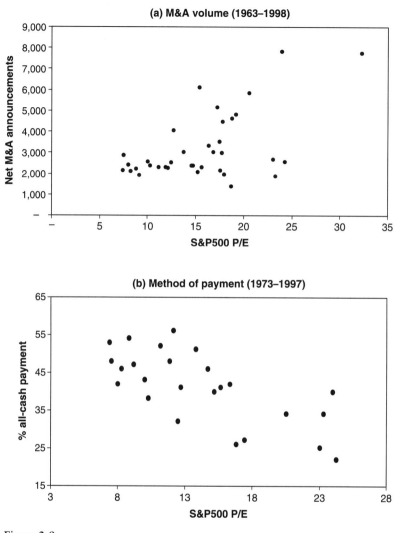

Figure 2.9
M&A volume, method of payment, and the stock market 1963–1998
Source: Caballero and Hammour (2000).

times when liquidity is plentiful. In fact, some of the major examples of asset restructuring during financial crises, such as Aguiar and Gopinath (2005) highlight for the East Asian crisis when foreign acquisitions rose sharply, often correspond to episodes where local liquidity may be scarce but global liquidity is abundant.

2.5   Institutional Impediments to Restructuring

For all practical purposes, some product or process innovation is taking place at every instant in time. Absent obstacles to adjustment, continuous innovation would entail infinite rates of restructuring. What are these obstacles to adjustment? The bulk of it is technological—adjustment consumes resources—but excessive regulation and other artificial institutional impediments are also a source of depressed restructuring. This is a theme I will discuss extensively through the perspective of different models. For now, I simply summarize a few empirical articles that hint at the nature of the connection between institutional factors and restructuring.

2.5.1   Labor Market Impediments and Restructuring

Effective Labor Regulation and Microeconomic Flexibility   In Caballero et al. (2004) we tested and found support for the hypothesis that labor market regulation hinders the process of creative destruction.

Our methodology builds on the simple partial-adjustment idea that larger adjustment costs are reflected in slower employment adjustment to shocks. Limited adjustment to these shocks creates a wedge over time between frictionless and actual employment, which is the main right-side variable in our approach. We make a series of assumptions that essentially reduce this wedge to a simple transformation of the difference between labor productivity and the wage rate, and pool data on labor market legislation with comparable employment and output data for a broad range of countries. In the tables that follow, the wedge is depicted as the variable *Gap*.

We use the extensive new data set on labor market regulation constructed by Djankov et al. (2003) and comparable cross-country sectoral data on employment and output from the United Nations Industrial Development Organization (UNIDO, 2002) dataset. We also emphasize the key distinction between effective and official labor market regulation because countries have different institutional ability and willingness to enforce regulations. Our attempt to measure effective labor regulation interacts existing measures of job security provision with measures of rule of law and government efficiency.

Our main job security index is the sum of four components, measured in 1997, each of which takes on values between 0 and 1: (1) grounds for dismissal protection, (2) protection regarding dismissal procedures, (3) notice and severance payments, and (4) protection of employment in the constitution. The four components of our job security index increase with the level of job security. We also measure job security using an index constructed by Heckman and Pagés (2003). This measure has the advantage of time variation, but the disadvantage of significantly fewer countries and a narrower measure of dismissal costs. The index computes the expected (at hiring) cost of a future dismissal and includes both the costs of advance notice legislation and firing costs, and is measured in units of monthly wages. Our proxies for institutional development include measures of the rule of law and government efficiency from Kaufmann, Kraay, and Zoido-Lobaton (1999). We interact these variables with our indices of job security, expecting labor market legislation to have a larger impact on adjustment costs in countries with a stronger rule of law and more efficient governments.

Tables 2.4 and 2.5 present our basic results. The first column of table 2.4 presents the estimated speed of adjustment from actual to desired

Table 2.4
The impact of effective job security

	(1)	(2)	(3)
Gap	0.600	0.603	0.607
	(0.009)	(0.008)	(0.012)
Gap × *JS*	—	−0.080	−0.015
		(0.037)	(0.051)
Gap × *JS* × *DSRL*	—	—	−0.514
			(0.068)

Source: Caballero et al. (2004).

Table 2.5
Productivity growth

Change in λc-quintile	Change in annual growth rate (%)
1st to 2nd	0.88
[0.325 to 0.457]	
2nd to 3rd	0.29
[0.457 to 0.527]	
3rd to 4th	0.23
[0.527 to 0.600]	
4th to 5th	0.28
[0.600 to 0.723]	
1st to 5th	1.68

Source: Caballero et al. (2004).

employment, the *Gap,* controlling for other variables. In the second column we observe that the adjustment speed drops as de jure job security (*JS*) increases. Finally, in the third column, we add effective job security (i.e., the interaction of *JS* and rule of law, *DSRL*). These results imply that job security regulation hampers the process of creative destruction, especially in countries where labor market regulations are likely to be enforced. Moving from the 20th to the 80th percentile in job security, in countries with strong rule of law, cuts the annual adjustment speed by a third.

By impairing worker migration from less to more productive units, effective labor protection reduces aggregate output and slows down economic growth. Developing a simple framework to quantify this effect, we arrive at an aggregate production function of the form $Y = AK$, where the productivity term A is an increasing function of the speed at which labor is reallocated to the most productive establishments (see Caballero et al. 2004 for additional details). Table 2.5 presents the productivity effects of different levels of the adjustment speed (λ_C). Combining these results with those in table 2.4 suggests that the cost of the microeconomic inflexibility caused by effective employment protection is large. In countries with a strong rule of law, moving from the 20th to the 80th percentile of job security lowers annual productivity growth by 1.7 percent.

Employment Protection, Flows, and Productivity: U.S. Evidence   Autor, Kerr, and Kluger (2006) exploit state and time variation in exceptions to employment-at-will to estimate the impact of employment regulation on productivity in the United States. While their identification strategy and data are entirely different from that in Caballero et al. (2004), their broad conclusions are qualitatively similar.

Employment-at-will is the legal presumption that workers and employers may terminate their employment relationships without advance notification, financial penalty or demonstrating any cause. Wrongful-discharge protections are exceptions to the employment-at-will doctrine in the United States, and since the late 1970s have been adopted to various degrees by state courts in America. Autor, Kerr, and Kluger (2006) classify the exceptions to the employment-at-will doctrine into three categories:

1. "Good faith exception," which prohibits employers from firing workers for bad cause (the actual definition of bad cause varies substantially by state, but the typical interpretation of bad cause concerns cases in which the employer fires the worker to avoid paying a promised benefit).
2. "Public policy exception," which covers cases in which workers' obligations under public policy conflict with employer demands (e.g., the exception may prohibit job termination due to absence for jury duty).
3. "Implicit contract exception," which deals with situations in which an employer implicitly promises not to terminate a contract without a good cause (e.g., by stating in a personnel manual that workers will be fired only for a just cause).

While forty-three American states currently recognize the public policy and implicit contract exceptions, only eleven state courts recognize the good faith exception. Autor, Kerr, and Kluger (2006) argue that the introduction of these exceptions increases both the level and the uncertainty of dismissal costs. They exploit the time and state variation in the introduction of these legal exceptions, and use sectoral and establishment data taken from the Annual Survey of Manufactures (ASM) and the Longitudinal Business Database. Their main results suggest that wrongful-discharge protections decrease employment flows, particularly in cyclically sensitive manufacturing sectors. More specifically, they use total factor productivity data to show that the adoption of "good faith exceptions" significantly decrease firm-level productivity. Finally, they also show that the firms most affected by exceptions raise their capital-labor ratios, conjecturing that this is one of the channels through which productivity is affected. (See chapters 8 and 9 for more evidence and models on capital deepening in response to increased labor protection.)

The Information Technology Revolution and Flexibility   More direct evidence can be gleaned from observing that American corporations seem to have been more efficient than their European counterparts in translating the IT revolution into productivity growth. One hypothesis is that excessive regulation in Europe may have limited the ability of firms to create and adapt technologies that demand organizational flexibility (e.g., Greenspan 2000; Feldstein 2001).

Two recent papers provide empirical evidence in support of this hypothesis. Gust and Marquez (2004) use a panel of thirteen industrial economies over the 1990s to document that labor market regulation retards IT adoption, which in turn has ramifications for productivity growth. Bloom, Sadun, and Van Reenen (2006) go further and show that these differences remain even in multinational corporations that operate in a common market (the United Kingdom). That is, establishments in Britain owned by American multinationals tend to have higher productivity and investment in IT than establishments owned by non-U.S. multinationals. It would seem that regulation in the home country of a multinational plays a significant role in the working practice inflexibilities of subsidiary firms regardless of the overall flexibility of the markets in which these operate.

2.5.2   Financial Market Impediments and Restructuring

The idea that well-functioning financial institutions and markets are important factors promoting economic growth is accepted (see, e.g., Levine, Loayza, and Beck 2000 for recent empirical evidence supporting this view). The process of creative destruction is likely to be a chief reason behind this link. Below I review two articles that find evidence of such a connection, one based on Japan's postbubble experience during the 1990s and the other on the mid-1980s French banking reforms.

Zombie Firms in Japan   In Caballero, Hoshi, and Kashyap (2006), we analyze the decade-long Japanese slowdown of the 1990s and early

2000s. Our analysis starts with the well-known observation that many large Japanese banks would have been out of business had regulators forced them to recognize all of their loan losses. Because of this, the banks kept many *zombie* firms alive by rolling over loans that they knew would not be collected (a process called ever-greening). Thus, the normal competitive outcome whereby the zombies would shed workers and lose market share was thwarted. The main idea in our article is that the counterpart to the congestion created by the zombies is a reduction in profits for potential and more productive entrants, which discourages their entry. In this context, even solvent banks saw no particularly good lending opportunities in Japan. Essentially Japan had reached the situation of having bankrupt banks lend to bankrupt firms, and in this environment the private sector struggled.

To identify zombie firms, we compared actual interest payments made by firms to a benchmark payment that would be expected for the firm given its borrowing. We studied all publicly traded manufacturing, construction, retail, wholesale (excluding nine general trading companies), and service-sector firms. The divergence between actual and benchmark interest payments is used as a proxy for a credit subsidy. The numbers are large: in 2002 roughly 30 percent of these firms were on life support from the banks and about 15 percent of assets resided in these firms.

The core of the study consists of firm-level regressions examining the interaction between the performance of nonzombie firms and the extent of the zombie problem in their corresponding industry at different points in time. We find clear evidence that expansion decisions in nonzombie companies were hampered by a significant presence of zombie firms in their industry.

These firm-level effects were strong enough to leave significant traces in aggregate data. Figure 2.10 shows the relationship between changes in the industry-level zombie index and changes in the rates of job creation and destruction, where all changes are measured relative to the pre-zombie era. Panel (a) of figure 2.10 shows, first, that the job destruction rate increased in every industry, as one would expect from a contractionary episode. More important, the figure also shows that the increase was smaller in the industries where more zombie firms appeared—the counterpart of the emergence of zombie firms is depressed destruction. The key result, however, is in panel (b) of

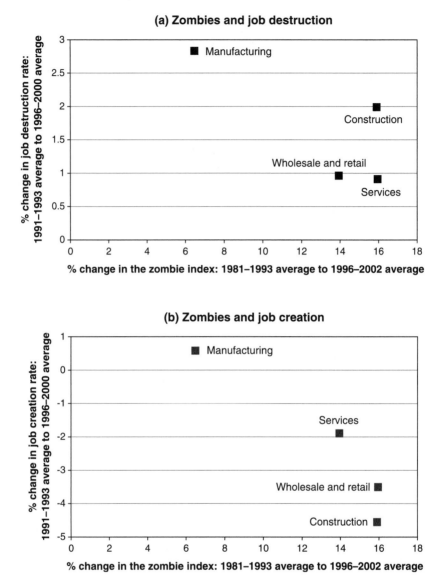

Figure 2.10
Zombies and restructuring in Japan
Source: Caballero, Hoshi, and Kashyap (2006).

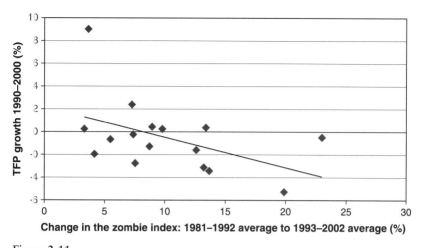

Figure 2.11
Zombies and TFP growth
Source: Caballero, Hoshi, and Kashyap (2006).

figure 2.10, which shows that the presence of zombie firms depresses job creation. Creation declined more in the industries that experienced sharper zombie firm growth. In manufacturing, which suffered the least from the zombie problem, job creation hardly changed. In sharp contrast, job creation exhibited extensive declines in nonmanufacturing sectors, particularly in the construction sector. That is, *both* destruction *and* creation, and hence restructuring, are relatively depressed by the presence of zombie companies.

Figure 2.11 is highly suggestive of the connection between depressed restructuring and productivity growth. It shows that total factor productivity growth slowed down significantly more in industries with severe zombie problems.

The French Banking Reforms of 1985   Bertrand, Schoar, and Thesmar (2004) further drive home the point that problems in the banking sector can have grave consequences for the health of the restructuring process. They use a differences-in-differences approach on detailed, firm-level data for the period 1977–1999 to analyze the impact of the mid-1980s banking reforms on firm and bank behavior. These reforms eliminated government interference in bank lending decisions, eliminated subsidized bank loans, and allowed French banks to compete more freely in the credit market.

Their main identification comes from the fact that different sectors have different degrees of banking dependence. They compare the behavior of firms before and after the banking reform across sectors with high and low banking dependence. They showed that after the reforms (1) bank debt declines, especially among the worst performing firms; (2) the interest rate spread between bad and good firms' loans rises significantly; and (3) the banks become more reluctant to extend credit to firms facing negative performance shocks. In summary, they find clear indication that the worst performing firms were protected before the banking reforms and much less so after the reforms.

They then go on to document the impact of the change in lending practices on the restructuring process. The reforms have a number of effects. (1) Firms' exit rates rise and in the more bank-dependent sectors, exits become more correlated with firms performance. (2) Within-sector reallocation of gross assets and employment increases in the bank-dependent sectors. This rise in reallocation is mainly driven by entry and exit decisions and by the increase in the market share of better performing firms. (3) There is an increase in value added per worker in the more bank-dependent firms.

All in all, Bertrand, Schoar, and Thesmar (2004) present evidence consistent with the discussion of the Japanese zombie firms in Caballero, Hoshi, and Kashyap (2006) and the deleterious effects of distortions in the banking sector on the restructuring process. Both papers corroborate the belief that a well-functioning financial sector is a crucial ingredient for a healthy creative-destruction process.

2.5.3 Trade Restrictions and Restructuring

The findings that labor reallocation is large, takes place within sectors, and accounts for a significant fraction of productivity growth have broad implications in several fields of economics. For example, traditional analyses of restructuring in the trade and development literature emphasize one dimension of the creative destruction process—namely, major shifts between the main sectors of the economy—but the empirical evidence does not support the importance of intersectoral labor reallocation. Bernard, Jensen and Schott (2006) and Wacziarg and Wallack (2004) present evidence that intersectoral labor reallocation did not increase significantly after trade liberalizations in the United States and in a group of developing and emerging economies, respectively. Instead, as hinted by the literature reviewed earlier in this chapter, there is a multitude of creation and destruction decisions driven by highly decentralized idiosyncratic factors that are affected by trade reforms. Levinsohn (1999), Eaton and Kortum (2002), and Melitz (2003) argue and provide evidence that a significant benefit of trade reform arises from factor reallocation toward more productive firms.

A natural approach for studying the effects of reallocation on restructuring and productivity is the analysis of changes in the degree of trade openness. Trefler (2004) concludes that there are significant productivity and reallocation effects from trade openness even in industrialized economies. To reach this conclusion, Trefler takes advantage of the Canada-U.S. Free Trade Agreement (FTA) to study the effects of a reciprocal trade agreement on Canada. He identifies the effects of the FTA by implementing a double-difference estimation in which he regresses changes in a number of variables between the pre- and post-FTA periods upon changes in the Canadian tariff reductions, changes in American tariffs, and a number of controls for trends, endogeneity, and business-cycle effects. He finds that for industries that experienced the deepest Canadian tariff reductions, the contraction of low-productivity plants reduced employment by 12 percent while raising industry-level labor productivity by 15 percent. Moreover, he finds that at least half of this increase is related to exit and/or contraction of low productivity plants. Finally, for industries that experienced the largest American tariff reductions, plant-level labor productivity soared by 14 percent.

Consistent with this evidence, Bernard, Jensen, and Schott (2006) find that in the United States, productivity growth is fastest in industries where trade costs (barriers) have declined the most. They exploit time series and cross-sectional (across industries) changes in trade costs to study the effects of trade barriers on firm productivity and restructuring. They use product-level trade data to construct a new measure of trade costs that is defined as the sum of ad valorem tariffs and transport costs. This measure varies substantially across industries and time, so they can use this source of variation to study the effect of trade costs on industry productivity. Their main findings are that (1) productivity growth is faster in

Box 2.3
Service offshoring and productivity

The share of service inputs imported into the United States (service offshoring) has grown by nearly two-thirds from 1992 to 2000, a period that has also seen a dramatic acceleration of productivity growth in U.S. manufacturing. Amiti and Wei (2006) study the connection between service offshoring and productivity growth. They argue that offshoring could affect productivity growth through several channels: (1) static efficiency—firms relocate their less efficient activities overseas and, consequently, average productivity increases by a compositional effect; (2) restructuring—firms may restructure as a response to offshoring; (3) learning externalities—firms may increase productivity by learning new technologies embodied in the imported services; and (4) variety effects—productivity could rise due to an increase in the variety of inputs.

They find that service offshoring has a positive and significant effect on productivity growth for ninety-six U.S. manufacturing sectors in the 1992–2000 period. The effects are robust to several estimation techniques and to the inclusion of several controls. Moreover, the effects are economically significant: service offshoring accounts for around 11 percent of labor productivity growth during the 1992–2000 period (as a benchmark, material-input offshoring accounts for only 5 percent of productivity growth, and the effects are not precisely estimated).

industries with falling trade costs, (2) plants in industries with falling trade barriers are more likely to exit or become exporters, and (3) in these industries existing exporters increase their shipments abroad.

Looking at developing economies, Pavcnik (2002) documents that trade liberalization significantly affected plant productivity in the case of Chile. This country underwent a substantial trade liberalization in the late 1970s and early 1980s, eliminating most nontariff barriers and reducing tariffs from rates usually above 100 percent to a uniform 10 percent ad valorem rate. This liberalization exposed domestic firms to foreign competition. Pavcnik identifies the impact of trade liberalization on plant productivity by comparing the performance of import-competing and nontradable goods sectors. She finds that plant productivity in import-competing sectors improved on average by between 3 percent to 10 percent more than those in the nontradable sector after the liberalization. Moreover, she finds that exiting plants were on average 8 percent less productive than continuing plants and that more productive plants increased their product market and input-use shares over the period. In particular, reallocation of resources toward more productive plants explains about two-thirds of the 19 percent increase in productivity during the 1979–1986 period.

2.5.4   Deregulation and Restructuring

Domestic deregulation of goods markets can have similar effects. For example, Olley and Pakes (1996) find that deregulation in the American telecommunications industry increased productivity predominantly through factor reallocation toward more productive plants rather than through intraplant productivity gains.

More broadly, Klapper, Laeven, and Rajan (2004) implement a differences-in-differences strategy to study the effect of entry regulation on firm behavior in a sample including firm-level data from Western and Eastern European countries. Their two dimensions are countries with high and low levels of entry regulation, and industries with high and low levels of *natural* entry. They identify the latter using entry rates in the United States, arguing that this country provides a valid benchmark because it has relatively low regulation of entry. The cross-country measures of entry regulation are from Djankov et al. (2002). Their findings support the notion that regulation affects firm entry: "naturally high-entry" industries have relatively lower entry in countries that have higher entry regulations. Moreover, *both* the growth rate and share of high-entry industries is depressed in countries with more stringent barriers to entry.

Finally, Fisman and Sarria-Allende (2004) extend the Klapper, Laevan, and Rajan study to countries outside Europe and include both industry- and firm-level data from the UNIDO and WorldScope databases. Their results nicely complement those of Klapper, Laevan, and Rajan (2004). Fisman and Sarria-Allende find that (1) industries with low natural barriers to entry operating in countries with high entry regulations have fewer and larger firms relative to less regulated economies, (2) operating margins are relatively high in industries with low natural entry barriers in countries with high entry regulations, and (3) the investment response to growth opportunities is stronger in countries with low entry regulations.

Box 2.4
An important caveat on measuring sclerosis from job flows

The cross-country evidence presented in this chapter shows that job flows (job creation and job destruction) are not significantly different across countries having very different labor market policies. For instance, job flows are roughly similar in the United States and continental Europe. At first glance, this evidence may seem inconsistent with the idea that restructuring is less efficient in regulation-burdened continental Europe than in the United States. However, this conclusion does not stand up to closer scrutiny. While throughout the book I develop models where this link can be made directly, in richer environments job flows are not a sufficient statistic for sclerosis. Importantly, worker flows in the United States are much larger than those observed for continental Europe (Pries and Rogerson [2005] document that worker flows are between 1.5 and 2.5 times larger in the United States than in Europe).

This difference is important because two economies with similar job flows can nevertheless have different productivity performances. If a relatively unproductive worker never leaves his or her own accord, maintaining a job for a given period of time is much more costly in terms of technological backwardness than if the firm can find the optimal complement for the machine at each point in time. Thus, in studying the impact of labor market regulation on sclerosis, one must be careful not to look at job flows exclusively. On the other hand, job flows are probably a good enough (although not perfect) measure to study the *cyclical* properties of sclerosis and restructuring.

Pries and Rogerson (2005) enrich a model of the type described in this book with an "experimentation" ingredient à la Jovanovic (1979). In the model, the quality of a worker-firm match is both an inspection good and an experience good. At the time of meeting, both parties have limited information about the match's quality, which is completely revealed only by engaging in production. In this economy, hiring practices play a key allocational role that can be severely distorted by labor market regulations. Workers and firms observe a signal about the match's true quality prior to deciding whether to form a match, and matches form only if the signal about quality exceeds a threshold level. True quality is revealed over time, but only if a match is formed. Labor market regulations affect worker turnover by affecting the level of the threshold signal. In an economy with policies such as a relatively high minimum wage or high dismissal costs, the threshold level for a match is higher.

Pries and Rogerson (2005) evaluate the individual and combined impact of four different regulations: (1) a 15 percent increase in the minimum wage, (2) a dismissal cost equivalent to three months of the lowest wage observed in the calibrated equilibrium, (3) an increase in unemployment benefits equivalent to 20 percent of the lowest wage observed in the calibrated equilibrium, and (4) a tax of 15 percent on expected output. Their results suggest that the increase in the minimum wage and the three-month dismissal costs have significant effects on worker turnover and productivity without affecting job destruction rates.

2.6   Conclusion

This introductory chapter has compiled empirical evidence from a wide variety of sources, countries, and sectors. Overwhelmingly, the evidence points to a massive and persistent process of ongoing restructuring, which takes place mostly within (rather than across) narrowly defined sectors. This process of factor reallocation is a chief determinant of aggregate productivity growth, which can be hampered by over-regulation, weak financial conditions and contractual weaknesses in a broader sense.

Liquidations are countercyclical but gross flows are mostly decoupled—in particular, job destruction rises but job creation falls during recessions. Moreover, and contrary to conventional wisdom, when one studies gross flows over a whole recession-recovery episode, restructuring turns out to be procyclical despite the rise in liquidations at the recession's onset. Similar patterns are observed in corporate assets restructuring.

The goal of the rest of the book is to provide a unified theoretical macroeconomic framework to understand these and related facts, as well as to characterize many of the positive and normative implications that follow from them.

References and Suggested Readings

Aguiar, Mark, and Gita Gopinath. 2005. "Fire-Sale FDI and Liquidity Crises." *Review of Economics and Statistics* 87(3): 439–452.

Amiti, Mary, and Shang-Jin Wei. 2006. "Service Offshoring and Productivity: Evidence from the United States." NBER Working Paper No. 11926.

Autor, David, William Kerr, and A. Kluger. 2006. "Do Employment Protections Reduce Productivity? Evidence from U.S. States." Mimeo., Massachusetts Institute of Technology.

Aw, Bee-Yan, and Geeta Batra. 2001. "Job Turnover and Total Factor Productivity Growth: Micro Evidence from Taiwan." Mimeo., Pennsylvania State University.

Aw, Bee-Yan, Sukkyun Chung, and Mark J. Roberts. 2003. "Productivity, Output, and Failure: A Comparison of Taiwanese and Korean Manufacturers." *Economic Journal* 113(8): F485–F510.

Baily, Martin N., Charles Hulten, and David Campbell. 1992. "Productivity Dynamics in Manufacturing Plants." *Brookings Papers on Economic Activity: Microeconomics* 1992: 187–249.

Barlevy, Gadi. 2002. "The Sullying Effect of Recessions." *Review of Economic Studies* 69(1): 65–96.

Bartelsman, Eric J., and Phoebus J. Dhrymes. 1994. "Productivity Dynamics: U.S. Manufacturing Plants, 1972–1986." Working paper, Finance and Economics Discussion Series 94-1, Board of Governors of the Federal Reserve System.

Bartelsman, Eric J., John C. Haltiwanger, and Stefano Scarpetta. 2004. "Microeconomic Evidence of Creative Destruction in Industrial and Developing Countries." Mimeo., University of Maryland.

Bernard, Andrew B., J. Bradford Jensen, and Peter K. Schott. 2006. "Survival of the Best Fit: Exposure to Low-Wage Countries and the (Uneven) Growth of U.S. Manufacturing Plants." *Journal of International Economics* 68(1): 219–237.

Bertrand, Marianne, Antoinette Schoar, and David Thesmar. 2004. "Banking Deregulation and Industry Structure: Evidence from the French Banking Reforms of 1985." CEPR Discussion Paper No. 4488.

Bloom, Nick, Raffaella Sadun, and John Van Reenen. 2006. "It Ain't What You Do It's the Way that You Do I.T.—Investigating the Productivity Miracle Using Multinationals." Mimeo., London School of Economics.

Bureau of Economic Analysis, United States Department of Commerce. http://www.bea.gov/bea/dnl.htm.

Caballero, Ricardo J., Kevin N. Cowan, Eduardo M. R. A. Engel, and Alejandro Micco. 2004. "Effective Labor Regulation and Microeconomic Flexibility." Mimeo., Massachusetts Institute of Technology.

Caballero, Ricardo J., and Mohamad L. Hammour. 1994. "The Cleansing Effect of Recessions." *American Economic Review* 84(5): 1350–1368.

Caballero, Ricardo J., and Mohamad L. Hammour. 1996. "On the Timing and Efficiency of Creative Destruction." *Quarterly Journal of Economics* 111(3): 805–852.

Caballero, Ricardo J., and Mohamad L. Hammour. 2000. "Institutions, Restructuring, and Macroeconomic Performance." Invited lecture, XII World Congress of the International Economic Association, Buenos Aires, Argentina.

Caballero, Ricardo J., and Mohamad L. Hammour. 2005. "The Cost of Recessions Revisited: A Reverse-Liquidationist View." *Review of Economic Studies* 72(2): 313–341.

Caballero, Ricardo J., Takeo Hoshi, and Anil K. Kashyap. 2006. "Zombie Lending and Depressed Restructuring in Japan." Mimeo., Massachusetts Institute of Technology.

Cox, W. Michael, and Richard Alm. 1992. "The Churn: The Paradox of Progress." In *1992 Annual Report*. Dallas, Tex.: Federal Reserve Bank of Dallas.

Davis, Steven J., R. Jason Faberman, and John C. Haltiwanger. 2005. "The Flow Approach to Labor Markets: New Data Sources, Micro-Macro Links and the Recent Downturn." IZA Discussion Paper No. 1639.

Davis, Steven J., and John C. Haltiwanger. 1999a. "Gross Job Flows." In David Card and Orley Ashenfelter, eds., *Handbook of Labor Economics*, 2711–2805. Amsterdam: North-Holland.

Davis, Steven J., and John C. Haltiwanger. 1999b. "On the Driving Forces behind Cyclical Movements in Employment and Job Reallocation." *American Economic Review* 89(5): 1234–1258.

Davis, Steven J., and John C. Haltiwanger. 2001. "Sectoral Job Creation and Destruction Responses to Oil Shocks." *Journal of Monetary Economics* 48(3): 465–512.

Davis, Steven J., John C. Haltiwanger, and Scott Schuh. 1998. *Job Creation and Destruction*. Cambridge, Mass.: The MIT Press.

Djankov, Simeon, Rafael La Porta, Florencio Lopez-de-Silanes, and Andrei Shleifer. 2002. "The Regulation of Entry." *Quarterly Journal of Economics* 117(1): 1–37.

Djankov, Simeon, Rafael La Porta, Florencio Lopez-de-Silanes, Andrei Shleifer, and Juan Botero. 2003. "The Regulation of Labor." NBER Working Paper No. 9756.

Doms, M., and T. Dunne. 1998. "Capital Adjustment Patterns in Manufacturing Plants." *Review of Economic Dynamics* 1(2): 409–429.

Eaton, Jonathan, and Samuel Kortum. 2002. "Technology, Geography, and Trade." *Econometrica* 70(5): 1741–1779.

Eisfeldt, Andrea L., and Adriano Rampini. 2006. "Capital Reallocation and Liquidity." *Journal of Monetary Economics* 53(3): 369–399.

Faberman, R. Jason. 2004. "Gross Job Flows over the Past Two Business Cycles: Not All 'Recoveries' Are Created Equal." BLS Working Paper No. 372.

Feldstein, Martin. 2001. "Comments and Analysis." *Financial Times* (June 28).

Fisman, Raymond, and Virginia Sarria-Allende. 2004. "Regulation of Entry and the Distortion of Industrial Organization." NBER Working Paper No. 10929.

Foster, Lucia, John C. Haltiwanger, and C. J. Krizan. 2001. "Aggregate Productivity Growth: Lessons from Microeconomic Evidence." In Edward Dean, Michael Harper, and Charles Hulten, eds., *New Developments in Productivity Analysis*, 303–363. Chicago, Ill.: University of Chicago Press.

Golbe, D., and L. White. 1987. "A Time-Series Analysis of Mergers and Acquisitions in the U.S. Economy." In A. Auerbach, ed., *Corporate Takeovers*, 265–302. Chicago, Ill.: University of Chicago Press.

Greenspan, Alan. 2000. "Technology and the Economy." Speech before the Economic Club of New York, January 13.

Gust, C., and J. Marquez. 2004. "International Comparisons of Productivity Growth: The Role of Information Technology and Regulatory Practices." *Labour Economics* 11: 33–58.

Haltiwanger, John, Adriana Kugler, Maurice Kugler, Alejandro Micco, and Carmen Pagés. 2004. "Effects of Tariffs and Real Exchange Rates on Job Reallocation: Evidence from Latin America." *Journal of Policy Reform* 7(4): 191–208.

Heckman, James, and Carmen Pagés. 2003. "Law and Employment: Lessons from Latin America and the Caribbean." NBER Working Paper No. 10129.

Inter-American Development Bank (IDB). 2003. *IPES 2004: Good Jobs Wanted: Labor Markets in Latin America.* Washington, D.C.: Inter-American Development Bank.

Job Openings and Labor Turnover Survey, Bureau of Labor Statistics, U.S. Department of Labor. http://www.bls.gov/jlt/.

Jovanovic, Boyan. 1979. "Job Matching and the Theory of Turnover." *Journal of Political Economy* 87(5): 972–990.

Jovanovic, Boyan. 1982. "Selection and the Evolution of Industry." *Econometrica* 50(3): 649–670.

Kaufmann, Daniel, Aart Kraay, and Pablo Zoido-Lobaton. 1999. "Governance Matters." World Bank Policy Research Department Working Paper No. 2196.

Klapper, Leora, Luc Laeven, and Raghuram Rajan. 2004. "Business Environment and Firm Entry: Evidence from International Data." NBER Working Paper No. 10380.

Kiyotaki, N., and Moore, John. 1997. "Credit Cycles." *Journal of Political Economy* 105(2): 211–248.

Levine, Ross, Norman Loayza, and Thorsten Beck. 2000. "Financial Intermediation and Growth: Causality and Causes." *Journal of Monetary Economics* 46(1): 31–77.

Levinsohn, James. 1999. "Employment Responses to International Liberalization in Chile." *Journal of International Economics* 47(2): 321–344.

Melitz, Marc J. 2003. "The Impact of Trade on Intra-Industry Reallocations and Aggregate Industry Productivity." *Econometrica* 71(6): 1695–1725.

Olley, Steve, and Ariel Pakes. 1996. "The Dynamics of Productivity in the Telecommunications Equipment Industry." *Econometrica* 64(6): 1263–1297.

Pavcnik, Nina. 2002. "Trade Liberalization, Exit, and Productivity Improvements: Evidence from Chilean Plants." *Review of Economic Studies* 69(1): 245–276.

Pries, Michael, and Richard Rogerson. 2005. "Hiring Policies, Labor Market Institutions, and Labor Market Flows." *Journal of Political Economy* 113(4): 811–839.

Ramey, Valerie A., and Matthew D. Shapiro. 1998. "Costly Capital Reallocation and the Effects of Government Spending." *Carnegie-Rochester Conference Series on Public Policy* 48: 145–194.

Schiantarelli, Fabio. 2005. "Product Market Regulation and Macroeconomic Performance: A Review of Cross-Country Evidence." IZA Discussion Paper No. 1791.

Schumpeter, Joseph A. 1942. *Capitalism, Socialism, and Democracy.* New York: Harper & Brothers.

Trefler, Daniel. 2004. "The Long and Short of the Canada-U.S. Free Trade Agreement." *American Economic Review* 94(4): 870–895.

United Nations Industrial Development Organization (UNIDO). 2002. *Industrial Statistics Database 2002 (3-digit level of ISIC code [Revision 2]).*

Wacziarg, Romain, and Jessica S. Wallack. 2004. "Liberalization and Intersectoral Labor Movements." *Journal of International Economics* 64(2): 411–439.

World Bank. 2004. *World Development Report 2005: A Better Investment Climate for Everyone.* Washington, D.C.: World Bank.

II

The Basics

3

The "Fundamental Transformation"

3.1 Introduction

An asset is specific to a relationship to the extent that its value is greater within the relationship than outside it. Economic specificity is a pervasive phenomenon. For example, it arises when a firm selects and invests in a worker; when the worker spends his learning years in a firm; when capital is invested in a unionized firm or industry; when a bank extends credit to an entrepreneur; when an upstream firm makes investments to serve downstream customers; when foreign direct investment flows into a country.[1]

Specificity in a relationship reduces the flexibility of separation decisions, which induces reluctance in the investment decision. This is the basic insight of the irreversible investment literature. But specificity acquires a potentially more troublesome dimension when combined with contracting difficulties. To the extent that it is irreversible, entering into a relationship creates specific quasi-rents that may not be divided ex post according to the parties' ex ante terms of trade. Avoiding this transformation from an ex ante competitive situation to an ex post bilateral monopoly—known in the literature as the "fundamental transformation" or the "holdup problem"—requires prior protection through comprehensive and enforceable long-term contracts. The problem is that such contracts are much closer to a methodological benchmark than a description of actual practice.

Relationship specificity, together with recognition of the difficulties involved in actual contracting, is a central building block in the modern economic theory of institutions (Klein, Crawford, and Alchian 1978;

Williamson 1979, 1985). Specificity as a central dimension of transaction description forms the basis of insightful theories of the firm and internal organization (e.g., Grossman and Hart 1986; Hart and Moore 1990), of financial structure (e.g., Williamson 1988; Hart and Moore 1994; Shleifer and Vishny 1996), of public choice institutions and their credibility (e.g., North and Weingast 1989; Thomas and Worrall 1994), and of a variety of other institutional arrangements. The common feature of these theories is the idea that an important function of institutional arrangements is to allow the transacting parties to partly circumvent the holdup problem.

The institutional literature generally acknowledges that, while institutions often help alleviate appropriability, they rarely resolve the problem entirely. From a macroeconomic perspective, the prevalence of unprotected specific rents is a potentially central factor in determining the functioning of the aggregate economy. Transactions in the labor, capital and goods markets are frequently characterized by some degree of specificity. The creation of a job, for example, typically involves relationship-specific investments by the firm and the worker (e.g., Becker 1964). Beyond its purely technological aspect, effective specificity may be increased by such institutional features as dismissal regulations (which devalue the firm's option of using its investment outside the relationship) or unionization (which narrows the firm's outside option to a sector outside the scope of the union). In partial equilibrium, unresolved opportunism results in reduced investment incentives, because the resulting specific quasi-rents may later be partly appropriated by others (e.g., Simons 1944; Grout 1984). In general equilibrium, as the problem of creating and sharing quasi-rents spreads throughout the economy, the market system adjusts to help compensate the appropriated factors, providing a highly inefficient macroeconomic "solution" to the unresolved microeconomic contracting problems. This general-equilibrium adjustment can affect major aspects of the aggregate functioning of the economy.

In this chapter I begin building a simple structure to characterize the first-order macroeconomic implications of the unresolved microeconomic holdup problem. Throughout the book I think of the problem as one where two (and later on, more) factors of production contemplate either committing to a partly irreversible joint production relationship, or

Box 3.1
Standard specificity examples in macroeconomics

Specificity and appropriable quasi-rents characterize a variety of transactions that are prevalent throughout the economy. A prime example concerns labor and capital. A special case of firm- and worker-specificity that has been studied extensively in the labor market literature is search costs expended by firms and workers, which, by their very nature, cannot be protected by ex ante contracting (see, e.g., Acemoglu 1996).

Specificity can have an important institutional origin in addition to its technological dimension. Consider, for example, the case of labor unions, whose power may derive from firm investments that are embodied in workers as a group—again, ultimately a contracting problem—or from legislation (see, e.g., Lindbeck and Snower 1986). In this context, appropriability finds its clearest expression in the phenomenon of strikes. The only reason strikes put any pressure on employers is that it is costly—for technological or legal reasons—to substitute outsiders for striking insiders, namely, capital has some degree of specificity with respect to labor. That is precisely the leverage used by insiders to improve their deal. With organized labor, it is not only worker-specific investments but potentially all invested capital that can become relationship-specific and enter the scope of the union. Legislation on dismissals provides another example of institutionally driven specificity.

Other examples of specific quasi-rents of particular macroeconomic relevance can be found in financial and goods markets. In an external financing transaction, the first factor may represent "management;" and the second factor represents the capital of outside financiers. The delegation of control rights over the firm's assets to management makes those assets partly management-specific (e.g., Williamson 1988; Hart and Moore 1994). If it withdraws from the relationship, management can in various ways cause serious damage to the firm's value—by withdrawing their inalienable human capital, by withholding vital information on the firm and its assets, or by undertaking highly disruptive acts of omission or commission.

Vertical relationships in the goods market provide a third example (e.g., Klein, Crawford, and Alchian 1978). The two factors would then represent the capital of upstream suppliers and of downstream customers, who may make mutually specific investments. An electric utility, for example, may invest in a plant that is specific to a supplier (by locating it near a coal mine, for example) or specific to a customer (by locating near an industrial complex). A special case is "customer markets," where the upstream supplier is a final-goods producer, and the downstream customer is a consumer (e.g., Phelps and Winter 1970).

Finally, a number of contributions have examined various implications of appropriable quasi-rents in general-equilibrium settings. For example,

Box 3.1
(continued)

> Makowski and Ostroy (1995) highlight the key role that "appropriation" plays in the efficiency of markets. Ramey and Watson (1996) analyze the interactions of the holdup problem and effort incentivization in a matching model. More applied examples are: MacLeod and Malcomson (1993), who study the macroeconomic effects of employment contract forms that attempt to avert investment holdup; Acemoglu (1996), who examines the effects of search-related incomplete contracting on human capital accumulation; and Robinson (1995), who looks at the economics and politics of labor market institutions when employment contracts are incomplete. Davis (2001) uses a labor-market search model to show that even when there is no specificity, there may be underinvestment in quality of jobs and employees as long as trade in the labor market is costly for both firms and workers.

remaining in "autarky." For illustrative purposes, I focus on the relationship between capital and labor through most of the book. After setting up a simple static model, in this chapter I highlight the basic macroeconomic features of this environment. The problem of appropriability implies that in general equilibrium, factors of production are underemployed and the market for the "appropriating" factor is segmented (i.e., it experiences involuntary unemployment). Despite the static nature of the model, it helps to understand a few business-cycle features that will remain present in dynamic models. At low levels of activity, labor is the factor that experiences market segmentation (i.e., there is involuntary labor unemployment), while at high levels of activity it is the market for capital that is segmented (i.e., there are labor shortages). Moreover, compared to an efficient economy, the cyclical response of the economy is excessively elastic when the labor market is segmented (recessions), and excessively rigid when the capital market is segmented (expansions).

3.2   Basic (Static-Single-Margin) Model

While the subjects developed in this book typically require a dynamic model with simultaneously active creation and destruction margins, a great deal of insight into these subjects can be obtained from a simple

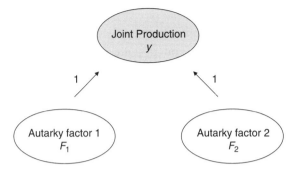

Figure 3.1
Joint Production and Autarky sectors

static model that temporarily removes all destruction decisions. Similarly, there are plenty of interactions between unresolved holdup problems and institutional as well as technological evolution, but for now I take both of these—institutions and technology—as given.

3.2.1   Production Structure

The model economy has one consumption good and two factors of production, denoted as factors 1 and 2. There is a unit mass of each of these factors, and they are identified with infinitesimal and fully specialized (just factor 1 or just factor 2) optimizing agents who derive linear utility from the consumption good. The latter is the numeraire.

The economy lasts for one period and is described in figure 3.1. Production takes place in two modes, identified with separate sectors of the economy. Factors 1 and 2 can either produce separately in their respective Autarky sectors, or combine in the Joint Production sector. For each factor i, U_i and E_i denote total employment in Autarky and in Joint Production, respectively.

Each factor's Autarky sector is perfectly competitive and characterized by an aggregate production function $F_i(U_i)$—in the case of decreasing returns, the rents accruing to these activities are allocated to fixed-supply renters, who are otherwise inessential for the discussion. In Joint Production, one unit of factor 1 combines with one unit of factor 2 in fixed proportions to produce y units of the consumption good. Let E denote the total number of production units and, for now, $E_i = E$ and $U_i = U = 1 - E$, for $i = 1, 2$.

3.2.2 Specificity and Incomplete Contracts

When factors join to form a production unit, they develop a degree of *specificity* with respect to each other, and a share $\phi_i \in [0, 1]$ of factors $i = 1, 2$ can no longer be used outside the production unit. If the factors separate, only $(1 - \phi_i)$ units of factor i can be used elsewhere. Specificity can be a pure aspect of technology or due to institutional factors. For example, capital specificity, $\phi_k > 0$, arises when the firm finances organizational or human capital embodied in the worker. Labor specificity, $\phi_l > 0$, may arise when the worker dedicates part of his lifetime learning opportunities to the acquisition of firm-specific knowledge.

Specificity creates quasi-rents equal to the difference between the value of the factors within the production unit and their value in their best outside use. To guarantee that specific quasi-rents are divided according to the factors' ex ante terms of trade, the factors must enter an ex ante contract that governs their participation in the production unit and the division of its surplus. Unfortunately, such ideal contracts are quite difficult to achieve once one considers the full complexity of concrete situations (see, e.g., Segal 1999). In practice, specific investments are typically made not once and for all, but incrementally throughout the life of a production unit. The plan for making such investments, the duration of the relationship, the rent-division mechanism, and the multiple dimensions that characterize each factor's participation, must be pre-specified from the start and made fully contingent on the future profitability of the production unit, on factors that determine its evolving prospects, and on the various events, both aggregate and idiosyncratic, that govern each factor's outside opportunity costs. A variety of problems of observability, verifiability, enforceability, and sheer complexity, make such ideal contracts rarely feasible. Thus, agents enter into arrangements—what one might loosely call "incomplete contracts"—that leave plenty of room for ex post discretion (for a discussion of incomplete contracts in the presence of specificity, see Hart (1995, chap. 4) and the references in box 3.2).

A simple transaction that would eliminate the need for contracting altogether is an exchange of factors that allows a single agent to own both factors in a production unit. In the labor and financial markets examples discussed in box 3.1, this solution is made impossible by the fact that one side of the transaction involves "inalienable" human capital. In the third

Box 3.2
Incomplete contracts in the presence of specificity

Even in the presence of specificity, one might try to mitigate the problem it induces by choosing the appropriate contractual form. There is an extensive and unresolved debate on how far contracts can go.

Hart (1995) shows that if the investment can be verified or the characteristics of the output can be described in advance, parties can write contracts that lead to the first-best level of investment. However, these conditions are quite restrictive since often, the investment has non-monetary components and the optimal output may vary according to the state of the world. Chung (1991) finds that simple contracts can achieve the *first-best* level of investment as long as they specify the parties' ex post bargaining positions. However, if this is not enforceable, one is back in an incomplete-contracts setting.

In fact, Segal (1999) argues that if renegotiation is possible a long-term contract does not solve the holdup problem, and the equilibrium level of investment under a long-term contract converges to that of incomplete contracting, where trade is contractible ex post but not ex ante.

Hart (1995) also argues that revenue- or cost-sharing does not solve the problem since either party can trigger the no-trade outcome with the intention of renegotiating. The point is that revenue- or cost-sharing contracts give each party an option to trade under the existing contract but do not force them to trade under this contract. Third parties may help under certain conditions if they are honest. However, there is an incentive for them to collude with one of the involved parties. If this is possible, the introduction of a third party achieves nothing.

Maskin and Tirole (1999) show that even if parties cannot foresee all states of nature, optimal contracting may still be achieved provided agents can probabilistically forecast their possible future payoffs. Hart and Moore (2004) also propose a contract under which parties agree now on a salary for a service that will be specified later as a way to mitigate the holdup problem. However, both of these results rely on the parties not being able to renegotiate ex post.

Guriev and Svasov (2005) argue that in a continuous-time setting, making contracts contingent on time may solve the holdup problem in the presence of specific investments. In their model the time dimension reduces the incompleteness of contracts by allowing the *duration* of contractual obligations to vary or by specifying the *advance notice* necessary for certain unilateral actions. However, their stark result applies only to environments where the seller has the opportunity of undertaking an investment that decreases his cost and increases the buyer's value. If instead there is bilateral investment, multidimensional investment, or investment opportunities with negative cross effects (that decrease the buyer's value as well as decreasing the seller's cost), then simply allowing a time dimension no longer leads to *first-best* contracting, although a time component might still be present in the optimal *second-best* contract.

Box 3.3
Holdup problems in colonial India

The harmful consequences of contract incompleteness are present in many economic activities. Kranton and Swamy (2005) analyze the case of textiles and opium in colonial India. Textiles were produced under the so-called Agency System. Under this arrangement, local weavers produced textiles that were sold to the East India Company (EIC), with local agents acting as intermediaries. The timing of transactions described in their paper is as follows:

• The intermediary assigns EIC capital—to be paid back in the future—to the weaver to produce textiles to be handed over in the future (the price to be paid contingent on quality).
• The weaver produces the textiles (she also decides the quality of the product).
• The weaver decides whether to sell the textiles to the EIC or to alternative buyers (even though the EIC had a monopoly to sell products to Britain, there were French, Dutch, and other merchants that could sell products to other countries).
• The intermediary verifies the quality and pays a price accordingly.
• The agent delivers the textiles to the EIC.

In a world with incomplete contracts (because institutions are not well developed), this arrangement has two implicit holdup problems: weavers may not uphold sale contracts and producers may not honor pricing arrangements. Kranton and Swamy show that in situations in which any of the agents has too much power, the transactions would not occur. As the historical experience of colonial Bengal shows, there may exist problems such as complaints by weavers that intermediaries abuse their position or complaints by the intermediaries that weavers are selling their output to outside buyers or producing poor quality textiles.

A key factor to explain why the Agency System existed was the lack of alternative arrangements and policies. Vertical integration was not available because it was not technically feasible to have a centralized production system. Reputation-building in a context of repeated interactions was not possible either, because there was a lot of uncertainty regarding the prospect of future transactions (e.g., low life expectancy, political turmoil, high mobility of EIC personnel).

Kranton and Swamy contrast this experience with the successful opium monopoly by the EIC some time later (in the late eighteenth century). The production arrangement was essentially similar to the Agency System. The main difference was that with the passage of time, the EIC had had more opportunity to invest in institution building. The EIC was able to monitor the abuse of intermediaries and, at the same time, to make sure that the producers were fulfilling their promises in terms of the quality of poppy. In addition, technical progress allowed for scientific evaluations of the quality of poppy (using chemical tests) that curtailed the freedom of intermediaries to use discretionary power to abuse producers.

All in all, these historical examples show how contract incompleteness may affect the efficiency of a productive process, and how the emergence of technical change and/or better institutions may produce a more efficient allocation of resources.

Box 3.4
Appropriability in capital-labor relations: Marx vs. Simons

In the context of capital-labor relations, the problem of appropriability of relationship-specific investment arose early in the history of economic thought. For Marx ([1867] 1967), in chapter 14 of *Das Kapital*, specificity for labor lies in the division of labor, through which "each workman becomes exclusively assigned to a partial function, and...for the rest of his life, his labor-power is turned into the organ of this detail function" (339). This form of labor specificity leads to ex post appropriation by capital, which constitutes "a refined and civilized method of exploitation" (364): "If, at first, the workman sells his labor-power to capital, because the material means of producing a commodity fail him, now his very labor-power refuses its services unless it has been sold to capital. Its functions can be exercised only in an environment that exists in the workshop of the capitalist after the sale. By nature unfitted to make anything independently, the manufacturing laborer develops productive activity as a mere appendage of the capitalist's workshop" (360–361).

Marx clearly saw the general nature of the appropriability problem: "This division of labor is a particular sort of cooperation, and many of its disadvantages spring from the general character of cooperation, and not from this particular form of it" (339).

Nearly eighty years later, with the progress achieved by organized labor, Simons (1944) took the opposite view that it is labor that takes advantage of specificity in order to appropriate capital: "Frankly, I can see no reason why strongly organized workers, in an industry where huge investment is already sunk in highly durable assets, should ever permit a return on investment sufficient to attract new capital or even to induce full maintenance of existing capital" (8).

He provided an early analysis of the resulting underinvestment: "The bias against new investment inherent in labor organization is important.... Investors now face...the prospect that labor organizations will appropriate most or all of the earnings....Indeed, every new, long-term commitment of capital is now a matter of giving hostages to organized sellers of complementary services" (17).

example, it is limited by span-of-control and other limits to the extent of vertical integration.

When precontracting is not possible, the division of specific quasi-rents must be determined ex post. It is well known that in this case the relationship between the two factors undergoes, in Williamson's (1985) turn of phrase, a "fundamental transformation" from an ex ante competitive setting to an ex post bilateral monopoly. To analyze the effect of incomplete contracting, let us distinguish between two extreme cases: the "efficient" equilibrium, where factors are able to engage in full contractual precommitment, and the "incomplete-contracts" equilibrium, where no precommitment is possible.

For concreteness, I henceforth refer to factors 1 and 2 as *capital* and *labor*, respectively. Joint Production consists of worker employment and capital investment within the firm. Autarky for workers corresponds to "unemployment"—voluntary or involuntary—or employment in sectors that are relatively immune to contracting problems; and Autarky for capital corresponds to investment abroad, or to consumption. Let us now study the factors' decisions as to whether to participate in Joint Production or remain in Autarky.

3.2.3   Factor Rewards

Capital and labor have their own idiosyncrasies, several of which I will incorporate into the discussion as the book progresses. For now, I simply use the fact that ex ante, capital is a substantially more flexible factor than labor is. In modern market-oriented economies, uncommitted capital is free to migrate across countries, industries, or uses. On the contrary, labor's mobility within each of these dimensions is often limited by skills and other human traits.

Let the Autarky technology for capital be linear, so that for any level of capital allocated to this sector its per unit return is $r > 0$. The Autarky sector for labor, on the other hand, experiences decreasing returns so the wage received by labor in that sector, v, is decreasing with respect to U, and hence increasing with respect to Joint Production employment:

$$v(E) = F'(1 - E), \qquad v'(E) = -F''(1 - E) > 0. \tag{3.1}$$

Turning to Joint Production, let π and w denote the unit compensation of capital and labor in a newly created production unit.

In the incomplete-contracts equilibrium, factor compensation in new production units is governed by their ex post opportunity cost $(1 - \phi_k)r$ and $(1 - \phi_l)v$. The specific quasi-rent s from such a production unit is the difference between the unit's revenue y and the ex post opportunity costs of its factors:

$$s = y - (1 - \phi_k)r - (1 - \phi_l)v. \tag{3.2}$$

The particular form of splitting this surplus is not central for the main qualitative message, as long as it is not fully determined by ex ante conditions, which would correspond to a complete-contracts environment. For simplicity, I adopt the 50/50 Nash bargaining solution for sharing the unit's revenue. That is, I assume that each factor gets its ex post opportunity cost plus half of the unit's bargainable surplus s:

$$\pi = (1 - \phi_k)r + \tfrac{1}{2}s, \tag{3.3}$$

$$w = (1 - \phi_l)v + \tfrac{1}{2}s. \tag{3.4}$$

An alternative specification of the "disagreement point" in bargaining yields the Shaked and Sutton (1984) sharing rule that allocates $\tfrac{1}{2}y''$ to each factor as long as neither factor $i = 1, 2$ receives less than $(1 - \phi_i)p_i$, where p_i denotes factor i's reward in autarky (see Binmore, Rubinstein, and Wolinsky 1986 for a discussion of the foundational differences between the two approaches). The discrete change in the way the opportunity cost $(1 - \phi_i)p_i$ enters the Shaked-Sutton rule makes it less attractive for an "aggregate" model. Otherwise, the main conclusions in this book do not depend on the specific sharing rule.

3.2.4 Free Entry

For uncommitted factors of production to participate in Joint Production, it must be the case that

$$\pi \geq r, \qquad w \geq v. \tag{3.5}$$

Since in the efficient—complete-contracts—case, resources are transferred to the factor whose participation constraint is not met for as long as there is any surplus left in Joint Production, the two entry conditions in (3.5) can be reduced to a single joint condition:

$$y \geq r + v. \tag{3.6}$$

This condition is not sufficient in the incomplete-contracts case, for there is no ex post transfer mechanism to ensure that *each* factor of production receives its ex ante opportunity cost. Thus, one needs to look into each factor's participation decision separately.

Let $\Delta^{(i)}$ denote the *net effective specificity* of factor i, so that

$$\Delta^{(k)} = \phi_k r - \phi_l v = -\Delta^{(l)}.$$

It is easy to show from equations (3.2), (3.3), and (3.4) that equation (3.5) is equivalent to

$$y \geq r + v + \Delta^{(k)}, \qquad y \geq r + v + \Delta^{(l)}. \tag{3.7}$$

The difference between the efficient entry condition (3.6) and this condition for factor i is the term $\Delta^{(i)}$. $\Delta^{(i)}$ is positive if i sinks in a greater value than the other factor, and negative otherwise. Since $\Delta^{(\neg i)} = -\Delta^{(i)}$, let us denote the absolute value by $\Delta \equiv |\Delta^{(i)}|$. Condition (3.7) for i requires that revenues y cover the two factors' outside opportunity costs plus the net effective specificity $\Delta^{(i)}$ that factor i would sink into the relationship. It is apparent that it is the entry condition of the factor with positive net specificity that is binding, so that, taken together for $i = k, l$, the two entry conditions (3.7) are equivalent to

$$y \geq r + v + \Delta. \tag{3.8}$$

3.3   Short-Run Macroeconomic Implications

A microeconomic situation in which one factor of production is open to appropriability by another, if widespread throughout the economy, results in offsetting macroeconomic adjustments to guarantee that appropriated factors obtain adequate returns in general equilibrium and satisfy their free-entry condition. This general-equilibrium response affects major aspects of the macroeconomy, which appear as symptoms of an inefficient macroeconomic "solution" to the unresolved appropriability problems. This section describes basic equilibrium implications for factor employment and business cycles.

3.3.1   Rationing, Unemployment, and Segmentation
Let us start by finding parameter conditions for the incomplete-contracts equilibrium to be efficient. The efficient case will be used as the bench-

mark throughout. It is easy to see that equations (3.6) and (3.8) coincide only when the specificity of capital and labor is balanced:

$$\phi_k r = \phi_l v \Rightarrow \Delta = 0, \tag{3.9}$$

which happens for strictly positive ϕ_k and ϕ_l if and only if

$$\frac{\phi_k}{\phi_l} = \frac{y - r}{r}. \tag{3.10}$$

Let us assume throughout that the equilibrium of the economy is interior. Then, away from the *balanced-specificity* scenario in condition (3.9), the incomplete-contracts economy exhibits *underemployment*. This can be easily derived from the free-entry condition

$$y = r + v(E) + \Delta. \tag{3.11}$$

Observe that irrespective of which factor is the appropriating or appropriated factor,

$$\frac{\partial(v(E) + \Delta)}{\partial E} \geq 0$$

because $\phi_l \in [0, 1]$. Then equation (3.11) implies that in equilibrium v (and E) must fall as Δ rises. It is the decline in E that reduces $v(E) + \Delta$, so that regardless of which factor is the appropriating or appropriated:

$$\Delta > 0 \Rightarrow E = v^{-1}(y - r - \Delta) < E^* = v^{-1}(y - r),$$

where the superscript $*$ denotes the value of a variable in the efficient equilibrium.

It is important to recognize that underemployment results from the decreased incentives of the appropriated factor to enter Joint Production, since it is that factor's entry condition that holds with equality. This determines the nature of the underemployment experienced by each factor of production.

For concreteness, let us assume until further notice that

$$\phi_k \gg \phi_l,$$

so that capital is the appropriated factor of production. In this case, at the margin capital is indifferent between participating in Joint Production or producing in Autarky, since

$$\pi = r.$$

On the other hand, labor is not indifferent, since

$$w = y - r > v = w - \Delta.$$

That is, net appropriation gives rise to *involuntary* unemployment of labor in Joint Production, which persists because that factor cannot commit to a compensation lower than equilibrium w. The "slots" open in Joint Production are determined by capital's free-entry condition, and are rationed among units of the appropriating factor. Labor in the Joint Production sector earns more than labor in Autarky. The labor market is *segmented* between these two sectors, and unemployment is involuntary.

3.3.2   Flat Effective Labor "Supply"

One of the main macroeconomic issues at business-cycle frequency is the lack of real wage adjustment to sharp rises in unemployment during recessions. This observation has motivated the many *flat quasi-labor supply* theories in macroeconomics.

Up to now the model developed is static and hence not well designed to address business-cycle issues, but it is enough to shed light on a potentially important mechanism for this debate. If capital is being appropriated in equilibrium, it is the elasticity of *capital* in the Autarky sector rather than that of labor in its Autarky sector that most influences employment. If uncommitted or Autarky-capital is more elastic than uncommitted labor, then employment fluctuates more than it would in an efficient economy.

To see this, simply replace $\Delta^{(k)} = \Delta$ in the equilibrium condition (3.11) to obtain

$$y = (1 + \phi_k)r + (1 - \phi_l)v, \qquad (3.12)$$

which contrasts with the efficient equilibrium condition,

$$y = r + v, \qquad (3.13)$$

by weighting the opportunity cost of capital disproportionately. Differentiating equation (3.12) yields

$$\frac{dE}{dy} = \frac{1}{(1 + \phi_k)\frac{dr}{dE} + (1 - \phi_l)v'}$$

$$= \frac{1}{(1 - \phi_l)v'} > \frac{1}{v'} > 0.$$

That is, in the incomplete-contracts economy any change in y must be accommodated by a proportionally larger change in E.

3.3.3 Bottlenecks during Booms and High Tobin's q

Up to now, we have focused primarily on the region where capital is the appropriated factor of production. However, for any given pair of ϕ_k and ϕ_l, the balanced specificity condition (3.10) shows that whether labor or capital is appropriated (left-hand side less than or greater than the right-hand side, respectively) also depends on aggregate conditions, y.

Let y^b denote the level of revenues at which there is zero net appropriation and the incomplete-contracts economy is efficient, for a given pair of $\{\phi_k, \phi_l\}$. From equation (3.10) it follows that

$$y^b = r\left(\frac{\phi_k}{\phi_l} + 1\right).$$

Since equilibrium employment is increasing with respect to y, one can write $v(E(y))$ with $dv/dy > 0$. Which, from

$$\Delta^{(l)} = \phi_l v - \phi_k r,$$

implies that capital is appropriated for $y < y^b$, the case I have emphasized up to now, but it is the appropriating factor for $y > y^b$. As the economy expands and crosses the level of activity y^b, it turns from a situation of involuntary labor unemployment and capital shortages for job creation to one of labor market shortages and segmentation in capital markets.

How should one interpret the possibility of segmented capital markets? It is a situation where capital could obtain a higher return if invested in Joint Production but is unable to find the requisite labor. In terms of the stock market valuation of Joint Production units, Tobin's q is one when $y < y^b$ and greater than one when $y > y^b$ (even though there are no explicit adjustment costs). Periods of labor market shortages are times of expensive stock market valuations.

Although the level of revenues y^b seems arbitrary, I argue in chapter 8 that, in the long run, institutional and technological evolution are likely to result in a situation where y^b is within the range of revenues in which the economy fluctuates. Over time, institutions are likely to respond in order to correct any imbalance in appropriation that causes macroeconomic inefficiency to rise beyond a certain point. Similarly, technologies are also likely to adapt to allow efficient production with new factor proportions that reduce this imbalance. On both counts, one does not expect y^b to be far removed from the economy's average level of output in the long run.

Recall from the previous section that when labor suffers from involuntary unemployment, the incomplete-contracts economy is more responsive to shocks than an efficient economy. In contrast, when labor is the scarce factor, the economy's cyclical response is more rigid than in the efficient case. Thus, appropriability exacerbates recessions and involuntary unemployment, while it constrains expansions by creating labor shortages that prevent sufficient investment in new jobs. The balanced-specificity level of employment E^b associated with y^b is, in a sense, analogous to the concept of a "natural rate." It is the level of employment at which the labor market functions effectively within the economy—it neither builds up the excessive slack of involuntary unemployment nor creates a shortage that constitutes a bottleneck for the rest of the economy.

The logic behind the "rigidification" of the economy during booms is symmetric to that of the flat quasi-labor supply in section 3.3.2. In the region of labor shortage,

$$y = (1 - \phi_k)r + (1 + \phi_l)v, \tag{3.14}$$

which contrasts with the efficient-equilibrium condition by weighting the opportunity cost of the inelastic factor of production, labor, disproportionately.

In summary, at low revenue levels it is new capital—the more elastic of the two factors—whose binding free-entry condition constrains labor employment and induces excessive elasticity in the economy's response to shocks; while at high revenue levels, it is labor—the less elastic factor—that constrains growth and induces a rigid response. This is reflected in figure 3.2 by the (relatively) more concave mapping of productivity onto E in the incomplete-contracts economy.

3.3.4 Asymmetric Business Cycles

Two interesting implications follow from the previous result. The first is a simple application of Jensen's inequality. Because of the asymmetry in the economy's cyclical responsiveness at low and high levels of activity, an increase in the volatility of aggregate shocks around y^b inefficiently

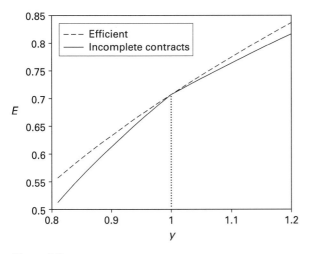

Figure 3.2
Efficient vs. incomplete-contracts equilibrium

lowers average Joint Production employment and output. This "level" effect can lead to high costs of macroeconomic instability.

Second, the economy exhibits an *asymmetric* cyclical response to a symmetric shock process. Figure 3.3 gives a stylized representation of the model's implications for a symmetric cycle in revenues around y^b (the figure was generated with the same parameter values as figure 3.2). The two curves represent the sequence of (static) equilibrium employment levels that correspond to each revenue level over the cycle, with the curves' averages shown as a straight line. The dashed curve represents the response of an efficient economy, which is symmetric around the average employment level E^b. The solid curve represents the response of the incomplete-contracts economy. It is asymmetric, with excessive elasticity at low activity levels and excessive rigidity at high activity levels, and exhibits lower average employment than the efficient economy. The resulting cyclical pattern is reminiscent of asymmetries documented for the U.S. business cycle, such as the apparent asymmetry in the economy's response to negative and positive oil price shocks. Sichel (1992), for example, characterizes postwar fluctuations in U.S. output as consisting of three phases: contractions, high-growth recoveries to pre-recession levels, and moderate-growth periods. The corresponding features in figure 3.3 are the relatively short and sharp recession-recovery

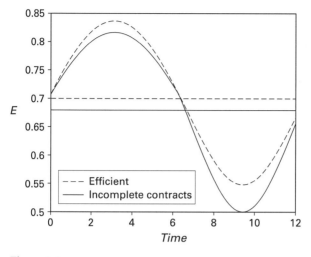

Figure 3.3
Quasi-cyclical response

phases below average E, and the shallow and more prolonged phase of moderate expansion above it.

3.4   The Destruction Margin

The previous section emphasized the *creation* side and how the anticipation of contractual problems leads to inefficient outcomes. Let us now turn to the *destruction* margin. In doing so, it is useful to split destruction (separation) decisions into three types: efficient, privately efficient but socially wasteful, and privately inefficient. Let us illustrate the first two using a single model, and then conclude with a simple extension that generates privately inefficient separations from a holdup problem similar to the one we have been discussing.

3.4.1   Sclerosis and Excessive Destruction

Let us enrich the previous model by adding a mass m of *existing* production units with a distribution of productivities $D(y^0)$ with $y^0 \in [0, y]$. The results I wish to emphasize for now do not depend on the effect of separation decisions on equilibrium prices; thus I will assume that m is infinitesimal.

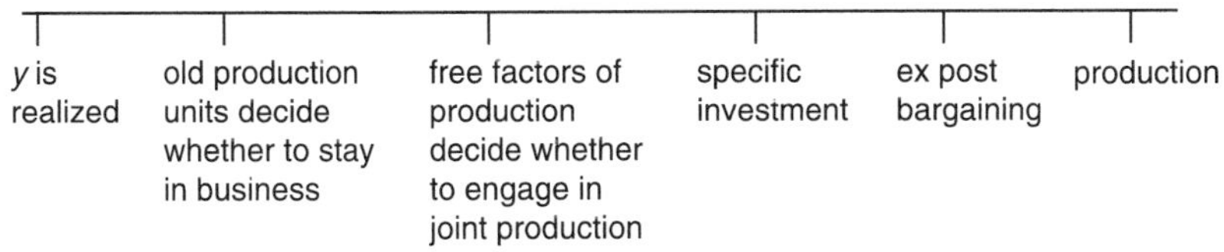

y is realized	old production units decide whether to stay in business	free factors of production decide whether to engage in joint production	specific investment	ex post bargaining	production

Figure 3.4
Timeline

Furthermore, since the goal here is to highlight the equilibrium implications of holdup problems on the creation side for the destruction decision, I will assume that factors of production in existing units have *no* specificity and are thus free to migrate without incurring any transaction costs. Any inefficiency that may arise in this decision is a result of distorted equilibrium prices and rationing rather than of microeconomic impediments on the destruction margin.

The timing is summarized in figure 3.4 and can be described as follows. The level of productivity for any new unit of Joint Production, y, is realized. At this point, existing production units anticipate the equilibrium described in the previous sections, and decide whether to scrap their production unit or not. Since there are no transaction costs, factors of production in old production units need only compare their current reward to their opportunity cost. In general, the latter depends upon whether the factor migrates to Autarky or to a new Joint Production unit after the separation. Later on I will discuss at length what determines the likelihood of one outcome or the other in equilibrium. For now, I simply assume that a factor of production that separates from an old unit has a probability $0 \leq \lambda < 1$ of ending up in a new Joint Production unit and $(1 - \lambda)$ of finishing in Autarky.

From these assumptions, it follows that the opportunity cost of capital and labor currently at an old production unit are, respectively,

$$\lambda \pi + (1 - \lambda)r,$$

$$\lambda w + (1 - \lambda)v.$$

Since separations are *privately efficient* (no specificity or holdups), we can combine these opportunity costs to conclude that destruction takes place whenever

$$y^0 \leq \lambda(\pi + w) + (1 - \lambda)(r + v). \tag{3.15}$$

Let $\bar{y}^0$ denote the productivity level that satisfies equation (3.15) with equality. By comparing the efficient threshold, $\bar{y}^{0*}$, with the incomplete-contracts economy threshold, $\bar{y}^0$, one can show that an important consequence of unresolved holdups on the creation side is that the economy becomes *sclerotic*: that is, production units that would not survive in the efficient economy do survive in the incomplete-contracts economy.

Concretely, in the efficient economy we have that $\pi^* = r$ and $w^* = v^*$. Replacing these back into equation (3.15) yields

$$\bar{y}^{0*} = r + v^*,$$

and since by the free-entry condition (3.6) y is also equal to $r + v^*$, we have that

$$\bar{y}^{0*} = y. \tag{3.16}$$

In contrast, in the incomplete-contracts economy the free-entry condition determines that

$$y = \pi + w = r + v + \Delta.$$

Replacing this expression back into equation (3.15) yields

$$\bar{y}^0 = y - (1 - \lambda)\Delta < y = \bar{y}^{0*}. \tag{3.17}$$

Sclerosis is an equilibrium consequence of depressed competition on the entry side. Reduced creation lowers the opportunity cost of factors of production with limited alternative uses in order to create space for rents. This reduction in opportunity cost alleviates the pressure on less efficient units to scrap.

Sclerosis is thus an expression of low opportunity costs due to inefficient resource allocation, which is tightly related to factor market segmentation. Coupled with underemployment, it is likely to constitute a powerful drag on economic growth.

Note that in the particular model illustrated here, labor is the only ex ante inelastic factor, and hence the drop in its opportunity cost, v, must absorb Δ in its entirety, *regardless* of what the appropriating factor is. Later on I will discuss more general models where relative elasticities depend upon the time horizon considered.

Somewhat paradoxically, the incomplete-contracts economy also exhibits *excessive destruction*. How can the economy simultaneously exhibit both sclerosis and excessive destruction? Sclerosis refers to a comparison with respect to the efficient economy. Excessive destruction, on the other hand, refers to the amount of destruction present in the incomplete-contracts economy *given* a depressed level of creation.

In order to see the excessive-destruction result, let us revisit the exit condition (3.15) and replace $(\pi + w)$ for $(r + v + \Delta)$ in it, to obtain

$$\bar{y}^0 = r + v + \lambda\Delta > r + v. \tag{3.18}$$

Note that $\lambda\Delta$ represents the probability that a factor of production exiting an old unit finds a match in a new Joint Production unit times the rent that the appropriating factor of production obtains in such a match. Therefore, while separations are privately efficient, they are *socially excessive*, as a component of the private opportunity cost of one of the factors of production is due to rent-seeking, which has no social value.

3.4.2 Privately Inefficient Separations

Regardless of whether the decision is *socially* efficient or not, the separation rule in equation (3.15) is *privately* efficient. That is, there is no private surplus left on the table—if such surplus exists, capital and labor find a way to split it without breaking up. For specific quasi-rents to give rise to the possibility of privately inefficient separations there must be some "non-transferability" problem. The classic illustration of privately inefficient separations is Hall and Lazear's (1984) diagram, shown in figure 3.5.

The worker is hired at a fixed wage w. The firm has the right to lay off the worker if productivity M falls below w, and the worker has the right to quit if there is an alternative job paying a wage A higher than w. If no renegotiation is possible, there is inefficient separation when the worker's productivity is higher than the opportunity cost of labor but lower than the contracted wage (inefficient layoffs during recessions), or when the opportunity cost of labor is lower than productivity but higher than the wage (inefficient quits during booms).

The key issue in this context is why renegotiation does not take place and solve the inefficiency. Part of the reason could be regulatory, as is the case with a minimum wage. Yet another is informational, as in Myerson and Satterthwaite (1983) or due to incentive issues, as in Ramey and Watson (1997).

Myerson and Satterthwaite (1983) show that in a bilateral trading problem, if the seller's valuation is distributed over the interval $[a, b]$,

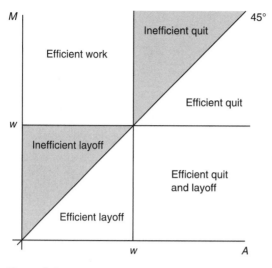

Figure 3.5
Privately inefficient separations as in Hall and Lazear (1984)
Source: Adapted from Hall and Lazear (1984).

and the buyer's valuation is distributed over $[c, d]$, and if the interiors of these intervals have a non-empty intersection, then no incentive-compatible, individually rational trading mechanism can be ex post efficient. This means that when valuations are private information, there is no mechanism that can ensure that there are no inefficient separations since both parties have an incentive to pretend to be of a lower type in order to get additional surplus.

Ramey and Watson (1997) model the employment relation as a repeated prisoner's dilemma where both parties have an incentive to misbehave at the expense of the other. In times of low productivity the available output may not be enough to sustain the relationship even though cooperation is still optimal. The diagrammatic representation of this is figure 3.6. Below the 45-degree line, the parties separate because the value of staying in the relationship is less than what can be earned subsequent to separation. Above the 45-degree line, separation is inefficient. Nevertheless, in the shaded region, the relationship will not continue because the benefits of cooperation are not large enough to induce individual agents to exert effort.

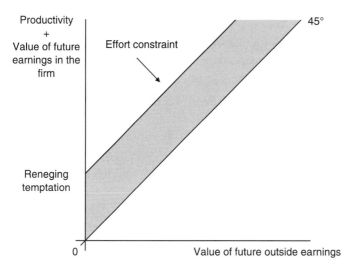

Figure 3.6
Privately inefficient separations as in Ramey and Watson (1997)
Source: Adapted from Ramey and Watson (1997).

In this case, although there are unlimited wage renegotiation opportunities, there are inefficient separations due to the impossibility of sustaining high effort when the rewards are too low.

Going back to the basic model developed in this chapter, one can easily introduce inefficient separations, building on the same insights behind inefficient creation. Recall that the source of private inefficiency in the creation decision is that physical and human capital investments cannot be protected from ex post opportunism. But the decision to preserve an existing unit often has many investment dimensions as well, which are also exposed to opportunism. For example, the decision to incur temporary losses in the face of transitory declines in demand is an investment decision, as is a worker's decision to take temporary wage cuts.

Suppose that in order to obtain *net* output y^0, capital must irreversibly inject additional resources of a, which allows the unit not only to continue but also to generate output $y^0 + ra$. It is apparent that in such a case nothing is affected in the efficient economy, and the cutoff net productivity remains:

$$\bar{y}^{0*} = y.$$

In contrast, the introduction of this investment decision does affect the incomplete-contracts economy if a cannot be protected. Now capital has to invest the quantity a, knowing that it will only recover half of its investment. For capital to be willing to preserve the production unit, the latter must generate enough surplus to compensate capital for such a loss.

Let me assume that if negotiations break down after investment of a, factors can still migrate to a new production unit and that equilibrium is such that capital is being appropriated (in a new production unit) so that $\pi = r$ and $w = v + \Delta$. Then the scrapping threshold becomes

$$\bar{y}^{0pi} = \bar{y}^0 + ra,$$

which ensures that capital is indifferent since

$$r + \frac{\bar{y}^{0pi} + ra - [r + \lambda w + (1 - \lambda)v]}{2} = r + \frac{\bar{y}^0 + 2ra - [r + v + \lambda\Delta]}{2}$$

$$= r + ra.$$

In this context, old production units with net productivity

$$\bar{y}^0 < y^0 \leq \bar{y}^{0pi}$$

are destroyed, leaving private surplus on the table. Workers would like to persuade capital not to destroy such units, but their inability to commit not to appropriate part of a makes their argument unpersuasive to capital.

For most of the book, I work with the case of socially inefficient but privately efficient separations. An important exception is chapter 6, where I separate capital from entrepreneurs and discuss financial frictions.

3.5   Conclusion

This chapter introduced the concept of the *fundamental transformation* and explored some of its implications for issues that concern macroeconomists. Despite the rudimentary nature of the model, it is enough to generate a rich set of predictions for the macroeconomy arising from the specificity inherent to most relationships. They are as follows: creation is depressed; when capital is appropriated, there is segmentation and involuntary unemployment in the labor market; the effective labor supply is flat during contractions and excessively steep during booms; business cycles are asymmetric, with contractions that are steeper than expansions; the restructuring process becomes sclerotic, but there is excessive destruction during contractions.

Before moving on, note that the simple model presented here has only one entry decision: whether to join or not. It is for this reason that efficiency can be achieved even if the two factors have positive specificity, as long as these cancel out. This would not be true in an environment with multiple decisions, such as in Davis (2001) where firms also decide on the quality of the job. Note, however, that even in the simple framework presented here larger gross specificity leads to larger net specificity and inefficiency for all levels of y not consistent with the balanced-specificity condition. Moreover, in chapter 8, I show that in some instances factor proportions can be adjusted to restore balanced specificity. In this case the economy exhibits productive inefficiency even when equilibrium net specificity is zero.

Finally, it should be apparent that at times I have interpreted a static model in such a way as to shed light on issues which are inherently dynamic in nature. The next chapters revisit many of the basic insights of this chapter in dynamic settings.

Note

1. This chapter is based on Caballero and Hammour (1996a, 1998b).

References and Suggested Readings

Acemoglu, Daron. 1996. "A Microfoundation for Social Increasing Returns in Human Capital Accumulation." *Quarterly Journal of Economics* 111(3): 779–804.

Ball, Laurence. 1996. "Disinflation and the NAIRU." In Christina D. Romer and David H. Romer, eds., *Reducing Inflation: Motivation and Strategy*, 167–185. Chicago, Ill.: University of Chicago Press.

Becker, Gary. 1964. *Human Capital*. New York: Columbia University Press.

Becker, Gary. 1983. "A Theory of Competition among Pressure Groups for Political Influence." *Quarterly Journal of Economics* 98(3): 371–400.

Binmore, Kenneth, Ariel Rubinstein, and Asher Wolinsky. 1986. "The Nash Bargaining Solution in Economic Modeling." *Rand Journal of Economics* 17(2): 176–188.

Blanchard, Olivier J., and Juan F. Jimeno. 1995. "Structural Unemployment: Spain versus Portugal." *American Economic Review* 85(2): 212–218.

Bulow, Jeremy I., and Lawrence H. Summers. 1986. "A Theory of Dual Labor Markets with Application to Industrial Policy, Discrimination, and Keynesian Unemployment." *Journal of Labor Economics* 4(3, pt. 1): 376–414.

Caballero, Ricardo J., and Mohamad L. Hammour. 1994. "The Cleansing Effect of Recessions." *American Economic Review* 84(5): 1350–1368.

Caballero, Ricardo J., and Mohamad L. Hammour. 1996a. "The Fundamental Transformation in Macroeconomics." *American Economic Review* 86(2): 181–186.

Caballero, Ricardo J., and Mohamad L. Hammour. 1996b. "On the Timing and Efficiency of Creative Destruction." *Quarterly Journal of Economics* 111(3): 805–852.

Caballero, Ricardo J., and Mohamad L. Hammour. 1996c. "On the Ills of Adjustment." *Journal of Development Economics* 51(1): 161–192.

Caballero, Ricardo J., and Mohamad L. Hammour. 1997. "Improper Churn: Social Costs and Macroeconomic Consequences." Mimeo., Massachusetts Institute of Technology.

Caballero, Ricardo J., and Mohamad L. Hammour. 1998a. "Jobless Growth: Appropriability, Factor Substitution and Unemployment." *Carnegie-Rochester Conference Series on Public Policy* 48: 51–94.

Caballero, Ricardo J., and Mohamad L. Hammour. 1998b. "The Macroeconomics of Specificity." *Journal of Political Economy* 106(4): 724–767.

Chung, Tai-Yeong. 1991. "Incomplete Contracts, Specific Investments, and Risk Sharing." *Review of Economic Studies* 58(5): 1031–1042.

Davis, Steven J. 2001. "The Quality Distribution of Jobs and the Structure of Wages in Search Equilibrium." NBER Working Paper No. 8434.

De Long, J. Bradford. 1990. "Liquidation Cycles: Old Fashioned Real Business Cycle Theory and the Great Depression." NBER Working Paper No. 3546.

De Long, J. Bradford, and Lawrence H. Summers. 1988. "How Does Macroeconomic Policy Affect Output?" *Brookings Papers on Economic Activity*, no. 2: 433–495.

Dow, Gregory K. 1993. "Why Capital Hires Labor: A Bargaining Perspective." *American Economic Review* 83(1): 118–134.

Grossman, Sanford J., and Oliver D. Hart. 1986. "The Costs and Benefits of Ownership: A Theory of Vertical and Lateral Integration." *Journal of Political Economy* 94(4): 691–719.

Grout, Paul A. 1984. "Investment and Wages in the Absence of Binding Contracts: A Nash Bargaining Approach." *Econometrica* 52(2): 449–460.

Guriev, Sergei, and Dmitriy Svasov. 2005. "Contracting on Time." *American Economic Review* 95(5): 1369–1385.

Hall, Robert E., and Edward P. Lazear. 1984. "The Excess Sensitivity of Layoffs and Quits to Demand." *Journal of Labor Economics* 2(2): 233–257.

Hart, Oliver. 1995. *Firms, Contracts and Financial Structure: Clarendon Lectures in Economics*. Oxford: Oxford University Press.

Hart, Oliver, and John Moore. 1988. "Incomplete Contracts and Renegotiation." *Econometrica* 56(4): 755–785.

Hart, Oliver, and John Moore. 1990. "Property Rights and the Nature of the Firm." *Journal of Political Economy* 98(6): 1119–1158.

Hart, Oliver, and John Moore. 1994. "A Theory of Debt Based on the Inalienability of Human Capital." *Quarterly Journal of Economics* 109(4): 841–880.

Hart, Oliver, and John Moore. 2004. "Agreeing Now to Agree Later: Contracts that Rule Out but Do Not Rule In." Harvard Institute of Economic Research Discussion Paper No. 2032.

Katz, Lawrence F., and Lawrence H. Summers. 1989. "Industry Rents: Evidence and Implications." *Brookings Papers on Economic Activity: Microeconomics* 1989: 209–275.

Klein, Benjamin, Robert G. Crawford, and Armen A. Alchian. 1978. "Vertical Integration, Appropriable Rents, and the Competitive Contracting Process." *Journal of Law and Economics* 21(2): 297–326.

Kranton, Rachel, and Anand Swamy. 2005. "Hold-Up and Exports: Textiles and Opium in Colonial India." Mimeo., University of Maryland.

Krueger, Alan B., and Lawrence H. Summers. 1988. "Efficiency Wages and the Inter-Industry Wage Structure." *Econometrica* 56(2): 259–293.

Lindbeck, Assar, and Dennis Snower. 1986. "Wage Setting, Unemployment and Insider-Outsider Relations." *American Economic Review* 76(2): 235–239.

MacLeod, W. Bentley, and James M. Malcomson. 1993. "Investments, Holdup, and the Form of Market Contracts." *American Economic Review* 83(4): 811–837.

Makowski, Louis, and Joseph M. Ostroy. 1995. "Appropriation and Efficiency: A Revision of the First Theorem of Welfare Economics." *American Economic Review* 85(4): 808–827.

Marx, Karl. [1867] 1967. *Capital: A Critique of Political Economy*. Ed. Frederick Engels. Trans. Samuel Moore and Edward B. Aveling (from 3rd German ed.). New York: International Publishers.

Maskin, Eric, and Jean Tirole. 1999. "Unforseen Contingencies and Incomplete Contracts." *Review of Economic Studies* 66(1): 83–114.

Myerson, Roger B., and Mark A. Satterthwaite. 1983. "Efficient Mechanisms for Bilateral Trading." *Journal of Economic Theory* 29(2): 265–281.

Noldeke, Georg, and Klaus M. Schmidt. 1995. "Option Contracts and Renegotiation: a Solution to the Hold-up Problem." *Rand Journal of Economics* 26(2): 163–179.

North, Douglass C., and Barry R. Weingast. 1989. "Constitutions and Commitment: The Evolution of Institutions Governing Public Choice in Seventeenth-Century England." *Journal of Economic History* 49(4): 254–283.

Organization for Economic Cooperation and Development (OECD). 1996. *Employment Outlook*. Paris: Organization for Economic Cooperation and Development.

Phelps, Edmund S., and Sidney G. Winter, Jr. 1970. "Optimal Price Policy under Atomistic Competition." In Edmund S. Phelps et al., *Microeconomic Foundations of Employment and Inflation Theory*, 309–337. New York: W. W. Norton.

Ramey, Garey, and Joel Watson. 1996. "Bilateral Trade and Opportunism in a Matching Market." U.C. San Diego Economics Discussion Paper No. 96-08.

Ramey, Garey, and Joel Watson. 1997. "Contractual Fragility, Job Destruction and Business Cycles." *Quarterly Journal of Economics* 112(3): 873–911.

Robinson, James A. 1995. "Incomplete Contracting, Capital Accumulation, and Labor Market Institutions." Mimeo., University of Southern California.

Robinson, James A. 1996. "The Dynamics of Labor Market Institutions." Mimeo., University of Southern California.

Roe, Mark J. 1994. *Strong Managers, Weak Owners: The Political Roots of American Corporate Finance*. Princeton, N.J.: Princeton University Press.

Segal, Ilya. 1999. "Complexity and Renegotiation: A Foundation for Incomplete Contracts." *Review of Economic Studies* 66(1): 57–82.

Shaked, A., and John Sutton. 1984. "Involuntary Unemployment as a Perfect Equilibrium in a Bargaining Model." *Econometrica* 52(6): 1351–1364.

Shleifer, Andrei, and Robert W. Vishny. 1996. "A Survey of Corporate Governance." NBER Working Paper No. 5554.

Sichel, Daniel E. 1992. "Inventories and the Three Phases of the Business Cycle." Economic Activity Working Paper No. 128, Board of Governors of the Federal Reserve System.

Simons, Henry C. 1944. "Some Reflections on Syndicalism." *Journal of Political Economy* 52(1): 1–25.

Thomas, Jonathan, and Tim Worrall. 1994. "Foreign Direct Investment and the Risk of Expropriation." *Review of Economic Studies* 61(1): 81–108.

Topel, Robert. 1990. "Specific Capital and Unemployment: Measuring the Costs and Consequences of Job Loss." *Carnegie-Rochester Conference Series on Public Policy* 33: 181–214.

Williamson, Oliver E. 1979. "Transaction-Cost Economics: The Governance of Contractual Relations." *Journal of Law and Economics* 22(2): 233–261.

Williamson, Oliver E. 1985. *The Economic Institutions of Capitalism*. New York: Free Press.

Williamson, Oliver E. 1988. "Corporate Finance and Corporate Governance." *Journal of Finance* 43(3): 567–591.

4

Efficient Restructuring

Let us now introduce dynamics and better characterize the process of creative destruction. In this chapter I focus on neoclassical aspects of such a process, highlighting the subtle connection between technology and the behavior of gross flows. In the next chapters I reintroduce inefficient opportunism and merge the insights of this and the previous chapter.[1]

The chapter contains two models. The first one is a dynamic extension of the complete-contracts economy presented in chapter 3, while the second one replaces the labor supply schedule with a search friction. Both models can explain the average pattern of the process of creative destruction, but neither is fully successful in accounting for the cyclical features of this process.

4.1 Basic (Dynamic) Model of Restructuring

The starting point is a dynamic extension of the efficient—complete-contracts—version of the model presented in the previous chapter.

4.1.1 Production Units: Distribution and Flows

A central aspect of any economic model of simultaneous creation and destruction is heterogeneity. In practice, there are many sources of heterogeneity across production units, and each of these sources creates its own dynamics. One particularly realistic and tractable dimension of heterogeneity is the vintage aspect of technology, which I discuss next.

The economy experiences exogenous technical progress. New production units that embody the most advanced techniques are continuously being created, and outdated ones are being destroyed. Because the creation process is costly, production units with different productivities coexist.

As in chapter 3, labor and capital combine in fixed proportions to form *production units*. A production unit created at time t_0 embodies the leading technology at t_0, and produces the same constant flow $A(t_0)$ of output throughout its lifetime. Technical progress makes the productivity $A(t)$ of the leading technology at time t grow at an exogenous rate $\gamma > 0$.

While in the model the creation process is interpreted as one of technology adoption, it could also be interpreted as one of product innovation. In the latter context, the space of goods may be modeled as a continuum of perfectly substitutable products that yield different utilities. In such a case, a production unit created at t_0 produces a unit flow of the most advanced product in existence at t_0, which yields utility $A(t_0)$.

Returning to the single good model, production units are created at different times (and thus may coexist) and fail *exogenously* at rate δ. Let

$$H(t-a)e^{-\delta a} \qquad \text{and} \qquad 0 \le a \le \bar{a}(t)$$

denote the cross-section density of surviving production units aged a at time t, where $\bar{a}(t)$ is the age of the oldest unit *in operation* at time t.

The boundary $H(t)$ is given by the rate at which new units are created, and the age $\bar{a}(t)$ at which units become obsolete is determined by the destruction process. The number of units of age a at any time t is equal to $e^{-\delta a}$ times the number of units that were created a years ago, for as long as that vintage does not become obsolete. In what follows, I assume that $H(t-a)$ and $\bar{a}(t)$ are continuous functions.

The distribution $H(t-a)e^{-\delta a}$ can be aggregated to obtain the total number (or "mass") of production units at any time t:

$$E(t) = \int_0^{\bar{a}(t)} H(t-a)e^{-\delta a}\, da. \qquad (4.1)$$

Because of fixed proportions, $E(t)$ is a measure of both employment and the capital stock in operation. Its evolution is linked to the creative destruction process through

$$\dot{E}(t) = H(t) - H(t-\bar{a}(t))(1-\dot{\bar{a}}(t))e^{-\delta\bar{a}(t)} - \delta E(t). \qquad (4.2)$$

The first term, $H(t)$, measures the creation rate of production units, the second measures the endogenous rate of destruction, and the third,

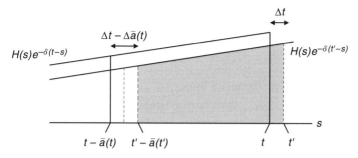

Figure 4.1
Evolution of the stock of existing production units

$\delta E(t)$, measures the exogenous rate of destruction. The endogenous rate of destruction has two components: $H(t - \bar{a}(t))e^{-\delta\bar{a}(t)}$ units are destroyed because they have reached the obsolescence age $\bar{a}$; and $-H(t - \bar{a}(t))e^{-\delta\bar{a}(t)}\dot{\bar{a}}(t)$ are destroyed because $\bar{a}$ changes over time. Let us assume henceforth that creation and endogenous destruction are always positive: $H(t) > 0$ and $\dot{\bar{a}}(t) < 1$, for all t.

Figure 4.1 portrays an example of the evolution of the distribution of active firms from t to t'. The shaded area represents the firms that remain active at time t'. The left end of the figure illustrates endogenous destruction, with part of it a result of the passage of normal obsolescence and another due to a cyclical decline in $\bar{a}$. Exogenous destruction is captured by the downward shift in the solid curve, while creation corresponds to the shaded area to the right of t.

4.1.2   Decisions and Equilibrium

Because the main arguments in this chapter do not depend on the presence or absence of uncertainty, let us assume perfect foresight for now.

Supply is determined by free entry and perfect competition. There is a cost $I_H(H(t))A(t)$ of creating a new production unit, with $I_{HH} \geq 0$. The creation cost depends on the creation rate to capture the possibility that, for the economy as a whole, fast creation may be costly and adjustment may not take place instantaneously. This can be true for different reasons. It can arise from features of the aggregate saving function, or from a concave production function in the sector producing the industry's capital stock, or from a congestion effect in the matching process characterizing the industry's labor market (e.g., Howitt and McAfee 1987), or from ex ante heterogeneity in the productivity of potential entrants (see, e.g., Barlevy 2004; Caballero and Hammour 2005). It can also arise from standard convex capital installation and labor training costs.

The operating cost of a production unit is composed of a wage, $v(t)A(t)$, and the cost of a unit of imported materials, $p_m(t)A(t)$. Let $p_m(t)$ be continuous and the only source of fluctuations in this chapter. Note that p_m admits many interpretations besides an input cost, such as the inverse of a demand or productivity shock. The profits generated at time t by a production unit of age a are

$$\pi(a,t) = A(t - a) - (p_m(t) + v(t))A(t). \qquad (4.3)$$

To see what determines exit note that whenever a unit is being destroyed, its profits have reached zero (more generally, its value has to be zero, but I assume below that there is no incentive to restart a unit that has generated losses). Since such a unit is the oldest in operation at that time, $\bar{a}(t)$ satisfies

$$A(t - \bar{a}(t)) = (p_m(t) + v(t))A(t). \qquad (4.4)$$

This condition relates the unit's operating costs to $\bar{a}(t)$. Let us now determine these costs. While $p_m(t)$ is an exogenous driving force, the wage $v(t)$ is determined from equilibrium in the labor market. As in chapter 3, let us assume that the labor supply

$$v(t) = v(E(t)) \qquad (4.5)$$

is increasing with respect to $E(t)$. Replacing in equation (4.4) yields an equilibrium exit condition

$$A(t - \bar{a}(t)) = (p_m(t) + v(E(t)))A(t). \qquad (4.6)$$

Now let us return to the creation margin and define $T(t)$ as the maximum lifetime of a unit created at t. As long as creation is taking place, free entry equates a unit's creation cost to the present discounted value of profits over its lifetime. That is, at any time t, the free-entry condition is

$$I_H(H(t))A(t)$$
$$= \int_t^{t+T(t)} \pi(s - t, t)e^{-(r+\delta)(s-t)} \, ds$$
$$= \int_t^{t+T(t)} [A(s - (s - t)) - (p_m(s) + v(E(s)))A(s)]e^{-(r+\delta)(s-t)} \, ds,$$

where r is the interest rate.

Substituting the exit condition (4.4) into the free-entry condition and dividing by $A(t)$ yields

$$I_H(H(t)) = \int_t^{t+T(t)} (1 - e^{-\gamma(\bar{a}(s)-s+t)}) e^{-(r+\delta)(s-t)} \, ds, \tag{4.7}$$

with

$$\bar{a}(t) = -\frac{1}{\gamma} \ln(p_m(t) + v(E(t))), \tag{4.8}$$

and

$$E(t) = \int_0^{\bar{a}(t)} H(t-a) e^{-\delta a} \, da. \tag{4.9}$$

Finally, by perfect foresight, the age of a marginal unit $T(t)$ periods from t must be equal to the maximum lifetime of a unit created at t:

$$\bar{a}(t + T(t)) = T(t). \tag{4.10}$$

An equilibrium in this economy is a path $\{H(t), \bar{a}(t), T(t), E(t)\}$ for $t \geq 0$ that satisfies equations (4.7)–(4.10).

4.1.3 Steady State

Before analyzing business-cycle fluctuations, it is instructive to characterize the economy's steady-state (or balanced-growth) equilibrium, assuming that the price of the intermediate input is constant over time at $\bar{p}_m^{SS}$.

In steady state the lifetime of production units is constant: $T(t) = \bar{a}(t) = \bar{a}^{SS}$, for all t; and the age distribution is invariant: $H(t-a)e^{-\delta a} = H^{SS}e^{-\delta a}$, for all t.

The creation rate and destruction age $(H^{SS}, \bar{a}^{SS})$, and equilibrium employment, E^{SS}, are jointly determined from the entry and exit conditions and the aggregate employment expression:

$$I_H(H^{SS}) = \frac{1}{r+\delta} + \left(\frac{1}{r+\delta-\gamma} - \frac{1}{r+\delta}\right) e^{-(r+\delta)\bar{a}^{SS}} - \frac{1}{r+\delta-\gamma} e^{-\gamma\bar{a}^{SS}}, \tag{4.11}$$

$$\bar{a}^{SS} = -\frac{1}{\gamma} \ln(\bar{p}_m^{SS} + v(E^{SS})), \tag{4.12}$$

$$E^{SS} = \frac{H^{SS}}{\delta}(1 - e^{-\delta\bar{a}^{SS}}). \tag{4.13}$$

Consider first the constant marginal cost of entry case, $I_{HH} = 0$, where the system becomes recursive. Assume $r + \delta > \gamma$. Since the left-hand side of equation (4.11) is a constant, and the right-hand side is an increasing function of $\bar{a}^{SS}$ only, it determines a unique $\bar{a}^{SS}$ that is independent of the remaining equilibrium variables. Given this value, the exit condition (4.12) determines employment, E^{SS}. And these quantities together determine H^{SS} through the employment equation (4.13).

Note that since $\bar{a}^{SS}$ is determined independently of $\bar{p}_m^{SS}$, varying the latter across steady states has no effect on $\bar{a}^{SS}$. This implies, from the exit condition (4.12), that any rise in $\bar{p}_m^{SS}$ must be accommodated *one for one* by a corresponding fall in the wage, v. Finally, the employment equation (4.13) reveals that the decline in employment takes place through a decline in creation, H^{SS}.

Later on we will see that for the constant marginal entry cost case, the recursive structure and its implications are preserved over the business cycle.

Suppose now that there are decreasing returns to entry, so that $I_{HH} > 0$. It should be apparent that the recursive structure breaks down in this case. As H^{SS} falls, the creation cost on the left side of the condition (4.11) falls. This implies that the destruction age falls as well, since the right side of the entry condition is increasing with respect to $\bar{a}^{SS}$. Moreover, because as $\bar{a}^{SS}$ falls the productivity of the marginal unit rises, the wage falls by less than the rise in $\bar{p}_m^{SS}$ (see the exit condition [4.12]).

It turns out that this general pattern of comovement between the rate of creation and the destruction age, and its implication for the behavior of wages, are preserved over the business cycle (see section 4.1.4).

4.1.4   Margins of Adjustment over the Business Cycle

Let us now turn to the response of the creative destruction process to cyclical fluctuations in $p_m(t)$. Purely from an accounting point of view, the economy or industry has two margins along which it can accommodate a fall in employment when $p_m(t)$ rises. It can either reduce the rate of creation $H(t)$ or increase the rate of endogenous destruction $H(t - \bar{a}(t))(1 - \dot{\bar{a}}(t))e^{-\delta \bar{a}(t)}$, which amounts to reducing the age $\bar{a}(t)$ at which units are destroyed. The issue is, which of these two margins— $H(t)$ or $\bar{a}(t)$—responds to fluctuations in $p_m(t)$, and to what extent?

The problem's difficulty stems from the interaction between two margins. For a given creation rate, a recession causes the most outdated units to become unprofitable and be scrapped. But if the recession is partly accommodated by a fall in the creation rate, units in place may not suffer the full impact of the downturn.

As in the steady-state analysis, the extent to which creation "insulates" existing units from business-cycle fluctuations depends on the costs of fast creation in the industry, namely, on I_{HH}. The insulating effect of creation is more complete the smaller is I_{HH}.

The "Insulation" Effect: An Extreme Case   The insulating effect of creation is isolated when the cost of creation I_H is a constant, independent of the rate of creation $H(t)$. In this case, as long as the nonnegativity constraint on $H(t)$ is not binding, the insulation effect is complete. Fluctuations in the business-cycle shock $p_m(t)$ are accommodated *exclusively* on the creation margin, and destruction does not respond.

To see why, note that there is a simple recursive way to solve equilibrium conditions (4.7)–(4.10) when I_H is constant, akin to that we used in the steady-state analysis. One first solves for $\bar{a}(t)$, using the free-entry condition (4.7) together with equation (4.10). Given that these equations do not depend on the path of $p_m(t)$, $H(t)$, or $E(t)$, they can be solved independently of the system's other equations. But since this is exactly what we did in the analysis of steady state, the solution a^* is the same constant "efficient lifetime" $\bar{a}^{SS}$ we obtained there.

Employment is then solved from the exit condition, equation (4.8):

$$E(t) = v^{-1}(e^{-\gamma\bar{a}^*} - p_m(t)).$$

Finally, the creation rate $H(t)$ has to satisfy the aggregate employment relation, equation (4.2):

$$\begin{aligned} H(t) &= H(t - \bar{a}^*)e^{-\delta\bar{a}^*} + \delta E(t) + \dot{E}(t) \\ &= H(t - \bar{a}^*)e^{-\delta\bar{a}^*} + \delta v^{-1}(.) - v^{-1'}(.)\dot{p}_m(t). \end{aligned}$$

In equilibrium, p_m fluctuations are fully accommodated by adjustments on the creation margin $H(t)$, while the destruction margin $\bar{a}(t)$ remains constant. By controlling the wage, the creation process neutralizes the effect of input price fluctuations, thus fully "insulating" existing units from changes in $p_m(t)$. Total costs continue to provide the right signal for production units to operate for the constant "efficient" lifetime $\bar{a}^*$.

Note that the previous analysis does not imply that the destruction rate is constant in equilibrium, but only that it does not respond to cost shocks through variations in the age $\bar{a}(t)$ at which units are destroyed. Variations in the destruction rate result, however, from an "echo" effect of the history of the created $H(t - \bar{a}^*)e^{-\delta\bar{a}^*}$ units that reach the age of obsolescence $\bar{a}^*$.

Finally, note that the logic behind full insulation is robust to any modification that preserves the independence of equations (4.7) and (4.10) from $p_m(t)$ and $H(t)$. In particular, it does not hinge on the perfect foresight (certainty) assumption, on perfect competition, or on the degree of industry-wide returns to scale. Perfect foresight is not necessary because as long as it is known that the nonnegativity constraint on $H(t)$ will never be binding, implementing equilibrium behavior does not require expectations of future business conditions. Fully accommodating business cycles on the creation side only requires knowledge of *current* conditions. Perfect competition is not necessary either, since a monopolist's first-order conditions would only add a markup to equations (4.7) and (4.8) and preserve the recursive structure of system (4.7)–(4.10). A similar argument applies to industry-wide increasing returns.

Creation and Destruction over the Cycle   The full insulation case is due to constant creation costs. More generally, the degree of insulation is determined by how costly fast creation is. If I_{HH} is positive insulation is only partial, and destruction also responds to business cycles.

Once I_H rises with $H(t)$, system (4.7)–(4.10) loses its analytic tractability and must be solved numerically. The solution method and the specific parameters are described in section 4.4. Essentially, one can transform the system (4.7)–(4.10) into one of time-varying delay differential equations in $(H(t), \bar{a}(t))$ (see Gorecki et al. 1989), use a "multiple shooting" method for finding an equilibrium solution for given *arbitrary* values of the path $\{\bar{a}(t)\}$, and then use an iterative procedure to converge to the right expectations for this path. Figure 4.2 depicts the response of creation and destruction to the cost cycle for the case when we have convex adjustment costs. Panel (a) reports the path of a "business-cycle" variable $b(t) \equiv -(p_m(t) - \bar{p}_m)$, which is positive during expansions and negative during recessions, where $\bar{p}_m$ is the average $p_m(t)$ over the cycle. Panels (b)–(d) show the path of the scrapping age, creation and destruction (as a percentage of total labor force), and employment.

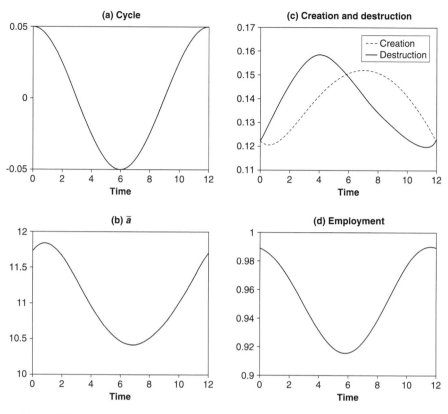

Figure 4.2
Business cycle in basic dynamic model with convex adjustment costs

With $I_{HH} > 0$, as creation drops with the onset of a recession, the cost of entry falls. From the entry condition (4.7), this implies that the present value of profits must fall as well, which is achieved with a fall in $\bar{a}(t)$. By the exit condition (4.8), the latter means that $p_m(t) + v(t)$ now rises. That is, the fall in the wage is no longer enough to fully offset the rise in intermediate input prices and hence to insulate the destruction margin. Part of the contraction has to take place on the destruction margin. From a purely formal point of view, destruction responds to demand because equations (4.7) and (4.10) are no longer independent of the path of $H(t)$ and $p_m(t)$.

The paths on the figure are realistic, although creation and destruction tend to be positively correlated. The next section contains an extensive

Box 4.1
Recession and industry shakeout: The U.S. motor vehicle industry, 1929–1933

Bresnahan and Raff (1991) provide a stark example of the effect of recessions on industry structure in their study of the American motor vehicles industry during the Great Depression. Using Census panel data, they find that the large contraction in automotive production was the occasion for a permanent structural change in the industry.

Table B4.1 presents production, employment, and labor productivity averages in 1929 and 1933 for plants open in both years ("continuing" plants), for plants open in 1929 but not in 1933 ("closing" plants), and for plants open in 1933 but not in 1929 ("newly opening" plants). At the beginning of the Great Depression, the diffusion of mass production techniques in manufacturing had only been partial, and a substantial segment of the industry was still based on skilled craftsmanship. Plant shutdown, which accounted for a third of the decline in industry employment during the Depression, was concentrated in smaller, less productive craft-production plants, while plants that had adopted the mass-production system had a competitive advantage that made them more likely to survive. The result was a true "shakeout" or cleansing of the productive structure, as most plant shutdowns were permanent. Interestingly, creation was still taking place alongside this massive destruction process, with a sizable number of new plants entering even during the depths of the Depression.

Table B4.1
Plant closing and continuation during the Great Depression

Plants	Closing 1929	Continuing 1929	Continuing 1933	Opening 1933
Number of plants	105	106	106	16
Avg. wage-earner months (WEM)	4931	20599	10538	3586
Avg. vehicles produced	13173	36564	16465	6128
Vehicles/WEM	1.36	2.09	1.50	1.14

Source: Bresnahan and Raff (1991).

discussion of this correlation. More important for now is the hidden assumption in the previous figure that the true labor supply is counterfactually elastic. Without the latter assumption, the wage would absorb all fluctuations, and neither creation nor destruction would be affected by business cycles. That is, the current model may offer a reasonable characterization of the average behavior of creation and destruction, but without assuming an implausibly large labor supply elasticity it is unlikely to account for the cyclical evidence on job flows presented in chapter 2 and the large fluctuations in unemployment observed in most economies.

4.2   An Opportunity Cost View of Recessions: Efficient Search

Before a worker and a firm meet, both parties spend time and resources searching for each other. Much of the modern theory of equilibrium unemployment builds upon the modeling of this process (see, e.g., Diamond 1982; Mortensen 1982; Pissarides 1985 for seminal work in this area). One of the appealing features of costly search is that it introduces unemployment without having to assume an unrealistically flat "true" labor supply schedule. Accordingly, while I continue to make assumptions so that equilibrium is efficient (see below), in this section I enrich the restructuring model discussed above to include search costs. I also set the value of leisure to zero and assume total labor supply is fixed at $\bar{L}$, which means unemployment is given by

$$U = \bar{L} - E. \tag{4.14}$$

It turns out that this widely used model offers a richer characterization of unemployment and flows, but it does *not* generate the right flow comovement. In this efficient search model, the rationale for destroying jobs and creating unemployment is to facilitate the reallocation of factors of production at a time when the opportunity cost of doing so is low— that is, during recessions. But this motive's implication is that creation must follow destruction quickly; otherwise there would be no reason to destroy jobs. Job creation and destruction move in tandem, which is not consistent with the evidence reviewed in chapter 2, where destruction rises sharply and creation falls during recessions.

4.2.1   Search Costs

In addition to $I_H(t)A(t)$, a firm must now incur a search cost, $\sigma(t)A(t)$, to create an extra production unit, with

$$\sigma = \sigma(H, U), \qquad \sigma_H \geq 0,\ \sigma_U \leq 0.$$

This flow search cost is the expenditure required to expect one hire per unit time and is (weakly) increasing with respect to aggregate hires H and decreasing with respect to unemployment U: when many firms are searching, there are congestion costs; when many workers are looking for a job, it is easier for firms to hire labor. This search-cost function can be derived from a constant vacancy-posting cost and a constant-returns-to-scale matching function:

$$H = H(U, V), \qquad H_U, H_V > 0,$$

where V denotes aggregate vacancies. To see this, let $\xi > 0$ denote the unit cost (in flow terms) of posting a vacancy, and invert the matching function to write $V = V(H, U)$. Then the unit flow cost of hiring a worker is

$$\sigma(H, U) = \xi V(H, U)/H.$$

The property $\sigma_H > 0$ requires that the matching function be less than unit elastic with respect to V; the property $\sigma_U < 0$ only requires that the matching function be increasing in U.

One could also introduce a search cost for the worker and even differentiate between on-the-job search and unemployed search (see, e.g., Mortensen and Nagypal 2005). However, the main points I want to make are best illustrated by keeping the workers' side costless and limiting search to the unemployed (of course, an employed worker can always quit and search while unemployed). Let us assume that all workers in new production units are hired from the unemployment pool, and all workers from destroyed production units return to this pool.

4.2.2   Decisions and Bargaining

Firms can freely enter the labor market at any time in order to hire workers. To create a production unit at time t a firm searches for a worker at the flow cost $\sigma(t)$ described earlier.

Because of its individual and ex ante nature, this search cost cannot be protected from opportunism (see, e.g., Acemoglu and Shimer 1999). As we discussed in chapter 3, this means that in equilibrium the production unit must be expected to generate enough surplus to compensate the firm both for these costs *and* for opportunism.

The surplus $S(t)$ is equal to the value the production unit creates above what the firm and the worker can claim as their best alternatives. For now, let us assume that the firm recovers $I_H(t)A(t)$ in its entirety if it drops out of the match. The worker's outside alternative is to become unemployed and search for another job. The flow opportunity cost of not doing so is the "shadow" wage $v(t)A(t)$. With this in mind, the appropriable surplus can be written as

$$S(t) = \int_{t}^{t+T(t)} [A(t) - (p_m(s) + v(s))A(s)]e^{-(r+\delta)(s-t)}\, ds - I_H(t)A(t). \quad (4.15)$$

The surplus is equal to the present value of the production unit's flow surpluses after subtracting the protected part of investment.

Let us now generalize the split of this surplus to situations different from that of the 50/50 split discussed in chapter 3. In particular, let the worker obtain a share $0 < \beta < 1$ of the surplus. In this context, the firms' free-entry condition amounts to

$$\sigma(t)A(t) = (1 - \beta)S(t), \quad (4.16)$$

which means that the firm's specific investment $\sigma(t)A(t)$ must be covered by its share of future rents $(1 - \beta)S(t)$.

Substituting in the expression for the appropriable surplus (4.15) and dividing both sides by $(1 - \beta)A(t)$ yields the following condition:

$$I_H(t) + \frac{1}{1-\beta}\sigma(t)$$
$$= \int_{t}^{t+T(t)} \left[1 - (p_m(s) + v(s))\frac{A(s)}{A(t)}\right]e^{-(r+\delta)(s-t)}\, ds. \quad (4.17)$$

This free-entry condition equates the firm's *effective* creation cost with the present value of flow surpluses (valued at opportunity cost rather than at actual wages). Note that in this condition the search cost is leveraged to reflect the fact that a fraction of the rents generated by this cost is extracted by workers in the form of wages that exceed the opportunity cost of labor.

On the worker side, the equilibrium shadow wage $v(t)A(t)$ is equal to the expected utility flow received by an unemployed worker, which is given by the flow probability $H(t)/U(t)$ of finding a job times the gain from capturing the worker's share of the associated appropriable surplus:

$$v(t)A(t) = \frac{H(t)}{U(t)} \beta S(t).$$

Together with the free-entry condition (4.16), this implies that

$$v(t) = \frac{H(t)}{U(t)} \frac{\beta}{1 - \beta} \sigma(t). \tag{4.18}$$

It is important to keep in mind that $v(t)A(t)$ measures an opportunity cost, while the *actual* flow of wage payments received by employed workers $w(t)A(t)$ exceeds $v(t)A(t)$ by the worker's share of appropriable specific quasi-rents. Later in this section I will add assumptions on how firms recover their nonspecific investment $I_H(t)A(t)$ over time, which allows us to compute the actual flow of wages the worker receives. However, the main results in this section do not depend on such details, which is why these are deferred for now.

Finally, note that the maximum planned lifetime of a unit created at time t is determined by the exit condition (4.6) combined with the perfect foresight condition (4.10):

$$A(t) - [p_m(t + T(t)) + v(t + T(t))]A(t + T(t)) = 0. \tag{4.19}$$

This condition states that exit is planned at the time $t + T(t)$ when value added from production no longer covers the worker's shadow wage. Note also that because I have assumed that *all* investments made at t embody technology $A(t)$, even nonspecific capital must be scrapped at $T(t)$ since the technology it embodies is no longer economically viable.

4.2.3   Efficient Equilibrium
Given a history $\{H(t)\}_{t<0}$ that determines the initial distribution of production units, an equilibrium for this economy is a path $\{\bar{a}(t), H(t), U(t)\}$ for $t \geq 0$ that satisfies the system of equations

$$I_H(t) + \frac{1}{1 - \beta} \sigma(t) = \int_t^{t+T(t)} (1 - e^{-\gamma(\bar{a}(s)-s+t)})e^{-(r+\delta)(s-t)} \, ds, \tag{4.20}$$

$$\bar{a}(t) = -\frac{1}{\gamma} \ln(p_m(t) + v(t)), \tag{4.21}$$

where

$$v(t) = \frac{H(t)}{U(t)} \frac{\beta}{1-\beta} \sigma(t), \tag{4.22}$$

as well as

$$\bar{a}(t + T(t)) = T(t), \tag{4.23}$$

and

$$U(t) = \bar{L} - \int_0^{\bar{a}(t)} H(t-a)e^{-\delta a}\, da. \tag{4.24}$$

Equation (4.23) gives the function $T(t)$ implicitly as a transformation of $\bar{a}(t)$, which holds as long as destruction is always taking place. It states that the age $\bar{a}(t)$ of the oldest job at t is equal to the maximum lifetime T that was planned for it at its time of creation $t - \bar{a}(t)$. Equation (4.24) gives unemployment as a function of hiring history and follows immediately from equations (4.1) and (4.14).

It is apparent from the free-entry condition (4.20) that the appropriability problem of search costs amplifies the effective cost of creating a production unit (this is what is behind the $1/(1-\beta)$ in front of the search cost), as in the simple static model in chapter 3. However, it turns out that when investment is appropriated due to search costs, it need not lead to an inefficient outcome. It is well known from Diamond (1982) and Hosios (1990) that despite the incomplete contract and holdup, this equilibrium is efficient if

$\beta =$ elasticity of search function with respect to unemployment.

This condition equates the private and social marginal costs of search, which in general are different because of the well-known "congestion" and "thick market" externalities of search models. Those two externalities operate as follows: (1) a decision to create a job and search for a worker makes searching costlier for other firms ($\sigma_H \geq 0$), and (2) a decision to destroy a job and add a worker to the unemployment pool makes searching cheaper for other firms ($\sigma_U \leq 0$). In this context it is optimal to give the worker some bargaining power even though all the sunk investments are incurred by the firms. This is because bargaining power raises workers' reservation wages and hence the unemployment rate, which in turn facilitates the matching process. Thus, as the matching

Box 4.2
Proof of the Diamond-Hosios condition

The planner in this economy maximizes the present value of total output (since the cost of labor is zero, and we ignore the value of production units that already exist at time zero):

$$\max \int_0^\infty \left(\int_t^{t+T(t)} [A(t) - p_m(s)A(s)]e^{-rs-\delta(s-t)} H(t)\, ds \right.$$
$$\left. - [I(H(t)) + H(t)\sigma(U(t), H(t))]A(t)e^{-rt} \right) dt$$

s.t. $U(t) = \bar{L} - \int_0^{\bar{a}(t)} H(t-a)e^{-\delta a}\, da$

$\bar{a}(t + T(t)) = T(t)$.

Using the Lagrange multipliers $\lambda(t)$ for the first restriction and $\mu(t)$ for the second yields the following first-order conditions:

$$H(t): \int_t^{t+T(t)} [A(t) - p_m(s)A(s)]e^{-(r+\delta)(s-t)}\, ds$$
$$= I_H(H(t))A(t) + \sigma(U(t), H(t))A(t) + H(t)\sigma_H(U(t), H(t))A(t)$$
$$+ e^{rt} \int_t^{t+T(t)} \lambda(s)e^{-\delta(s-t)}\, ds.$$

$U(t): H(t)\sigma_U(U(t), H(t))A(t)e^{-rt} + \lambda(t) = 0.$

Combining these two conditions yields

$$\int_t^{t+T(t)} \left[1 - [p_m(s) - H(s)\sigma_U(s)]\frac{A(s)}{A(t)} \right] e^{-(r+\delta)(s-t)}\, ds$$
$$= I_H(H(t)) + \sigma(t) + H(t)\sigma_H(t).$$

Recall that in the decentralized problem, $H(t)$ was determined according to the following condition:

$$\int_t^{t+T(t)} \left[1 - [p_m(s) + \upsilon(s)]\frac{A(s)}{A(t)} \right] e^{-(r+\delta)(s-t)}\, ds = I_H(H(t)) + \frac{1}{1-\beta}\sigma(t).$$

For the two conditions to be the same for every t, it is sufficient that

$$\upsilon(t) = -H(t)\sigma_U(t) = \frac{H(t)}{U(t)}\frac{\beta}{1-\beta}\sigma(t),$$

$$\frac{1}{1-\beta}\sigma(t) = \sigma(t) + H(t)\sigma_H(t).$$

These expressions can be rewritten as

$$\frac{\beta}{1-\beta} = -U(t)\frac{\sigma_U(t)}{\sigma(t)}$$

and $\dfrac{\beta}{1-\beta} = H(t)\dfrac{\sigma_H(t)}{\sigma(t)}.$

Box 4.2
(continued)

> It follows, first, that efficiency can be achieved only if the matching function has constant-returns-to-scale since
>
> $$H(t)\sigma_H(t) + U(t)\sigma_U(t) = 0.$$
>
> This implies that $\sigma(U, H)$ is homogeneous of degree zero, which means that $H(U, V)$ and $V(H, U)$ must be homogeneous of degree one.
>
> Since $\sigma = \xi V(H, U)/H$, it follows that $\sigma_H = \xi V_H/H - \xi V/H^2$, and $\sigma_U = \xi V_U/H$. Replacing these in any of the previous expressions for β yields
>
> $$\beta = -\frac{UV_U}{HV_H} = H_U \frac{U}{H}.$$
>
> That is, in order to achieve the optimal allocation, β must be equal to the elasticity of the matching function with respect to unemployment.

function becomes more sensitive with respect to unemployment, the efficient level of workers' bargaining power rises. Since my concern in this chapter is with efficient outcomes, I will assume throughout that the Diamond-Hosios condition holds.

If unemployment is positive, the shadow wage rate $v(t)$ is equal to the reduction $\sigma_U(t)$ in total search costs that would result were the worker to remain unemployed. Of course, if unemployment is zero, and the constraint $U(t) \geq 0$ is binding, the shadow wage is higher—equal to the value needed in equation (4.21) to reach full employment. The only beneficial function unemployment plays in this efficient economy is to reduce the search costs of creation. Note that if $\lim_{U \searrow 0} \sigma_U = \infty$, then there is always a small enough positive value of U that satisfies equation (4.21), so it is always efficient to have some unemployment. If, on the other hand, $\sigma_U \equiv 0$ and unemployment does not facilitate the creation process, then there is full employment $U = 0$ as long as $p_m(t)$ is low enough to guarantee a minimum level of profitability (which I assume).

4.2.4 Steady State

Let us now characterize the economy's steady state when the price of the intermediate input is constant at $\bar{p}_m^{SS}$.

In steady state, $T(t) = \bar{a}(t) = \bar{a}^{SS}$, $H(t) = H^{SS}$, $U(t) = U^{SS}$, $v(t) = v^{SS}$ and $\sigma(t) = \sigma^{SS}$, for all t. These values are determined jointly from

$$I_H(H^{SS}) + \frac{\sigma^{SS}}{1-\beta} = \frac{1}{r+\delta} + \left(\frac{1}{r+\delta-\gamma} - \frac{1}{r+\delta}\right)e^{-(r+\delta)\bar{a}^{SS}}$$

$$-\frac{1}{r+\delta-\gamma}e^{-\gamma\bar{a}^{SS}}, \tag{4.25}$$

$$\bar{a}^{SS} = -\frac{1}{\gamma}\ln(\bar{p}_m^{SS} + v^{SS}), \tag{4.26}$$

$$v^{SS} = \frac{H^{SS}}{U^{SS}}\frac{\beta}{1-\beta}\sigma^{SS}, \tag{4.27}$$

$$U^{SS} = \bar{L} - \frac{H^{SS}}{\delta}(1 - e^{-\delta\bar{a}^{SS}}), \tag{4.28}$$

$$\sigma^{SS} = \xi V\left(1, \frac{U^{SS}}{H^{SS}}\right). \tag{4.29}$$

It is apparent that this system is no longer recursive even if $I_{HH} = 0$, since H affects the optimal choice of $\bar{a}$ through the search cost σ; equation (4.25) depends on H not only through I_H, but also through σ. As we can see from equation (4.29), a higher H raises search costs, which requires firms to survive for a longer period of time in order to recover these costs.

We can simplify the expression for v^{SS} by substituting equation (4.29) into equation (4.27) to get

$$v^{SS} = \frac{H^{SS}}{U^{SS}}\frac{\beta}{1-\beta}\frac{\xi}{H^{SS}}V(H^{SS}, U^{SS}),$$

and by noting that at the efficient β,

$$\frac{\beta}{1-\beta} = \frac{-V_U U}{V_H H + V_U U} = \frac{-V_U U}{V},$$

we find that

$$v^{SS} = -\xi V_U(H^{SS}, U^{SS}).$$

Note that since we have assumed the value of leisure (or Autarky's marginal product of labor) is zero, there is no direct labor cost. Rather, v captures the search-cost-reduction benefit of unemployment. If unemployment did not facilitate matching, that is, if $\sigma_U = V_U = 0$ and $\beta = 0$ by the Hosios condition, then there would be no unemployment. In contrast, if we let σ_U and V_U go to zero but keep β constant (and strictly positive), we recover the type of inefficient unemployment discussed in chapter 3. I return to the discussion of inefficient unemployment in the next chapter. For now it suffices to emphasize that search models often bundle (and occasionally confuse) two types of unemployment: unemployment that is efficient and facilitates matches, and unemployment that is inefficient and arises from opportunism and appropriability. I continue to focus on efficient unemployment in this chapter.

4.2.5 Synchronized Flows

The only role unemployment plays in this efficient economy, therefore, is to facilitate labor reallocation. If job creation entails only investment but no search costs, efficient-equilibrium unemployment is zero. In this case aggregate shocks are entirely absorbed by fluctuations in the shadow wage rate, while all quantities, including labor market flows and stocks, remain unaffected.

Let us now consider business cycles when search costs are positive. Figure 4.3 simulates the path of an efficient economy with linear investment costs and positive search costs, with $I_H > 0$, $I_{HH} = 0$, $\sigma > 0$, and $\sigma_U < 0$. As before, business cycles are generated by a deterministic sine wave in $-p_m(t)$. Panel (a) shows one full business cycle in $b(t)$ with its trough in the middle of the diagram. Panels (b)–(d) present the path of output (where detrended output is $q(t) = \int_0^{\bar{a}(t)} \frac{A(t-a)}{A(t)} H(t-a)e^{-\delta a}\,da$), creation and destruction, and unemployment.

In this efficient search environment, the dynamics are driven by the optimal timing of restructuring. In particular, since the *opportunity cost* of creating unemployment is lowest at the depths of a recession when production is least profitable, it is efficient to concentrate the unemployment rate needed to facilitate reallocation near the trough of a recession and to enhance the process of creative destruction. This point is emphasized by Davis (1987) and Davis and Haltiwanger (1990) in a similar context and by, for example, Hall (1991), Galí and Hammour (1992), and Aghion and Saint-Paul (1998) in other contexts.

As shown in the figure, recessions are characterized by a sharp increase in destruction that throws workers into unemployment, followed promptly by a large spurt of creation, which peaks at the same time as unemployment does. Sharp recessions in this economy are a preparation

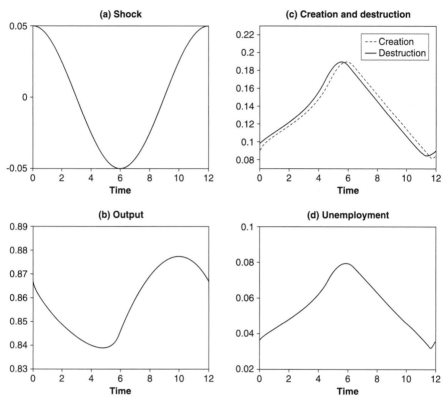

Figure 4.3
Business cycle in search model with linear adjustment costs

for strong recoveries. Creation, destruction, and unemployment are thus tightly synchronized and *positively* correlated.

The strong intertemporal substitution incentive to concentrate reallocation near a recession's trough may be counteracted by an incentive to smooth the creation process. If marginal investment costs are now increasing ($I_{HH} > 0$), creation must be smoothed, as it becomes expensive to vary the intensity of creation over the business cycle. Figure 4.4 presents the path of an efficient economy with both increasing marginal investment costs and search costs.

The figure contains an important message: since the sole purpose of destruction and unemployment in the efficient economy is subsequent creation, the two remain synchronized with creation, which now also requires smoothing. This strong, joint smoothing behavior is another as-

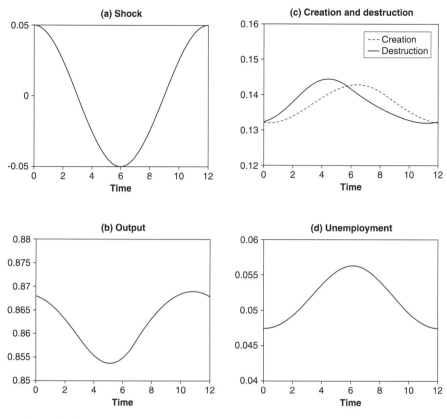

Figure 4.4
Business cycle in search model with convex adjustment costs

pect of the coupling of creation and destruction in an efficient economy. In chapter 5, I return to this extreme synchronization on the efficient path to argue that its absence in the data is likely to reflect the presence of the sort of inefficiency described in chapter 3.

4.2.6   Determining the Path of Wages

For completeness, before concluding this chapter let us characterize one possible path of actual wages in the efficient economy.

For a job created at t_0, the present value of *actual* wages $w(t)A(t)$ at t_0 exceeds the shadow wage $v(t)A(t)$ by the worker's share of appropriable quasi-rents, equal to $\beta S(t_0)$. To determine the exact path for wages that support the renegotiation-proof agreement one needs to specify how the firm recovers the protected part of its investment if it decides to part with the worker. Let us assume that in the event of a break the firm can use its nonspecific capital (the value of which deteriorates over time) in a relationship with another worker, for which it needs to incur the search cost again.

Note that the present value of remaining wage payments at any time $t \in [t_0, t_0 + T(t_0)]$ for a unit created at t_0 can be expressed as

$$\int_t^{t_0+T(t_0)} w(s; t_0)A(s)e^{-(r+\delta)(s-t)} \, ds$$

$$= \int_t^{t_0+T(t_0)} v(s)A(s)e^{-(r+\delta)(s-t)} \, ds + \beta S(t; t_0).$$

The path of wages follows from differentiating this expression with respect to t.

Numerically, this can be done by setting $w(t_0 + T(t_0); t_0) = v(t_0 + T(t_0))$ and then solving backward for $t \in [t_0, t_0 + T(t_0))$ using the expression $w(t; t_0) = v(t) + \beta[S(t; t_0) - S(t + 1; t_0)]/A(t)$, which can be derived from a discrete approximation of the previous expression. However, to do this, one needs an expression for the rent component $\beta S(t; t_0)$.

Let $t^*(t_0) \in [t_0, t_0 + T(t_0)]$ denote the first time the value of the unit's nonspecific capital reaches zero. In the event of a premature separation at time t, the firm finds it profitable to replace the worker if and only if $t < t^*(t_0)$: that is, if the search costs the firm needs to incur in order to find a new worker can be covered by the firm's share of the future stream of profits. At $t = t^*(t_0)$ the firm is exactly indifferent between looking for a new worker or closing down, which means $t^*(t_0)$ is given by

$$A(t^*(t_0))\sigma(t^*(t_0))$$

$$= (1 - \beta) \int_{t^*(t_0)}^{t_0+T(t_0)} [A(t_0) - (p_m(s) + v(s))A(s)]e^{-(r+\delta)(s-t^*(t_0))} \, ds.$$

Thus, for $t \in [t^*(t_0), t_0 + T(t_0)]$ the rent component is given by

$$S(t; t_0) = \pi(t; t_0),$$

where $\pi(t; t_0) = \int_t^{t_0+T(t_0)} [A(t_0) - (p_m(s) + v(s))A(s)]e^{-(r+\delta)(s-t)} \, ds.$

For $t \in [t_0, t^*(t_0)]$ one has to take into account that the firm has a positive outside option, which means the rent component is given by

$$S(t; t_0) = \pi(t; t_0) - [\pi(t; t_0) - \beta S(t; t_0) - A(t)\sigma(t)]$$

$$= \beta S(t; t_0) + A(t)\sigma(t)$$

$$= \frac{1}{1 - \beta} A(t)\sigma(t),$$

where $\beta S(t; t_0)$ is the worker's loss and $A(t)\sigma(t)$ is the firm's loss in the event of separation.

Since the expressions are equal at $t = t^*(t_0)$, one can use a single expression for all $t \in [t_0, t^*(t_0)]$ and $t \in [t^*(t_0), t_0 + T(t_0)]$:

$$S(t; t_0) = \min\left[\frac{1}{1 - \beta} A(t)\sigma(t), \pi(t; t_0)\right].$$

Figure 4.5 presents a simulation of the detrended path of actual wages for the search model with linear adjustment costs. The top panel displays

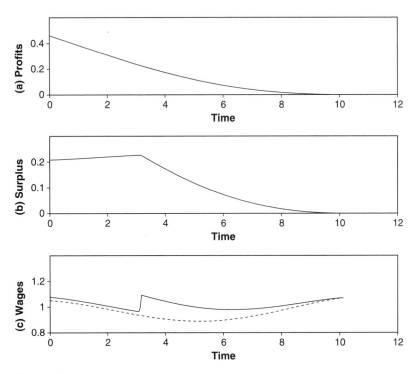

Figure 4.5
Distribution of surplus in search model with linear adjustment costs, starting at the peak of the cycle

the net present value of the firm's future profits at each point in time. The middle reports the total surplus, the detrended value of which is roughly constant until $t^*(t_0)$ and is decreasing afterward. The bottom panel reports the opportunity cost of labor with the dotted line and the actual wage with the solid line. The actual wage rate tracks the opportunity cost of wages closely up to $t^*(t_0)$. After $t^*(t_0)$ the actual wage rate jumps as the worker's ability to extract rents rises, owing to the fact that he or she cannot be replaced by the firm.

4.3 Conclusion

At the end of this chapter, we find ourselves with either limited unemployment and quantity fluctuations for reasonable elasticity values of the true labor supply schedule (first model), or with the right amplitude but wrong comovement of job flows (efficient search model). In the next chapters I show how reintroducing the appropriability problems we discussed in chapter 3 solves both problems.

4.4 Appendix: Numerical Computations

All numerical computations use a creation cost function of the form

$$I_H(H) = c_0 + c_1 H, \qquad \text{with } c_0, c_1 \geq 0,$$

and a sinusoidal business-cycle function

$$p_m(t) = p + \alpha \sin(t).$$

The solution procedure consists of making an initial guess for the path of one of the variables, computing the values for the other variables consistent with this guess, and then updating the initial guess until reaching a fixed point.

4.4.1 Numerical Calculations for the Basic Dynamic Model of Restructuring with Convex Creation Costs

For the first model in this section the labor supply takes the form

$$v(E) = kE^{\eta}.$$

The parameters are $c_0 = 0.08$, $c_1 = 1.5$, $\gamma = 0.021$, $\delta = 0.094$, $r = 0.016$, $p = 0.275$, $\alpha = 0.05$, $\eta = 2$, and $k = 0.57$.

The system begins with the path of E corresponding to the steady-state value for employment. I then find the opportunity cost of labor using the labor supply function, and then $\bar{a}$ can be calculated using this information and the exit condition (4.8). The next step is to compute the path for T using the perfect-foresight condition (4.10), after which a guess for the path of H follows from the entry condition (4.7). A new initial guess for employment is obtained by taking the average of the initial guess and the employment path that follows from equation (4.1). This procedure is repeated until the updated employment path is arbitrarily close to the input path.

4.4.2 Numerical Calculations for the Opportunity Cost View of Recessions Model

The search cost function takes the form

$$\sigma(H, U) = c_2 \left(\frac{H}{U}\right)^{\eta/(1-\eta)}, \qquad \text{with } 0 \leq \eta < 1 \text{ and } c_2 \geq 0,$$

which can be derived from the constant-returns, Cobb-Douglas matching function $H = \xi U^{\eta} V^{1-\eta}$.

Numerical Calculations for the Opportunity Cost View of Recessions with Linear Creation Costs The parameters are $c_0 = 0.23$, $c_1 = 0$, $c_2 = 0.04$, $\gamma = 0.021$, $\delta = 0.094$, $r = 0.016$, $\eta = 0.5$, $\rho = 0.275$, and $\alpha = 0.05$.

This system can be solved in two blocks. The first block uses equations (4.20)–(4.23) and yields a path for H/U, while the second takes the latter path as given and finds H and U separately from equation (4.24).

I start off with an initial guess for the path of σ equal to the steady-state value for σ^* when $\bar{p}_m = p$. I then compute the path for H/U using the search function, for v using condition (4.22), for $\bar{a}$ using the exit condition (4.21) and for T using the perfect-foresight condition (4.23). Next an updated value for sigma is computed using the entry condition (4.20), since the investment costs do not depend on H. Iteration over σ proceeds until a fixed point is reached.

Numerical Calculations for the Opportunity Cost View of Recessions with Convex Creation Costs The parameters are $c_0 = 0.02$, $c_1 = 1.5$,

$c_2 = 0.04$, $\gamma = 0.021$, $\delta = 0.094$, $r = 0.016$, $\eta = 0.5$, $\rho = 0.275$, and $\alpha = 0.05$.

With convex investment costs one can no longer solve the two blocks separately, since equations (4.20)–(4.23) depend not only on the ratio H/U, but also on H. This means one has to iterate on the whole system jointly.

Given an initial guess for the path of v, the path for $\bar{a}$ follows from the exit condition (4.21), that of T from the perfect-foresight condition (4.23) and that of the opportunity cost of labor v from the exit condition (4.21).

The ratio H/U and σ are computed using the free-entry condition (4.22), the Hosios condition and the functional form for search costs specified earlier, which allow us to write

$$\frac{H}{U} = \left(\frac{v}{c_2}\right)^{1-\eta},$$

$$\sigma = \frac{v}{H/U}\frac{1-\eta}{\eta}.$$

Next, I compute H using the entry condition (4.20), unemployment using equation (4.24), and the opportunity cost of labor v using the search cost function.

Finally, to improve convergence properties, it is useful to take a weighted average of the initial guess and the updated value for v to make a new guess and repeat the whole procedure until the updated value is arbitrarily close to the initial guess.

Note

1. This chapter is based on Caballero and Hammour (1994, 1996).

References and Suggested Readings

Acemoglu, Daron, and Robert Shimer. 1999. "Holdups and Efficiency with Search Frictions." *International Economic Review* 40(4): 827–850.

Aghion, Philippe, and Peter Howitt. 1992. "A Model of Growth through Creative Destruction." *Econometrica* 60(2): 323–352.

Aghion, Philippe, and Peter Howitt. 1994. "Growth and Unemployment." *Review of Economic Studies* 61(3): 477–494.

Aghion, Philippe, and Gilles Saint-Paul. 1998. "Virtues of Bad Times." *Macroeconomic Dynamics* 2(3): 322–344.

Baily, Martin N., Charles Hulten, and David Campbell. 1992. "Productivity Dynamics in Manufacturing Plants." *Brookings Papers on Economic Activity: Microeconomics* 1992: 187–249.

Barlevy, Gadi. 2004. "On the Timing of Innovation in Stochastic Schumpeterian Growth Models." NBER Working Paper No. 10741.

Bartelsman, Eric J., and Phoebus J. Dhrymes. 1994. "Productivity Dynamics: U.S. Manufacturing Plants, 1972–1986." Working paper, Finance and Economics Discussion Series 94-1, Board of Governors of the Federal Reserve System.

Binmore, Kenneth, Ariel Rubinstein, and Asher Wolinsky. 1986. "The Nash Bargaining Solution in Economic Modeling." *Rand Journal of Economics* 17(2): 176–188.

Blanchard, Olivier J., and Peter A. Diamond. 1989. "The Beveridge Curve." *Brookings Papers on Economic Activity*, no. 1: 1–60.

Blanchard, Olivier J., and Peter A. Diamond. 1990. "The Cyclical Behavior of the Gross Flows of U.S. Workers." *Brookings Papers on Economic Activity*, no. 2: 85–143.

Bresnahan, Timothy F., and Daniel M. G. Raff. 1991. "Intra-Industry Heterogeneity and the Great Depression: The American Motor Vehicles Industry, 1929–35." *Journal of Economic History* 51(2): 317–331.

Bresnahan, Timothy F., and Daniel M. G. Raff. 1992. "Technological Heterogeneity, Adjustment Costs, and the Dynamics of Plant-Shutdown Behavior: The American Motor Vehicle Industry in the Time of the Great Depression." Mimeo., Stanford University.

Caballero, Ricardo J., and Mohamad L. Hammour. 1994. "The Cleansing Effect of Recessions." *American Economic Review* 84(5): 1350–1368.

Caballero, Ricardo J., and Mohamad L. Hammour. 1996. "On the Timing and Efficiency of Creative Destruction." *Quarterly Journal of Economics* 111(3): 805–852.

Caballero, Ricardo J., and Mohamad L. Hammour. 2005. "The Cost of Recessions Revisited: A Reverse-Liquidationist View." *Review of Economic Studies* 72: 313–341.

Coase, Ronald. 1937. "The Nature of the Firm." *Economica* 4(4): 386–405.

Cooper, Russell, and John C. Haltiwanger. 1993. "The Aggregate Implications of Machine Replacement: Theory and Evidence." *American Economic Review* 83(3): 360–380.

Cox, W. Michael, and Richard Alm. 1992. "The Churn: The Paradox of Progress." In *1992 Annual Report*. Dallas, Tex.: Federal Reserve Bank of Dallas.

Davis, Steven J. 1987. "Fluctuations in the Pace of Labor Reallocation." *Carnegie-Rochester Conference Series on Public Policy* 27: 335–402.

Davis, Steven J., and John C. Haltiwanger. 1990. "Gross Job Creation and Destruction: Microeconomic Evidence and Macroeconomic Implications." In

Olivier J. Blanchard and Stanley Fischer, eds., *NBER Macroeconomics Annual 1990*, vol. 5, 123–168. Cambridge, Mass.: The MIT Press.

Davis, Steven J., and John C. Haltiwanger. 1992. "Gross Job Creation, Gross Job Destruction and Employment Reallocation." *Quarterly Journal of Economics* 107(3): 819–864.

Davis, Steven J., and John C. Haltiwanger. 1999. "On the Driving Forces behind Cyclical Movements in Employment and Job Reallocation." *American Economic Review* 89(5): 1234–1258.

Diamond, Peter A. 1982. "Wage Determination and Efficiency in Search Equilibrium." *Review of Economic Studies* 49(2): 217–227.

Diamond, Peter A. 1994. *On Time*. Cambridge, UK: Cambridge University Press.

Galí, Jordi, and Mohamad L. Hammour. 1992. "Long Run Effects of Business Cycles." Mimeo., Columbia University.

Gorecki, Henryk, S. Fuksa, P. Grabowski, and A. Korytowski. 1989. *Analysis and Synthesis of Time Delay Systems*. New York: Wiley.

Greenwood, Jeremy, Zvi Herkowitz, and Per Krusell. 1992. "Macroeconomic Implications of Investment-Specific Technological Change." Institute for International Economic Studies Seminar Paper No. 527.

Grossman, Gene M., and Elhanan Helpman. 1991. *Innovation and Growth in the Global Economy*. Cambridge, Mass.: The MIT Press.

Grout, Paul A. 1984. "Investment and Wages in the Absence of Binding Contracts: A Nash Bargaining Approach." *Econometrica* 52(2): 449–460.

Hall, Robert E. 1991. "Labor Demand, Labor Supply, and Employment Volatility." In Olivier J. Blanchard and Stanley Fischer, eds., *NBER Macroeconomics Annual 1991*, vol. 6, 17–47. Cambridge, Mass.: The MIT Press.

Hart, Oliver, and John Moore. 1988. "Incomplete Contracts and Renegotiation." *Econometrica* 56(4): 755–786.

Hosios, Arthur J. 1990. "On the Efficiency of Matching and Related Models of Search and Unemployment." *Review of Economic Studies* 57(2): 279–298.

Howitt, Peter, and R. Preston McAfee. 1987. "Costly Search and Recruiting." *International Economic Review* 28(1): 89–107.

Hulten, Charles R. 1992. "Growth Accounting When Technical Change Is Embodied in Capital." *American Economic Review* 82(4): 964–980.

Johansen, Leif. 1959. "Substitution versus Fixed Production Coefficients in the Theory of Economic Growth: A Synthesis." *Econometrica* 27(2): 157–176.

Johnson, George, and Richard Layard. 1987. "The Natural Rate of Unemployment: Explanation and Policy." In Orley Ashenfelter and Richard Layard, eds., *Handbook of Labor Economics*, 921–999. Amsterdam: North-Holland.

Katz, Lawrence F. 1986. "Efficiency Wage Theories: A Partial Evaluation." In Stanley Fischer, ed., *NBER Macroeconomics Annual 1986*, vol. 1, 235–276. Cambridge, Mass.: The MIT Press.

Klein, Benjamin, Robert G. Crawford, and Armen A. Alchian. 1978. "Vertical Integration, Appropriable Rents, and the Competitive Contracting Process." *Journal of Law and Economics* 21(2): 297–326.

Layard, Richard, Stephen Nickell, and Richard Jackman. 1991. *Unemployment: Macroeconomic Performance and the Labor Market.* Oxford: Oxford University Press.

Lindbeck, Assar, and Dennis Snower. 1986. "Wage Setting, Unemployment and Insider-Outsider Relations." *American Economic Review* 76(2): 235–239.

Mortensen, Dale T. 1978. "Specific Capital and Labor Turnover." *Bell Journal of Economics* 9(2): 572–586.

Mortensen, Dale T. 1982. "Property Rights in Mating, Races, and Related Games." *American Economic Review* 72(5): 968–979.

Mortensen, Dale T. 1994. "The Cyclical Behavior of Job and Worker Flows." *Journal of Economic Dynamics and Control* 18(6): 1121–1142.

Mortensen, Dale T., and E. Nagypal. 2005. "More on Unemployment and Vacancy Fluctuations." NBER Working Paper No. 11692.

Mortensen, Dale T., and Christopher Pissarides. 1993. "The Cyclical Behavior of Job Creation and Job Destruction." In J. C. Ours, G. A. Pfann, and G. Ridder, eds., *Labor Demand and Equilibrium Wage Formation*, 201–222. Amsterdam: North-Holland.

Mortensen, Dale T., and Christopher A. Pissarides. 1994. "Job Creation and Job Destruction in the Theory of Unemployment." *Review of Economic Studies* 61(3): 397–415.

Phelps, Edmund S. 1963. "Substitution, Fixed Proportions, Growth and Distribution." *International Economic Review* 4(3): 265–288.

Pissarides, Christopher. 1985. "Short-Run Equilibrium Dynamics of Unemployment, Vacancies, and Real Wages." *American Economic Review* 75(4): 676–690.

Pissarides, Christopher. 2000. *Equilibrium Unemployment Theory*, 2nd ed. Cambridge, Mass.: The MIT Press.

Saint-Paul, Gilles. 1993. "Productivity Growth and the Structure of the Business Cycle." *European Economic Review* 37(4): 861–883.

Salter, Wilfred. 1960. *Productivity and Technical Change.* Cambridge, U.K.: Cambridge University Press.

Schumpeter, Joseph A. 1942. *Capitalism, Socialism, and Democracy.* New York: Harper and Brothers.

Sheshinski, Eytan. 1967. "Balanced Growth and Stability in the Johansen Vintage Model." *Review of Economic Studies* 34(2): 239–248.

Solow, Robert M. 1960. "Investment and Technical Progress." In Kenneth J. Arrow, S. Karlin and P. Suppes, eds., *Mathematical Methods in Social Sciences*, 89–104. Stanford, Calif.: Stanford University Press.

Stiglitz, Joseph. 1993. "Endogenous Growth and Cycles." NBER Working Paper No. 4286.

Von Hayek, F. A. 1931. *Prices and Production*. London: George Routledge and Sons.

Williamson, Oliver E. 1979. "Transaction-Cost Economics: The Governance of Contractual Relations." *Journal of Law and Economics* 22(2): 233–261.

Williamson, Oliver E. 1985. *The Economic Institutions of Capitalism*. New York: Free Press.

Young, Alwyn. 1992. "A Tale of Two Cities: Factor Accumulation and Technical Change in Hong Kong and Singapore." In Olivier J. Blanchard and Stanley Fischer, eds., *NBER Macroeconomics Annual 1992*, vol. 7, 13–54. Cambridge, Mass.: The MIT Press.

III

Inefficient Restructuring

5

Inefficient Restructuring

This chapter integrates the relationship specificity discussed in chapter 3 with chapter 4's exploration of technological specificity and restructuring. In particular, it highlights the implications of incomplete contracts for the average and cyclical behavior of job flows, unemployment, and vacancies.[1]

5.1 Search Frictions and Bargaining

I first explore search inefficiencies and their implications for flows observed over the business cycle before developing the chapter's main theme. As I discussed before, search costs naturally yield an incomplete-contracts problem, since these costs are incurred before the bargaining parties meet. But the standard macroeconomic search model also comes bundled with other components primarily linked to the matching function, which dominate the cyclical features of these models. I contend that, at least for the cyclical aspects of flows, it is the incomplete-contracts aspect of the problem rather than the matching friction that seems most relevant and hence ought to be emphasized. This is one of the main messages of this chapter.

Let us continue building the "opportunity cost" model developed in section 4.2. I use the functional forms for creation costs and search costs given in section 4.4, which are

$$I_H(H) = c_0 + c_1 H, \qquad \text{with } c_0, c_1 \geq 0,$$

$$\sigma(H, U) = c_2 \left(\frac{H}{U}\right)^{\eta/(1-\eta)}, \qquad \text{with } 0 \leq \eta < 1 \text{ and } c_2 \geq 0.$$

Importantly, I relax the Diamond-Hosios efficiency condition so that $\beta \neq \eta$.

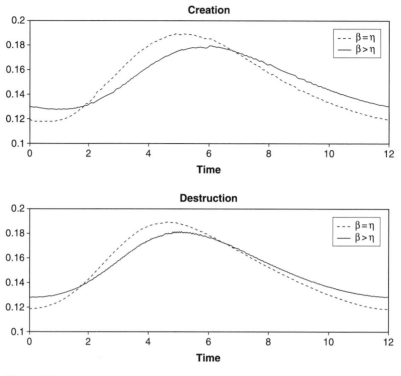

Figure 5.1
Distorted volatility

Figure 5.1 compares an efficient economy with linear adjustment costs to the corresponding inefficient economy with $\beta > \eta$. The top panel compares these two economies' cyclical creation responses, and the bottom one compares their respective destruction responses. It is clear that in both the efficient and inefficient economies creation and destruction are concentrated near the trough of a recession, but not to the same extent. While the same intertemporal substitution incentives are at work in both economies, these incentives are distorted in the inefficient one. When workers (insiders) are too strong ($\beta > \eta$), economic restructuring is inefficiently low during recessions (the case shown in the figure); when workers are too weak ($\beta < \eta$) the opposite situation happens, and the economy restructures excessively during recessions.

The reason why stronger-than-efficient insiders lead to insufficient restructuring during recessions is that a large worker share β of the bargainable surplus $S(t)$ means that only a small share of that surplus enters the free-entry condition (4.16). This dampens the effect of cyclical fluctuations on the entry condition and the related intertemporal substitution incentive. Moreover, the shadow wage rate (4.18) is excessively responsive to H/U, and overly accommodates fluctuations in profitability. The opposite happens when β is too low.

To summarize, in search-based models of creative destruction—such as the one developed by Mortensen and Pissarides (1993)—the economy's response to transitory aggregate fluctuations in profitability is driven by intertemporal substitution incentives to concentrate *both* creation and destruction near the trough of a recession. What search inefficiencies mostly disrupt is the extent to which restructuring is concentrated during cyclical downturns.

Of course, this does not mean that one cannot generate negative comovement across flows within a search model, but simply that some additional components will be responsible for that negative comovement. For example, Mortensen (1994) shows how adding an on-the-job search component recovers some of the negative comovement between job creation and destruction present in the data. Also, the rightly celebrated Mortensen and Pissarides (1994) model can generate negative comovement, but this feature depends on a delicate timing assumption: they assume that workers whose jobs are destroyed at time t only join the unemployment pool (and enter the matching function) at time $t + \Delta t$. Thus, a negative shock that increases destruction this period only leads to high unemployment and cheaper creation in the next period. This leads firms to delay creation from this period until the next, giving rise to a *negative* contemporaneous correlation between creation and destruction, an effect that is present even in an efficient economy. The "synchronization" between creation and destruction I have highlighted in this chapter lies in the *positive* correlation Mortensen and Pissarides (1993) document between destruction at t and creation at $t + \Delta t$. The issue of how small Δt is relative to the sampling frequency then becomes very important, which is an unpleasant modeling feature. In contrast, the continuous-time/continuous sample path model described in this chapter ignores this mechanism by construction, and hence allows us to focus on more robust features behind flows' comovement.

Finally, if η is reduced to zero while keeping $\beta > 0$, then the negative comovement between flows can be recovered, as demonstrated by Caballero and Hammour (1996) and Rogerson and Cole (1998). But in this case there is no longer a useful role for unemployment in facilitating microeconomic reallocation; hence unemployment is exclusively the result of incomplete contracts as described in chapter 3. This is the model I discuss next.

5.2   Decoupled Restructuring

The problem of incomplete contracts has implications for the economy's cyclical response that go beyond the distorted intertemporal-substitution incentives related to search inefficiencies. Incomplete contracting problems can derail the reallocation process over the course of the business cycle and *decouple* the connection between creation and destruction, both in terms of synchronization and joint smoothing. In the inefficient economy characterized by incomplete contracts, recessions become times of wasteful unemployment not associated with greater reallocation activity.

In order to see this inefficient restructuring most clearly, let us return to $\beta = 1/2$ and ignore search costs for a while. In this situation there is neither unemployment nor economic fluctuations if there is no appropriability problem, so let us reintroduce unprotected specificity and set $\phi > 0$. That is, part of the firm's investment in creating the job is sunk in the relationship (e.g., training costs).

With these modifications, the appropriable surplus can be written as

$$S(t) = \int_t^{t+T(t)} [A(t) - (p_m(s) + v(s))A(s)]e^{-(r+\delta)(s-t)} \, ds$$
$$- (1 - \phi)I_H(t)A(t). \tag{5.1}$$

Since workers and firms split the quasi-rents equally, the firm's free-entry condition requires that

$$\phi I_H(t)A(t) = \frac{1}{2}S(t),$$

which translates into

$$(1 + \phi)I_H(t) = \int_t^{t+T(t)} \left[1 - (p_m(s) + v(s))\frac{A(s)}{A(t)}\right]e^{-(r+\delta)(s-t)} \, ds. \tag{5.2}$$

The equilibrium shadow wage rate $v(t)A(t)$ is now

$$v(t)A(t) = \frac{H(t)}{U(t)}\frac{1}{2}S(t) = \frac{H(t)}{U(t)}\phi I_H(t)A(t). \tag{5.3}$$

In the basic model set forth in chapter 4, whether it is creation or destruction that responds most strongly to the business cycle depends on the characteristics of creation costs. In particular, if c_1 is small, and there is little motive to smooth creation over the business cycle, the economy exhibits a strong response along its creation margin. If, on the contrary, c_1 is relatively large, then the economy responds mostly on its destruction margin.

Figure 5.2 illustrates two cases with the same average adjustment cost but different functional forms. The top panel depicts the behavior of flows with linear adjustment costs (large c_0 and small c_1). In this case there is a

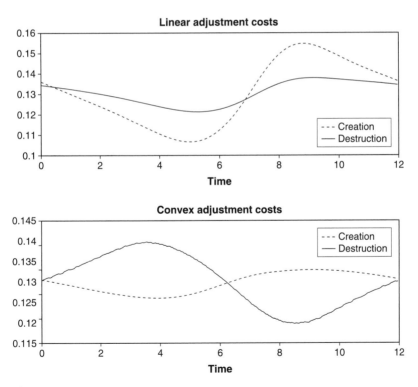

Figure 5.2
Business cycles in an inefficient economy

strong reaction on the creation margin at the bottom of the cycle, which also leads to a milder rise in destruction when these firms become obsolete. The bottom panel depicts the convex adjustment cost case, in which there is an incentive to smooth creation and destruction absorbs most of the inefficient adjustment.

Recently, a vigorous new debate has arisen on whether it is creation or destruction that is mainly responsible for the buildup in unemployment during recessions (see box 5.1). Based on evidence from the United States, the emerging consensus seems to be that earlier American business cycles have been driven by destruction, but that creation and destruction played equal parts during the recession of the early 2000s. Whether this is a permanent pattern change or something specific to the last recession is still unknown. Either way, the figure shows clearly that the generic implication of the appropriability problem is to break the synchronization between creation and destruction; it is this decoupling that is responsible for the inefficient rise in involuntary unemployment during recessions, as hinted in chapter's 3 static model.

5.3   Covert and Overt Rigidity

The decoupling between creation and destruction is ultimately due to the fact that incomplete contracting induces a form of rigidity in shadow wages, which requires the quantity movements of lower creation and higher unemployment for wages to fall during a recession. Yet the extent of those quantity effects may be such that little trace of the underlying rigidity remains on the equilibrium path of the shadow (and actual) wage rate. The extreme case of this result comes about when marginal creation costs are constant ($c_1 = 0$). In this instance, the cyclical response of the creation margin induces a one-to-one response in the shadow wage rate to cyclical fluctuations in $p_m(t)$, thus fully insulating the destruction margin. Although the shadow wage rate varies as much as it would in an efficient economy, it harbors a hidden form of rigidity in the quantity movements required to induce this wage response. That is, wage rigidity is covert.

When marginal costs of creation are increasing, there is an incentive to smooth H fluctuations and the shadow wage rate does not display a one-

Box 5.1
On the cyclical behavior of job flows: Is it job creation or destruction?

The conventional wisdom of the 1990s, that a sharp rise in job destruction rather than a drop in job creation is the main culprit for net job losses during recessions (see, e.g., Darby, Haltiwanger, and Plant 1986; Blanchard and Diamond 1990; Davis and Haltiwanger 1990, 1992) appears to be in contradiction with the recent work by Shimer (2005a, 2005b) and Hall (2005). The latter have documented that in the United States there are substantial procyclical fluctuations in unemployed workers' job finding probability, while the separation probability is mainly acyclic.

Although the empirical and theoretical work of Shimer and Hall is stimulating and insightful, I believe it has been misinterpreted. It offers useful complementary facts and points to fruitful dimensions along which models should be enriched, but it has little to say about the relative importance of job creation and destruction over the business cycle. First, the evidence refers to workers rather than job flows. Second, much of the cyclicality of the job finding rate comes *not* from the hiring in the numerator, but from the unemployment in the denominator. The view that the initial burst in unemployment is triggered by job destruction that finds an unresponsive job creation side is perfectly consistent with a very procyclical job finding rate and a relatively acyclic separation rate (which is divided by less volatile employment rather than by unemployment and contains countercyclical quits which are not part of job destruction). In fact, I ran simple regressions with manufacturing job flows data to proxy for economy-wide job flows and found that the job finding probability is negatively correlated with job destruction and *uncorrelated* with job creation.

These points and beyond have been made by Davis (2005) and by Kennan (2005), both commenting on Hall (2005). Davis argues that in order to explain the increase in worker flows during recessions, there must either be a significant increase in job destruction or an increase in the probability that separated workers move into unemployment. He then shows that during recessions there is an increase in *both* the flow of workers from unemployment to employment $(U \rightarrow E)$ *and* from employment to unemployment $(E \rightarrow U)$. He argues through simulations that a decrease in the monthly job-finding probability of the type observed in the data during recessions cannot replicate the flows. In particular, the simulated $(E \rightarrow U)$ flows increase very modestly relative to what we observe during U.S. recessions, and the $(U \rightarrow E)$ flows exhibit the wrong sign. He concludes that one needs to add a sizeable increase in the job destruction rate in order to match the facts.

Davis also presents evidence that (1) the ratio of layoffs to quits exhibits strong countercyclical behavior and (2) layoffs comove with the countercyclical job destruction rate but not with the job creation rate.

Box 5.1
(continued)

> Kennan (2005) focuses on the timing of worker flows. He argues that if the job finding probability rather than job destruction were the main factor driving an increase in unemployment during recessions, then it should decrease at the very beginning of a recession while the $(E \to U)$ transition should increase later. He then tests and rejects this implication using data from unemployment insurance claims during the 2001 U.S. recession. This is strong evidence in favor of the job-destruction-driven view, since it is generally accepted that the 2001 recession is unrepresentative: the usual spike in job destruction was less of a factor this time than in the average U.S. recession over the period since the 1970s.
>
> Fujita and Ramey (2006) use CPS worker flow data to calculate the cyclical component of the job loss hazard rate. They show that this component spikes during recessions, which provides further evidence for a separation-driven view of the business cycle.
>
> It is certain that we have not witnessed the conclusion of this debate. However, the messages that structural models should pay attention to both margins and that constant-returns matching models à la Mortensen-Pissarides (1994) have a hard time explaining why the job finding rate plummets during recessions, when hiring is cheap, are sound. Moreover, these concerns are consistent with the discussion and type of models developed in this book, where both margins interact through equilibrium prices, and with the central role played by the concept of *decoupling* in the central, incomplete-contracts scenario. Nonetheless, these facts also highlight an important omission of this book, which is the large component of worker flows not related to job flows.

to-one response to changes in $p_m(t)$. This causes a cyclical response on the destruction margin. In this situation, the shadow wage rate exhibits a mixture of "covert" and "overt" rigidity.

5.4   The Slope of the Beveridge Curve

Let us return to the more general model being developed and reintroduce search costs with workers' bargaining parameter β. The surplus must now cover the appropriable component of capital and the search cost:

$$(\phi I_H(t) + \sigma(t))A(t) = (1 - \beta)S(t),$$

which translates into

$$\left(1 + \frac{\phi\beta}{1-\beta}\right)I_H(t) + \frac{\sigma(t)}{1-\beta}$$

$$= \int_t^{t+T(t)}\left[1 - (p_m(s) + v(s))\frac{A(s)}{A(t)}\right]e^{-(r+\delta)(s-t)}\,ds.$$

Therefore, following the same procedures as in chapter 4, an equilibrium for this economy is a path $\{\bar{a}(t), H(t), U(t)\}_{t\geq 0}$ that satisfies the following equations:

$$c(t) = \int_t^{t+T(t)}(1 - e^{-\gamma(\bar{a}(s)-s+t)})e^{-(r+\delta)(s-t)}\,ds, \tag{5.4}$$

$$\bar{a}(t) = -\frac{1}{\gamma}\ln(p_m(t) + v(t)), \tag{5.5}$$

$$v(t) = \frac{H(t)}{U(t)}\beta\frac{S(t)}{A(t)} = \frac{H(t)}{U(t)}\frac{\beta}{1-\beta}(\phi I_H(t) + \sigma(t)), \tag{5.6}$$

where

$$c(t) = \left(1 + \frac{\phi\beta}{1-\beta}\right)I_H(t) + \frac{\sigma(t)}{1-\beta},$$

$$\bar{a}(t + T(t)) = T(t), \tag{5.7}$$

$$U(t) = \bar{L} - \int_0^{\bar{a}(t)} H(t-a)e^{-\delta a}\,da. \tag{5.8}$$

The next two sections will characterize the implications of efficient search unemployment and inefficient incomplete contracts for the slope of the Beveridge curve. While in each of these models the slope of the Beveridge curve depends on parameter values, the main point is that search unemployment has a tendency to produce an upward-sloping Beveridge curve, while incomplete contracts unemployment naturally yields a downward-sloping curve, as observed in the data. The main force behind the downward-sloping tendency of the incomplete-contracts model is the decoupling of job flows emphasized previously.

5.4.1 Efficient Unemployment

In the current model, efficient unemployment can only arise if search costs are positive. Figure 5.3 plots the behavior of an efficient economy with linear adjustment costs on the left panels and convex adjustment costs on the right panels.

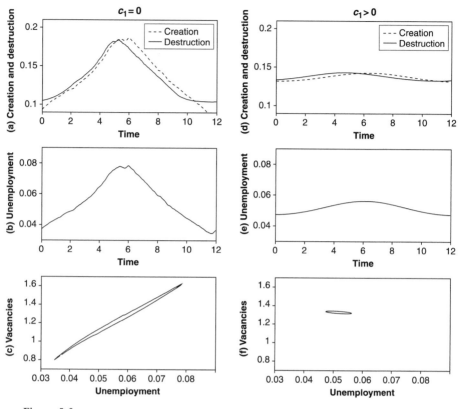

Figure 5.3
Beveridge curves in efficient economy

The panels on the left reveal the strong synchronizing incentives for gross flows and of unemployment's role as a reallocation device in an efficient economy. In this example, not only does creation rise as unemployment rises—which could be the direct result of higher unemployment in the matching function—but creation efforts (vacancy posting) also rise. The result is an upward-sloping Beveridge curve.

The synchronization incentives still remain when convex adjustment costs are reintroduced (shown on the right panels), but as these rise the efficient economy essentially shuts down the cyclical aspects of restructuring, as the incentive to smooth creation also implies an incentive to smooth destruction (the opposite of what happens in the inefficient economy). In this case, with sufficient convexity, the Beveridge curve can turn into a downward-sloping curve, as illustrated in panel (f), but

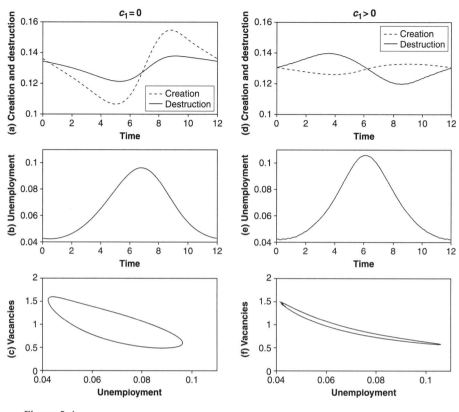

Figure 5.4
Beveridge curves in inefficient economy

the dominant feature is the absence of significant fluctuations rather than
the slope of the curve.

5.4.2   Inefficient Unemployment

As we have already seen, unemployment can arise in an incomplete-
contracts economy even if there are no search costs (which I again
suppress here). Figure 5.4 plots the behavior of an economy with linear
adjustment costs on the left panels and convex adjustment costs on
the right panels. The message is clear: now the Beveridge curve is
downward-sloping, regardless of the convexity of adjustment costs.

Appropriability decouples creation and destruction not only in terms
of timing, but also in terms of amplitude. Recall that in an efficient

economy with search and convex adjustment costs, there is a motive to smooth creation over the business cycle, and the efficient economy also smooths destruction. This joint smoothing behavior breaks down in the presence of appropriability. Incomplete contracting not only disrupts the precise timing of destruction being followed by immediate creation, but also breaks their joint smoothing pattern. The right panels in figure 5.4 show that by limiting the cyclical responsiveness of the shadow wage rate, creation smoothing exacerbates rather than dampens the volatility in destruction and leads to asymmetries in their respective volatilities. In this inefficient case, destruction is too volatile and occurs too early relative to creation, leading to an unnecessarily prolonged and volatile period of (inefficient) unemployment accumulation.

There is substantial evidence that the Beveridge curve is downward-sloping in most countries where such a curve has been plotted (see, e.g., Johnson and Layard 1987; Layard, Nickell, and Jackman 1991). In the literature on the relative importance of reallocation versus aggregate shocks during recessions, it has been taken for granted that aggregate shocks ought to generate a downward-sloping Beveridge curve. The point of this section, however, is to argue that such a slope probably reflects not only the relative importance of aggregate shocks, but also the presence of a labor market inefficiency, perhaps of the appropriability type highlighted in chapter 3. Absent this inefficiency, or of an equivalent flat, quasi-labor supply mechanism, aggregate shocks tend to generate a counterfactual upward-sloping Beveridge curve as in the efficient search economy portrayed in figure 5.3.

This is not to say that technological frictions alone cannot generate a downward-sloping Beveridge curve. For example, Shimer (2005c) has recently proposed a complementary view where unemployment occurs when the number of workers attached to an occupation in a given location is higher than the number of jobs available to them. Furthermore, firms and workers move randomly between different labor markets. Although the assumption that no voluntary mobility occurs (either geographical or between jobs) is a bit extreme, this alternative model captures the downward slope of the Beveridge curve extremely well. It is interesting to note, however, that the technological assumptions in Shimer's model resemble the rationing results that emerge from specificity and incomplete contracts, and in this sense part of his framework

Box 5.2
The reallocation vs. aggregate shocks debate

Lilien (1982) argues that shocks to the desired allocation of employment across sectors (reallocation shocks) can cause a fall in aggregate employment and an increase in unemployment if there are substantial frictions in the reallocation of factors across sectors. He supports his claim with the observed positive correlation between the unemployment rate and the dispersion of employment growth across sectors in the United States. He argues that about 50 percent of the variance of unemployment over the postwar period is related to changes in the unemployment due to the slow adjustment across sectors. Abraham and Katz (1986) question the existence of a causal relationship from sectoral shifts to aggregate unemployment. They argue that Lilien's finding could be obtained from purely aggregate shocks as long as sectors have different cyclical sensitivity. Moreover, they point out that if reallocation shocks are the driving force of unemployment fluctuations, then the Beveridge Curve should be upward-sloping, which is not the case in the United States.

Much work has followed the original debate (see, e.g., Campbell and Kuttner 1996; Haltiwanger and Schuh 1999; Caballero 1998) with most of the evidence and modeling pointing against a significant contribution of reallocation shocks to unemployment fluctuations.

The models and mechanisms discussed in this chapter are consistent with the Abraham-Katz explanation—with the additional insight that the observed downward-sloping shape of the Beveridge curve is probably not only a symptom of the relative importance of aggregate shocks, but also of the inefficient nature of employment adjustment over the cycle.

may well be a reduced form characterization of the underlying institutional impediments to mobility.

5.5   Average Distortions in Restructuring and Unemployment

Let us now use the dynamic model developed in this chapter to return to studying the effect of incomplete contracts on the pace of creative destruction sketched in chapter 3. Under what conditions will the restructuring of the productive system be excessively slow and result in technological "sclerosis"? When will restructuring be, on the contrary, wastefully rapid and result in what one might call technological "hyperkinesis"? It turns out that regardless of whether insider workers are excessively weak or strong, inefficiency in either direction always leads to sclerosis.

5.5.1 Weak and Strong Insiders

In order to study the pace of creative destruction, let us assume away aggregate shocks and focus on the model's steady state. Since differentiating between c_1 and c_0 is much less interesting in steady state than over the business cycle, let us assume the simpler case with $I_{HH} = 0$ for all steady-state calculations in this chapter.

Let us first derive an "equivalence" result that will be useful in the subsequent analysis. There is a form of steady-state equivalence between the two insider bargaining parameters ϕ and β, which allows us to compensate insiders for a reduction in one parameter by increasing the other. One can thus divide the parameter space into two well-defined regions where insiders are too "weak" or too "strong" relative to the efficient configuration. This enables rankings to be made across elements (ϕ, β) of the parameter space even when one parameter value appears weak and the other parameter value appears strong (e.g., $\beta < \eta$ together with $\phi > 0$).

Let "SS" denote the value of a variable in steady state. A steady state is an equilibrium path with constant $(\bar{a}^{SS}, H^{SS}, U^{SS})$ and requires a constant path for the exogenous variable $\bar{p}_m^{SS}$. In steady state, the economy's equilibrium conditions (5.4)–(5.8) become

$$e^{-\gamma \bar{a}^{SS}} - [\bar{p}_m^{SS} + v^{SS}] = 0, \tag{5.9}$$

$$c^{SS} = PV(\bar{a}^{SS}), \tag{5.10}$$

$$U^{SS} = \bar{L} - H^{SS} \frac{1 - e^{-\delta \bar{a}^{SS}}}{\delta}, \tag{5.11}$$

where

$$v^{SS} = \frac{H^{SS}}{U^{SS}} \frac{\beta}{1 - \beta} [\phi I_H^{SS} + \sigma^{SS}], \tag{5.12}$$

$$c^{SS} = \left(1 + \frac{\beta}{1 - \beta} \phi \right) I_H^{SS} + \frac{1}{1 - \beta} \sigma^{SS}, \tag{5.13}$$

c^{SS} is the shadow cost of creating a new production unit, and

$$PV(\bar{a}^{SS}) = \frac{[1 - e^{-(r+\delta)\bar{a}^{SS}}]}{r + \delta} - \frac{[e^{-\gamma \bar{a}^{SS}} - e^{-(r+\delta)\bar{a}^{SS}}]}{r + \delta - \gamma}. \tag{5.14}$$

The equivalence result can now be stated. Consider an economy with positive search costs ($c_2 > 0$). Consider any pair $(\phi_0, \beta_0) \in [0, 1] \times (0, 1)$,

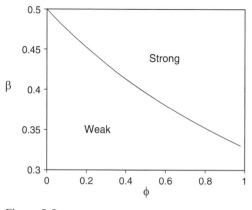

Figure 5.5
Weak vs. strong insiders

and the steady state $(\bar{a}_0^{SS}, H_0^{SS}, U_0^{SS})$ that corresponds to $(\phi, \beta) = (\phi_0, \beta_0)$. Then one can find a (weakly) decreasing function $f_0(\phi)$ over $[0, 1]$ such that, for any $\phi \in [0, 1]$, the corresponding steady state to $(\phi, \beta) = (\phi, f_0(\phi))$ is $(\bar{a}_0^{SS}, H_0^{SS}, U_0^{SS})$. Naturally, one must have $f_0(\phi_0) = \beta_0$.

Another way to state the result is that any steady-state outcome $(\bar{a}_0^{SS}, H_0^{SS}, U_0^{SS})$ corresponds to a whole schedule $(\phi, f_0(\phi))$ of bargaining-position parameters. Quite intuitively, this schedule is decreasing because a rise in one bargaining parameter must be offset by a fall in the other if one is to keep insiders' bargaining position and the steady-state outcome unchanged. It is in this sense that the parameters ϕ and β are "equivalent" *in steady state* (but not over the cycle).

This result allows us to divide the bargaining-position parameter space into two clearly delineated regions of excessively "weak" and "strong" insiders. The solid line in figure 5.5 traces an "efficient" schedule $(\phi, f^E(\phi))$ that corresponds to the efficient steady state. This schedule crosses the β-axis at the point $(\phi, \beta) = (0, \eta)$. All equivalence schedules that start below this point correspond to weaker insiders and remain below the efficient schedule. Note that equivalence schedules cannot cross because each is drawn for a different steady-state equilibrium. All schedules that start above the efficient point correspond to stronger-than-efficient insiders and remain above the efficient schedule. Thus the efficient schedule divides the parameter space into two regions: a region below it where insiders are weak, and a region above it where they are strong.

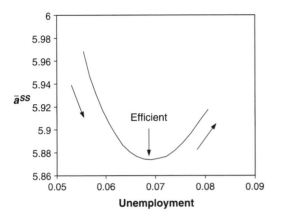

Figure 5.6
Effects of increasing β in steady state

5.5.2   Unemployment and Sclerosis

With the preceding classification of the insiders' bargaining position in steady state, the direction of inefficiency in the two regions can be characterized straightforwardly. It is clear from equations (5.9)–(5.11) that $(U^{SS}, \bar{a}^{SS})$ are sufficient statistics to describe a steady state, since H^{SS} can then be obtained from the unemployment equation (5.11). Let us focus on these two variables.

Under- and Overemployment   Figure 5.6 depicts the curve in $(U^{SS}, \bar{a}^{SS})$ space that is traced out as β increases (the arrows indicate the direction of movement as β increases). The trough of the curve corresponds to the efficient value $\beta = f^E(\phi)$. It is clear that unemployment is increasing with β. In other words, the strong-insiders region is characterized by underemployment, and the weak-insiders region by overemployment. This is what one would expect, given that strong insiders take an excessively large share of quasi-rents and discourage labor demand, while weak insiders take an excessively small share and encourage labor demand. The economy offsets a stronger insider bargaining position with an endogenous rise in unemployment that weakens the outside opportunities of employed workers and restores adequate firm profitability.

Given the equivalence result stated in section 5.5.1, we can focus on the case where $\phi = 0$ and vary β without loss of generality.

Let us define the hiring intensity as $X^{SS} \equiv H^{SS}/U^{SS}$. Replacing v^{SS} from equation (5.12) in exit condition (5.9) and differentiating yields

$$-\gamma e^{-\gamma \bar{a}^{SS}} \, d\bar{a}^{SS} = \frac{\beta \sigma^{SS}}{(1-\beta)(1-\eta)} dX^{SS} + \frac{X^{SS} \sigma^{SS}}{(1-\beta)^2} d\beta.$$

Replacing c^{SS} from equation (5.13) in free-entry condition (5.10) and differentiating yields

$$PV'(\bar{a}^{SS}) \, d\bar{a}^{SS} = \frac{\eta}{1-\eta} \frac{\sigma^{SS}/X^{SS}}{1-\beta} dX^{SS} + \frac{\sigma^{SS}}{(1-\beta)^2} d\beta.$$

Using these two conditions to solve for $d\bar{a}^{SS}$, we get

$$\frac{dX^{SS}}{d\beta} = -\frac{X^{SS}(1-\eta)[PV'(\bar{a}^{SS})X^{SS} + \gamma e^{-\gamma \bar{a}^{SS}}]}{\eta(1-\beta)[(\beta/\eta)PV'(\bar{a}^{SS})X^{SS} + \gamma e^{-\gamma \bar{a}^{SS}}]},$$

which is strictly negative since $PV'(\bar{a}^{SS}) > 0$.

Solving for dX^{SS} rather than $d\bar{a}^{SS}$, we get

$$\frac{d\bar{a}^{SS}}{d\beta} = \frac{\sigma^{SS} X^{SS} (\beta - \eta)}{(1-\beta)^2 [\beta PV'(\bar{a}^{SS})X^{SS} + \eta \gamma e^{-\gamma \bar{a}^{SS}}]}.$$

Thus, $\bar{a}^{SS}$ decreases as the insiders' bargaining position improves when insiders are weak, and the insiders' bargaining position decreases when insiders are strong. A minimum $\bar{a}^{SS}$ is reached at the efficient level of β.

We are now ready to characterize the behavior of unemployment. Differentiating equation (5.11) yields

$$\frac{dU^{SS}}{d\beta} = -\frac{(U^{SS})^2}{\bar{L}} \left[\frac{1 - e^{-\delta \bar{a}^{SS}}}{\delta} \frac{dX^{SS}}{d\beta} + X^{SS} e^{-\delta \bar{a}^{SS}} \frac{d\bar{a}^{SS}}{d\beta} \right].$$

This expression is clearly positive in the weak-insiders region since both X^{SS} and $\bar{a}^{SS}$ decrease as the position of insiders improves. In the strong-insiders region, the effect is ambiguous, but numerical examples suggest that it is positive as well. Furthermore, it is also positive near $\beta = \eta$ since at this point, $dX^{SS}/d\beta < 0$ and $d\bar{a}^{SS}/d\beta \simeq 0$.

Technological Sclerosis   Returning to the scrapping age $\bar{a}^{SS}$, figure 5.6 and the previous equations show that it is minimized at the efficient level of β. Thus, unlike unemployment, the economy exhibits the *same* direction of inefficiency for $\bar{a}^{SS}$ in the regions of weak *and* strong insiders: $\bar{a}^{SS}$ is above its efficient value in both regions. Inefficiencies in both directions always lead to sluggish restructuring and technological sclerosis.

Sclerosis is thus a state of affairs that any economic policy program will most likely have to face. Note that a related result can be found in the search literature: when job matching is stochastic, the "reservation productivity" is maximized at the efficient parameter configuration (see Pissarides 2000).

To gain intuition for this result, let us calculate the aggregate welfare of an economy in steady state. Welfare at time t is given by

$$W(t) = \int_t^\infty \{Q(s) - (I_H(s) + \sigma(s))H(s)A(s) - p_m(s)E(s)A(s)\}e^{-r(s-t)}\,ds,$$

(5.15)

where the first term corresponds to total output $Q(t) = \int_0^{\tilde{a}(t)} A(t-a)H(t-a)e^{-\delta a}\,da$ at each point in time, the second accounts for creation costs and the third for the cost of imported goods.

Detrending and adding and subtracting the shadow price signals yields

$$\frac{W(t)}{A(t)} = \int_t^\infty \{q(s) - [p_m(s) + v(s)]E(s) - c(s)H(s)\}e^{-(r-\gamma)(s-t)}\,ds$$

$$+ \int_t^\infty \{c(s) - I_H(s) - \sigma(s)\}H(s)e^{-(r-\gamma)(s-t)}\,ds$$

$$+ \int_t^\infty v(s)E(s)e^{-(r-\gamma)(s-t)}\,ds,$$

(5.16)

where $q(t) \equiv Q(t)/A(t)$.

The first term in equation (5.16) is equal to the shadow quasi-rents $K_0^{SS}(t)$ attributable to the owners of the initial distribution of production units. To see this, use the expressions for employment and output to obtain

$$\int_t^\infty \{q(s) - [p_m(s) + v(s)]E(s)\}e^{-(r-\gamma)(s-t)}\,ds$$

$$= \int_t^\infty \left\{ \int_0^{\tilde{a}(s)} [e^{-\gamma a} - p_m(s) - v(s)]H(s-a)e^{-\delta a}\,da \right\}e^{-(r-\gamma)(s-t)}\,ds$$

$$= \int_t^{t+T(t)} \left\{ \int_{s-t}^{\tilde{a}(s)} [e^{-\gamma a} - p_m(s) - v(s)]H(s-a)e^{-\delta a}\,da \right\}e^{-(r-\gamma)(s-t)}\,ds$$

$$+ \int_t^\infty \left\{ \int_0^{\min(s-t,\tilde{a}(s))} [e^{-\gamma a} - p_m(s) - v(s)]H(s-a)e^{-\delta a}\,da \right\}e^{-(r-\gamma)(s-t)}\,ds$$

$$= K_0^{SS}(t) + \int_t^\infty c(s)H(s)e^{-(r-\gamma)(s-t)}\,ds$$

by the free-entry condition.

The second term in equation (5.16) is equal to the detrended shadow wage received by the unemployed. Since $c(s) = I_H(s) + \frac{1}{1-\beta}\sigma(s)$ and $\sigma(s) = v(s)\frac{U(s)}{H(s)}\frac{1-\beta}{\beta}$, we have that

$$\{c(s) - I_H(s) - \sigma(s)\}H(s) = v(s)U(s). \tag{5.17}$$

Putting everything together, we get the final expression for social welfare:

$$\frac{W(t)}{A(t)} = K_0^{SS}(t) + \int_t^\infty v(s)U(s)e^{-(r-\gamma)(s-t)}\,ds + \int_t^\infty v(s)E(s)e^{-(r-\gamma)(s-t)}\,ds$$

$$= K_0^{SS}(t) + \int_t^\infty v(s)\overline{L}e^{-(r-\gamma)(s-t)}\,ds.$$

In steady state,

$$W^{SS}(t) = \left[K_0^{SS} + \frac{v^{SS}\overline{L}}{r-\gamma}\right]A(t). \tag{5.18}$$

This equation expresses welfare in terms of the *shadow income* flows attributable to different factors of production. The first term K_0^{SS} corresponds to the present value of income that goes to the owners of the *initial* distribution of production units. The second term is the discounted value of shadow income that flows to the workers ($v^{SS}\overline{L}$). Note that the shadow wage goes to both employed and unemployed workers, because the latter also receive an expected flow v^{SS} based on the probability of finding a job (see equation [5.12]).

Next, one needs to compare W^{SS} across steady states that correspond to different configurations of (ϕ, β). The problem is that in order to talk meaningfully about the parameters (ϕ, β) that maximize W^{SS}, one needs to start from the same initial distribution of jobs. But this means that the starting point generally does not correspond to a steady state. For this reason, despite the fact that the results are quite general, let us confine the discussion to the limiting case where $(r - \gamma)$ goes to zero, so that initial conditions do not matter and one can ignore the term K_0^{SS}.

In this case, equation (5.18) shows that the bargaining parameters that maximize welfare are the ones that maximize the shadow wage v^{SS}. But exit condition (5.9), which can be rewritten as

$$v^{SS} = e^{-\gamma\bar{a}^{SS}} - p_m^{SS},$$

implies that maximizing v^{SS} amounts to minimizing $\bar{a}^{SS}$. Thus the efficient parameter configurations are the ones that *minimize* $\bar{a}^{SS}$.

Intuitively, sclerosis in this economy—whether insiders are weak or strong—results from the undervaluation and misuse of labor as a factor of production. It is when labor has the highest shadow value that the exit pressure is highest on outdated techniques and the pace of restructuring is fastest. When insiders are weak, the reason for labor's undervaluation of labor is direct and clear. When workers are strong, their shadow wage rate should be high in partial equilibrium. But in general equilibrium, strong insiders discourage job creation, raising unemployment and depressing the shadow wage rate.

Note that this discussion is about shadow wages, not *average* wage flows. In fact, one can show that—with continuous Nash bargaining—average wage payments are generally maximized in the interior of the strong-insider region. Politically, labor may thus find it advantageous to push for an outcome where insiders have greater-than-efficient bargaining power. I return to these implications in chapter 8.

5.6   Economic Policy

What kind of economic policies improve the pace and cyclical features of the creative destruction process? What would be the effect of those policies on unemployment and sclerosis? A simple answer is to recommend that governments implement institutional reform in the labor market to fix the problems at their source. However, often there is little the government can do when the problem is one of incomplete contracting at the microeconomic level. On the other hand, when appropriability is brought into existence by legislation itself, reform may either be politically infeasible or slow at best. In this section, I abstract from any institutional improvements and instead study two classes of macroeconomic policies—production and creation incentives—that can provide at least a partial cure for the economy's ills. These two types of policies affect the economy's unemployment and sclerosis problems rather differently and could actually be combined optimally to bring the economy to its efficient outcome.

5.6.1   Production and Creation Incentives

At first glance, policies that directly encourage creation (e.g., an investment tax credit) and those that directly encourage production (e.g., a reduction in the corporate income tax) may appear equivalent. As long as their benefits are the same in present-value terms, should they not affect investment in the same way? In the presence of two margins, however, this line of argument ignores important differences in the way those policies affect destruction. Creation incentives directly affect the decision to invest and, through more intense hiring in the labor market, indirectly prop up wage pressures on existing jobs. Production incentives not only affect investment decisions, but also directly encourage firms to keep outdated production units in operation for longer. Of course distinguishing between production and creation incentives can be quite tricky in practice. Consider an investment tax credit. Although it is primarily a creation incentive, it can act simultaneously as a production incentive if, through a Keynesian-multiplier effect, it leads to an aggregate demand expansion. As a second example, consider a tax holiday for new investments. This policy acts effectively as a creation incentive if it lasts for less than a production unit's lifetime, but as a production incentive if it lasts for more. I abstract from these practical considerations here.

Let $i_p(t)A(t)$ represent a production subsidy that is subtracted from a production unit's operating costs, while $i_c(t)A(t)$ represents a creation subsidy that is subtracted from the unit's effective creation cost. Depending on the way it is designed, the creation subsidy could be appropriable or not. Let us assume the former. Decentralized equilibrium conditions (5.4) and (5.5) become

$$A(t - \bar{a}(t)) - (p_m(t) + v(t) - i_p(t))A(t) = 0, \tag{5.19}$$

$$[c(t) - i_c(t)]A(t)$$
$$= \int_t^{t+T(t)} [A(t) - (p_m(s) + v(s) - i_p(s))A(s)]e^{-(r+\delta)(s-t)}\, ds. \tag{5.20}$$

What are the effects of these policies on the economy's steady state in terms of the sufficient statistics $(U^{SS}, \bar{a}^{SS})$? In steady state, equations (5.19)–(5.20) become

$$e^{-\gamma \bar{a}^{SS}} - [p_m^{SS} + v^{SS} - i_p^{SS}] = 0, \tag{5.21}$$

$$c^{SS} - i_c^{SS} = PV(\bar{a}^{SS}). \tag{5.22}$$

Production Incentives   Differentiating equations (5.21)–(5.22), and taking equations (5.12)–(5.13) into account, we have

$$\frac{d\bar{a}^{SS}}{di_p^{SS}} = \frac{e^{\gamma\bar{a}^{SS}}}{\gamma} \left[1 - \frac{\beta}{1-\beta} \left(\phi I_H^{SS} + \frac{\sigma^{SS}}{1-\eta} \right) \frac{dX^{SS}}{di_p^{SS}} \right] \tag{5.23}$$

and

$$\frac{dX^{SS}}{di_p^{SS}} = \frac{1-\eta}{\eta} \frac{X^{SS}}{\sigma^{SS}} (1-\beta) PV'(\bar{a}^{SS}) \frac{d\bar{a}^{SS}}{di_p^{SS}}. \tag{5.24}$$

Since $PV'(\bar{a}^{SS}) > 0$, the second condition implies that $\frac{dX^{SS}}{di_p^{SS}}$ and $\frac{d\bar{a}^{SS}}{di_p^{SS}}$ must have the same sign. But this is only consistent with the first expression if they are both positive. Thus sclerosis rises with production incentives.

Using this result and differentiating equation (5.11) shows that unemployment decreases with subsidy i_p^{SS}:

$$\frac{dU^{SS}}{di_p^{SS}} = -\frac{(U^{SS})^2}{\bar{L}} \left\{ \frac{(1-e^{-\delta\bar{a}^{SS}})}{\delta} \frac{dX^{SS}}{di_p^{SS}} + X^{SS} e^{-\delta\bar{a}^{SS}} \frac{d\bar{a}^{SS}}{di_p^{SS}} \right\} < 0.$$

Creation Incentives   Replacing (5.12) in (5.21) and differentiating with respect to i_c^{SS} yields

$$\frac{d\bar{a}^{SS}}{di_c^{SS}} = -\frac{e^{\gamma\bar{a}^{SS}}}{\gamma} \frac{\beta}{1-\beta} \left[\phi I_H^{SS} + \frac{\sigma^{SS}}{1-\eta} \right] \frac{dX^{SS}}{di_c^{SS}}.$$

Substituting (5.13) in (5.22), differentiating with respect to i_c^{SS} and substituting $\frac{d\bar{a}^{SS}}{di_c^{SS}}$ from the previous expression yields

$$\frac{dX^{SS}}{di_c^{SS}} = (1-\beta) \left[\frac{\eta}{1-\eta} \frac{\sigma^{SS}}{X^{SS}} + \frac{e^{\gamma\bar{a}^{SS}}}{\gamma} PV'(\bar{a}^{SS}) \beta \left(\phi I_H^{SS} + \frac{\sigma^{SS}}{1-\eta} \right) \right]^{-1} > 0.$$

This implies that creation incentives reduce sclerosis:

$$\frac{d\bar{a}^{SS}}{di_c^{SS}} < 0.$$

In contrast, the response of unemployment to creation incentives cannot be unambiguously signed.

Steady-State Effects   We have just shown that an increase in the production incentive i_p^{SS} increases the hiring intensity H^{SS}/U^{SS}, reduces unemployment U^{SS}, but increases the scrapping age $\bar{a}^{SS}$. The subsidy i_p^{SS} to profit margins protects outdated production units by absorbing the cost pressures to destroy them, including those from increased hiring in-

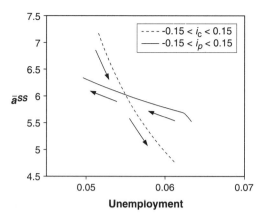

Figure 5.7
Increases in production and creation incentives

tensity. The impact of creation incentives is quite different. An increase in i_c^{SS} raises the hiring intensity H^{SS}/U^{SS}, reduces the scrapping age $\bar{a}^{SS}$, while its effect on unemployment U^{SS} is ambiguous. A creation subsidy leads to greater hiring intensity, which increases wage pressures to destroy outdated production units. Its effect on unemployment depends upon the degree to which higher destruction offsets the positive effect of increased creation on employment.

Figure 5.7 illustrates the steady-state effects of production and creation incentives. The solid and dashed lines represent the steady states that correspond to a range of values for i_p^{SS} and i_c^{SS} respectively (subsidies are positive and taxes are negative). The two lines intersect at the point where $i_p^{SS} = i_c^{SS} = 0$. As i_p^{SS} increases we move leftward along the solid line, and as i_c^{SS} increases we move downward along the dashed line.

Equations (5.23) and (5.24) indicate that as the search cost becomes smaller, the two lines become more orthogonal. As this happens, the production subsidy acts as a tool to reduce steady-state unemployment with little effect on $\bar{a}^{SS}$, while the creation subsidy is a tool to reduce sclerosis with little effect on unemployment.

5.6.2 Expansionary Policy, Liquidationism, and Accelerationism

What are the welfare implications of these two policy instruments? Let us concentrate on the strong-insiders region, where the economy suffers from high unemployment and technological sclerosis, and study the welfare effects of introducing a small production or creation incentive.

Production Incentives and the "Liquidationist" View of Recessions   In the strong-insiders region, the welfare effect of expanding the economy through a production subsidy appears, at first glance, to be ambiguous. While economic expansion can relieve the unemployment problem, conversely it can exacerbate the state of technological sclerosis. Could the second effect dominate the first and make the expansion undesirable on the whole? In this case, what the economy really needs would be a recession that "cleanses" its productive structure—an idea reminiscent of the pre-Keynesian "liquidationist" view (see, e.g., De Long 1990 and chapter 6).

To address this question, let us first look at the steady-state welfare effects of a small production subsidy di_p^{SS} starting from $i_p^{SS} = i_c^{SS} = 0$. As discussed in section 5.5.2, a meaningful welfare comparison across steady states can only be undertaken in the limiting case in which $(r - \gamma)$ goes to zero, so that initial conditions do not matter.

Define the steady-state flow of welfare as $\omega^{SS} A(t) \equiv \lim_{r \to \gamma} (r - \gamma) W^{SS}(t)$. Using equation (5.15), we can write $\omega^{SS} = q^{SS} - (I_H^{SS} + \sigma^{SS}) H^{SS} - p_m^{SS}(\bar{L} - U^{SS})$. Define the cost of creating a unit as $C^{SS} \equiv (I_H^{SS} + \sigma^{SS}) H^{SS}$. Let $-C_U^{SS}$ be the social shadow value of an unemployed worker in steady state, and C_H^{SS} be the social shadow cost of hiring a worker in steady state. We can think of the steady-state equations (5.21)–(5.22) as determining the pair (H^{SS}, U^{SS}), with $\bar{a}^{SS}$ implicitly determined by equation (5.11). With this in mind, one can write the effect of the policies on welfare as follows:

$$d\omega^{SS} = (q_H^{SS} - C_H^{SS}) dH^{SS} + (q_U^{SS} + p_m^{SS} - C_U^{SS}) dU^{SS}. \tag{5.25}$$

Differentiate $q^{SS} = H^{SS}[1 - e^{-(\gamma+\delta)\bar{a}^{SS}}]/(\gamma + \delta)$ with respect to H^{SS} and U^{SS} using the partial derivative of $\bar{a}^{SS}$ implicitly defined by equation (5.11) to obtain

$$q_H^{SS} = \frac{1}{H^{SS}}[q^{SS} - (p_m^{SS} + v^{SS} - i_p^{SS})E^{SS}],$$

$$q_U^{SS} = -(p_m^{SS} + v^{SS} - i_p^{SS}).$$

Using condition (5.14) with $r = \gamma$ and free-entry condition (5.22), one can rewrite the first expression as $q_H^{SS} = c^{SS} - i_c^{SS}$. Replacing in equation (5.25) yields

$$d\omega^{SS} = (c^{SS} - i_c^{SS} - C_H^{SS})\, dH^{SS} - (v^{SS} - i_p^{SS} + C_U^{SS})\, dU^{SS}. \tag{5.26}$$

In the neighborhood of $i_c^{SS} = i_p^{SS} = 0$, we have $(c^{SS} - C_H^{SS}) = \frac{U^{SS}}{H^{SS}}(v^{SS} + C_U^{SS})$. To see this, recall from the proof of the Hosios condition in chapter 4 that $\frac{\beta}{1-\beta} = H(t)\frac{\sigma_H(t)}{\sigma(t)}$ and $\frac{\beta}{1-\beta} = -U(t)\frac{\sigma_U(t)}{\sigma(t)}$. This means that $C_H^{SS} = I_H^{SS} + \sigma^{SS} - \frac{U^{SS}}{H^{SS}}C_U^{SS}$, which together with equation (5.17) proves the claim.

Thus, the change in the *flow* of steady-state welfare in response to policy can be expressed in terms of the response of the hiring intensity H^{SS}/U^{SS}:

$$d\omega^{SS} = (v^{SS} + C_U^{SS})U^{SS}\frac{d(H^{SS}/U^{SS})}{H^{SS}/U^{SS}}. \tag{5.27}$$

It is easy to see from equation (5.6) that when insiders are strong, their decentralized equilibrium shadow wage v^{SS} is always greater than their social shadow wage $-C_U^{SS}$. Since we are comparing v^{SS} and $-C_U^{SS}$ for the *same* aggregate quantities, this statement corresponds to the simple partial equilibrium result that the shadow wage is increasing in the bargaining position of insiders. Since a production incentive always increases H^{SS}/U^{SS}, equation (5.27) shows that a small production subsidy is *always* welfare-improving in the strong-insiders region. Conversely, one can show that, in the weak-insiders region, $(v^{SS} + C_U^{SS}) < 0$, and a small production *tax* is welfare-improving.

Going back to exit condition (5.19), we see why the liquidationist view cannot hold in the strong-insiders case. The "cleansing" that results from reducing economic activity amounts to moving a worker from a job at the destruction margin to the unemployment pool. Since the exiting worker produces v^{SS} on the job but has a social value of only $-C_U^{SS}$ in the unemployment pool, this produces a social loss of $(v^{SS} + C_U^{SS}) > 0$. This intuition carries over to temporary recessions as well, since the inequality $-C_U^{SS} < v^{SS}$ also holds outside steady state.

Creation Incentives and "Accelerationist" Policies   Let us now turn to the steady-state welfare effect of a small creation subsidy di_c^{SS} starting

Box 5.3
Singapore: A case of hyperkinesis?

> The case of Singapore as documented by Young (1992) seems to closely match a pattern of government-induced high investment and excess restructuring. In the 1970s and 1980s aggregate investment in Singapore reached phenomenal levels as a share of GDP, peaking at 43 percent in 1984. High investment was to a great extent related to a combination of tax incentives and widespread government participation in the financing of local companies (financed primarily by labor income taxation and forced saving). Not surprisingly, during the same period the economy was undergoing one of the world's highest rates of structural change in manufacturing, moving from one industry specialization to the next at a very fast pace. Young's assessment of the Singaporean economy is that it invested and restructured at excessively high rates. Compared to a laissez-faire economy like Hong Kong, it reached a similar growth rate at a much higher cost.

from $i_p^{SS} = i_c^{SS} = 0$. In the strong-insiders region, this policy would provide a partial cure for sclerosis by reducing $\bar{a}^{SS}$. Although its effect on unemployment is ambiguous, we know by equation (5.27) that since it increases H^{SS}/U^{SS}, it must be welfare-improving.

Naturally, a creation subsidy can only be beneficial up to a point. When the subsidy becomes too large, the economy suffers from a state of "hyperkinesis" with restructuring happening at an excessively fast and costly pace. Government intervention can thus give rise to a new phenomenon of excessively *low* $\bar{a}^{SS}$, which was shown to be impossible in our decentralized economy without government (see box 5.3 for the case of Singapore).

5.6.3   Optimal Dynamic Policy
Production and creation subsidies affect the economy's creation and destruction margins differently. This raises the question as to whether a judicious combination of the two policies can correct the price signals that distort the two margins and restore full efficiency.

In fact, the solution to this problem is quite simple. Efficiency can be restored by using the creation subsidy to correct the distortion in the effective creation-cost signal, and the production subsidy to correct the shadow wage signal. In other words, one needs to set

$$i_c(t) = \frac{\beta\phi}{1-\beta} I_H(t) + \frac{\beta - \eta}{(1-\eta)(1-\beta)} \sigma(t), \tag{5.28}$$

$$i_p(t) = \frac{H(t)}{U(t)} i_c(t). \tag{5.29}$$

It is straightforward to verify that equilibrium conditions (5.19)–(5.20) for the decentralized economy subject to these subsidies (5.28)–(5.29) are identical to equilibrium conditions (4.20)–(4.21) for the corresponding efficient economy.

Consider what this implies for a strong-insiders economy in steady state. Such an economy suffers from high unemployment and sclerosis. In terms of figure 5.7, it is desirable to move the economy in a southwest direction. This can be achieved through a combination of *positive* production and creation subsidies. The former mainly reduces unemployment (westward movement), and the latter mainly relieves sclerosis (southward movement). Thus, the presence of strong insiders requires that firms be compensated via a combination of creation and production subsidies. The opposite policy mix is required when insiders are weak.

In addition to the level effects, equations (5.28)–(5.29) also allow us to solve for the cyclical aspect of optimal policy design. In order to isolate this cyclical dimension, let us remove level effects by focusing on cases where (ϕ, β) lie along the efficient steady-state equivalence curve described in section 5.5.1. This guarantees that in steady state, insiders are neither too strong nor too weak. It does not guarantee that the same is true *on average* in an economy with ongoing fluctuations, because of possible nonlinearities in the response to shocks. However, figure 5.8 shows that this difference is of minor importance.

Figure 5.8 presents optimal dynamic policies for the economy with linear costs simulated in figure 5.3. The business-cycle variable $b(t)$ is shown in panel (a), the optimal path of creation incentives in panel (b), and the optimal path of production incentives in panel (c). The last two panels present curves for different configurations of bargaining-position parameters (ϕ, β) along the efficient equivalence curve. The efficient parameter configuration is $(\phi, \beta) = (0, 1/2)$ (since $\eta = 1/2$), and calls for no government intervention. As the parameter configuration gives more weight to the appropriability parameter ϕ, optimal creation and production subsidies become increasingly countercyclical. The shadow wage rate becomes increasingly rigid as the appropriability problem worsens.

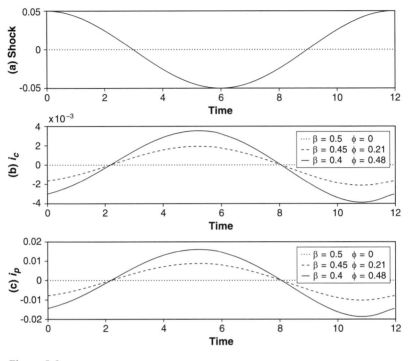

Figure 5.8
Optimal countercyclical policies

Relative to the efficient economy, insiders become excessively strong during recessions, when wages do not fall enough and unemployment is too high, and too weak during expansions for the opposite reason. It follows that firms must be given incentives during recessions and taxed during expansions to promote an efficient path of unemployment and restructuring over the business cycle.

5.7   Conclusion

The decoupling between creation and destruction, and to some extent the downward-sloping nature of the Beveridge curve, are ultimately due to the fact that incomplete contracting induces a form of "rigidity" in shadow wages—which requires the "quantity" movements of lower creation and higher unemployment for wages to fall in a recession. Yet the extent of those quantity effects may be such that they leave little trace of the underlying rigidity on the equilibrium path of wages. In general, the economy exhibits a mixture of covert and overt rigidity.

Incomplete contracting also affects the average functioning of the economy, which typically exhibits structural involuntary unemployment and, more pervasively, sclerosis.

In principle, both the cyclical and structural consequences of incomplete contracts can be addressed at the macroeconomic level with a suitable combination of production and creation incentives: the former being a better tool to address the unemployment problem, while the latter is an adequate tool to reduce the sclerosis problem. In practice, there are several problems that affect implementation of such policy packages, which make them (in limited amounts) suitable as complements to structural changes rather than a full cure.

5.8 Appendix: Numerical Computations

All numerical computations use a creation cost function of the form

$$I_H(H) = c_0 + c_1 H, \qquad \text{with } c_0, c_1 \geq 0,$$

and a sinusoidal business-cycle function

$$p_m(t) = \rho + \alpha \sin(t).$$

The search cost function takes the form

$$\sigma(H, U) = c_2 \left(\frac{H}{U}\right)^{\eta/(1-\eta)}, \qquad \text{with } 0 \leq \eta < 1 \text{ and } c_2 \geq 0,$$

which can be derived from the constant-returns, Cobb-Douglas matching function $H = \xi U^\eta V^{1-\eta}$.

The solution procedure consists of making an initial guess for the path of one of the variables, computing the values for the other variables consistent with this guess, and then updating the initial guess until reaching a fixed point.

5.8.1 Numerical Calculations for Section 5.1
Figure 5.1 was generated with the following parameters: $r = 0.016$, $\gamma = 0.021$, $\delta = 0.094$, $\eta = 0.5$, $\rho = 0.275$, $\alpha = 0.025$, and $\bar{L} = 1$; the creation-cost parameters are $c_0 = 0.1$, $c_1 = 0$, and $c_2 = 0.08$; $\beta = 0.5$ in the efficient economy and $\beta = 0.8$ in the inefficient one.

5.8.2   Numerical Calculations for Section 5.2

Figure 5.2 was generated with the following parameters: $r = 0.016$, $\gamma = 0.021$, $\delta = 0.094$, $\beta = \eta = 0.5$, $\rho = 0.275$, $\alpha = 0.225$, and $\bar{L} = 1$; the creation-cost parameters are $c_0 = 0.48$, $c_1 = 0$, and $c_2 = 0$ in the top panel and $c_0 = 0.19$, $c_1 = 0.8$, and $c_2 = 0$ in the bottom panel.

5.8.3   Numerical Calculations for Section 5.4

Figure 5.3 was generated with the same parameters as figures 4.3 and 4.4: $\gamma = 0.021$, $\delta = 0.094$, $r = 0.016$, $\eta = 0.5$, $\rho = 0.275$, and $\alpha = 0.05$; the creation-cost parameters are $c_0 = 0.23$, $c_1 = 0$, and $c_2 = 0.04$ for the left panels and $c_0 = 0.02$, $c_1 = 1.5$, and $c_2 = 0.04$ for the right panels.

Figure 5.4 was generated with the same parameters as figure 5.2, with the linear adjustment costs on the left panels and convex adjustment costs on the right.

5.8.4   Numerical Calculations for Section 5.5

Figure 5.5 was generated with the following parameters: $r = 0.03$, $\gamma = 0.04$, $\delta = 0.03$, $\eta = 0.5$, $p^* = 0.275$, and $\bar{L} = 1$; the creation-cost parameters are $c_0 = 0.4$, $c_1 = 0$, and $c_2 = 0.06$.

The parameters for figure 5.6 are $r = 0.03$, $\gamma = 0.04$, $\delta = 0.03$, $\eta = 0.5$, $p^* = 0.275$, and $\bar{L} = 1$; the creation-cost parameters are $c_0 = 0.4$, $c_1 = 0$, and $c_2 = 0.06$; the bargaining-position parameters are $\phi = 0.5$ and $0.005 \leq \beta \leq 0.9$.

5.8.5   Numerical Calculations for Section 5.6

Figure 5.7 was generated with the following parameters: $r = 0.03$, $\gamma = 0.04$, $\delta = 0.03$, $\eta = 0.5$, $p^* = 0.275$, and $\bar{L} = 1$; the creation-cost parameters are $c_0 = 0.4$, $c_1 = 0$, and $c_2 = 0.06$; the bargaining-position parameters are $\phi = 0$ and $\beta = 0.5$.

Figure 5.8 presents optimal dynamic policies for the economy with linear costs simulated in figure 5.3.

Note

1. This chapter is based on Caballero and Hammour (1996).

References and Suggested Readings

Abraham, Katharine G., and Lawrence F. Katz. 1986. "Cyclical Unemployment: Sectoral Shifts or Aggregate Disturbances?" *Journal of Political Economy* 94(3): 507–522.

Aghion, Philippe, and Peter Howitt. 1992. "A Model of Growth through Creative Destruction." *Econometrica* 60(2): 323–352.

Aghion, Philippe, and Peter Howitt. 1994. "Growth and Unemployment." *Review of Economic Studies* 61(3): 477–494.

Aghion, Philippe, and Gilles Saint-Paul. 1998. "Virtues of Bad Times." *Macroeconomic Dynamics* 2(3): 322–344.

Baily, Martin N., Charles Hulten, and David Campbell. 1992. "Productivity Dynamics in Manufacturing Plants." *Brookings Papers on Economic Activity: Microeconomics* 1992: 187–249.

Bartelsman, Eric J., and Phoebus J. Dhrymes. 1994. "Productivity Dynamics: U.S. Manufacturing Plants, 1972–1986." Working paper, Finance and Economics Discussion Series 94-1, Board of Governors of the Federal Reserve System.

Binmore, Kenneth, Ariel Rubinstein, and Asher Wolinsky. 1986. "The Nash Bargaining Solution in Economic Modeling." *Rand Journal of Economics* 17(2): 176–188.

Blanchard, Olivier J., and Peter A. Diamond. 1989. "The Beveridge Curve." *Brookings Papers on Economic Activity*, no. 1: 1–60.

Blanchard, Olivier J., and Peter A. Diamond. 1990. "The Cyclical Behavior of the Gross Flows of U.S. Workers." *Brookings Papers on Economic Activity*, no. 2: 85–143.

Bresnahan, Timothy F., and Daniel M. G. Raff. 1991. "Intra-Industry Heterogeneity and the Great Depression: The American Motor Vehicles Industry, 1929–35." *Journal of Economic History* 51(2): 317–331.

Bresnahan, Timothy F., and Daniel M. G. Raff. 1992. "Technological Heterogeneity, Adjustment Costs, and the Dynamics of Plant-Shut-Down Behavior: The American Motor Vehicle Industry in the Time of the Great Depression." Mimeo., Stanford University.

Caballero, Ricardo J. 1998. "Job Reallocation and the Business Cycle: New Facts For An Old Debate: Discussion." In J. C. Fuhrer and S. Schuh, eds., *Beyond Shocks: What Causes Business Cycles?*, 338–348. Conference Series No. 42. Boston: Federal Reserve Bank.

Caballero, Ricardo J., and Mohamad L. Hammour. 1994. "The Cleansing Effect of Recessions." *American Economic Review* 84(5): 1350–1368.

Caballero, Ricardo J., and Mohamad L. Hammour. 1996. "On the Timing and Efficiency of Creative Destruction." *Quarterly Journal of Economics* 111(3): 805–852.

Campbell, J. R., and K. N. Kuttner. 1996. "Macroeconomic Effects of Employment Reallocation." *Carnegie-Rochester Conference Series on Public Policy* 44: 87–116.

Coase, Ronald. 1937. "The Nature of the Firm." *Economica* 4(4): 386–405.

Cooper, Russell, and John C. Haltiwanger. 1993. "The Aggregate Implications of Machine Replacement: Theory and Evidence." *American Economic Review* 83: 360–380.

Cox, W. Michael, and Richard Alm. 1992. "The Churn: The Paradox of Progress." In *1992 Annual Report*. Dallas, Tex.: Federal Reserve Bank of Dallas.

Darby, Michael, John C. Haltiwanger, and Mark Plant. 1986. "The Ins and Outs of Unemployment: The Ins Win." NBER Working Paper No. 1997.

Davis, Steven J. 1987. "Fluctuations in the Pace of Labor Reallocation." *Carnegie-Rochester Conference Series on Public Policy* 27: 335–402.

Davis, Steven J. 2005. "Comment: Job Loss, Job Finding, and Unemployment in the U.S. Economy over the Past Fifty Years." In Mark Gertler and Kenneth Rogoff, eds., *NBER Macroeconomics Annual 2005*, vol. 20, 139–157. Cambridge, Mass.: The MIT Press.

Davis, Steven J., and John C. Haltiwanger. 1990. "Gross Job Creation and Destruction: Microeconomic Evidence and Macroeconomic Implications." In Olivier J. Blanchard and Stanley Fischer, eds., *NBER Macroeconomics Annual 1990*, vol. 5, 123–168. Cambridge, Mass.: The MIT Press.

Davis, Steven J., and John C. Haltiwanger. 1992. "Gross Job Creation, Gross Job Destruction and Employment Reallocation." *Quarterly Journal of Economics* 107(3): 819–864.

Davis, Steven J., and John C. Haltiwanger. 1999. "On the Driving Forces behind Cyclical Movements in Employment and Job Reallocation." *American Economic Review* 89(5): 1234–1258.

De Long, J. Bradford. 1990. "Liquidation Cycles: Old-Fashioned Real Business Cycle Theory and the Great Depression." NBER Working Paper No. 3546.

Diamond, Peter A. 1982. "Wage Determination and Efficiency in Search Equilibrium." *Review of Economic Studies* 49(2): 217–227.

Diamond, Peter A. 1994. *On Time*. Cambridge, UK: Cambridge University Press.

Fujita, Shigeru, and Garey Ramey. 2006. "The Cyclicality of Job Loss and Hiring." Federal Reserve Bank of Philadelphia Working Paper 06-17.

Galí, Jordi, and Mohamad L. Hammour. 1992. "Long Run Effects of Business Cycles." Mimeo., Columbia University.

Greenwood, Jeremy, Zvi Herkowitz, and Per Krusell. 1992. "Macroeconomic Implications of Investment-Specific Technological Change." Institute for International Economic Studies Seminar Paper No. 527.

Grossman, Gene M., and Elhanan Helpman. 1991. *Innovation and Growth in the Global Economy*. Cambridge, Mass.: The MIT Press.

Grout, Paul A. 1984. "Investment and Wages in the Absence of Binding Contracts: A Nash Bargaining Approach." *Econometrica* 52(2): 449–460.

Hall, Robert E. 1991. "Labor Demand, Labor Supply, and Employment Volatility." In Olivier J. Blanchard and Stanley Fischer, eds., *NBER Macroeconomics Annual 1991*, vol. 6, 17–47. Cambridge, Mass.: The MIT Press.

Hall, Robert E. 2005. "Job Loss, Job Finding, and Unemployment in the U.S. Economy over the Past Fifty Years." In Mark Gertler and Kenneth Rogoff, eds., *NBER Macroeconomics Annual 2005*, vol. 20, 101–137. Cambridge, Mass.: The MIT Press.

Haltiwanger, John C., and Scott Schuh. 1999. "Gross Job Flows Between Plants and Industries." *New England Economic Review* (March): 41–64.

Hart, Oliver, and John Moore. 1988. "Incomplete Contracts and Renegotiation." *Econometrica* 56: 755–786.

Hart, Oliver, and John Moore. 1994. "A Theory of Debt Based on the Inalienability of Human Capital." *Quarterly Journal of Economics* 109(4): 841–880.

Hosios, Arthur J. 1990. "On the Efficiency of Matching and Related Models of Search and Unemployment." *Review of Economic Studies* 57(2): 279–298.

Hulten, Charles R. 1992. "Growth Accounting When Technical Change Is Embodied in Capital." *American Economic Review* 82(4): 964–980.

Johansen, Leif. 1959. "Substitution versus Fixed Production Coefficients in the Theory of Economic Growth: A Synthesis." *Econometrica* 27(2): 157–176.

Johnson, George, and Richard Layard. 1987. "The Natural Rate of Unemployment: Explanation and Policy." In Orley Ashenfelter and Richard Layard, eds., *Handbook of Labor Economics*, 921–999. Amsterdam: North-Holland.

Jovanovic, Boyan. 1979. "Job Matching and the Theory of Turnover." *Journal of Political Economy* 87(5): 972–990.

Katz, Lawrence F. 1986. "Efficiency Wage Theories: A Partial Evaluation." In Stanley Fischer, ed., *NBER Macroeconomics Annual 1986*, vol. 1, 235–276. Cambridge, Mass.: The MIT Press.

Kennan, John. 2005. "Comment: Job Loss, Job Finding, and Unemployment in the U.S. Economy over the Past Fifty Years." In Mark Gertler and Kenneth Rogoff, eds., *NBER Macroeconomics Annual 2005*, vol. 20, 159–164. Cambridge, Mass.: The MIT Press.

Klein, Benjamin, Robert G. Crawford, and Armen A. Alchian. 1978. "Vertical Integration, Appropriable Rents, and the Competitive Contracting Process." *Journal of Law and Economics* 21(2): 297–326.

Layard, Richard, Stephen Nickell, and Richard Jackman. 1991. *Unemployment: Macroeconomic Performance and the Labor Market*. Oxford: Oxford University Press.

Lilien, David M. 1982. "Sectoral Shifts and Cyclical Unemployment." *Journal of Political Economy* 90(4): 777–793.

Lindbeck, Assar, and Dennis Snower. 1986. "Wage Setting, Unemployment and Insider-Outsider Relations." *American Economic Review* 76(2): 235–239.

Mortensen, Dale T. 1978. "Specific Capital and Labor Turnover." *Bell Journal of Economics* 9(2): 572–586.

Mortensen, Dale T. 1994. "The Cyclical Behavior of Job and Worker Flows." *Journal of Economic Dynamics and Control* 18(6): 1121–1142.

Mortensen, Dale T., and Christopher Pissarides. 1993. "The Cyclical Behavior of Job Creation and Job Destruction." In J. C. Ours, G. A. Pfann, and G. Ridder, eds., *Labor Demand and Equilibrium Wage Formation*, 201–221. Amsterdam: North-Holland.

Mortensen, Dale T., and Christopher Pissarides. 1994. "Job Creation and Job Destruction in the Theory of Unemployment." *Review of Economic Studies* 61(3): 397–416.

Phelps, Edmund S. 1963. "Substitution, Fixed Proportions, Growth and Distribution." *International Economic Review* 4(3): 265–288.

Pissarides, Christopher. 2000. *Equilibrium Unemployment Theory*, 2nd ed. Cambridge, Mass.: The MIT Press.

Pries, Michael, and Richard Rogerson. 2005. "Hiring Policies, Labor Market Institutions, and Labor Market Flows." *Journal of Political Economy* 113(4): 811–839.

Rogerson, Richard D., and H. Cole. 1998. "Can the Mortensen-Pissarides Matching Model Match the Business Cycle Facts?" *International Economic Review* 40(4): 933–959.

Saint-Paul, Gilles. 1993. "Productivity Growth and the Structure of the Business Cycle." *European Economic Review* 37(4): 861–883.

Salter, Wilfred. 1960. *Productivity and Technical Change*. Cambridge, UK: Cambridge University Press.

Schumpeter, Joseph A. 1942. *Capitalism, Socialism, and Democracy*. New York: Harper and Brothers.

Sheshinski, Eytan. 1967. "Balanced Growth and Stability in the Johansen Vintage Model." *Review of Economic Studies* 34(2): 239–248.

Shimer, Robert. 2005a. "The Cyclical Behavior of Equilibrium Unemployment and Vacancies." *American Economic Review* 95(1): 25–49.

Shimer, Robert. 2005b. "The Cyclicality of Hires, Separations, and Job-to-Job Transitions." Mimeo., University of Chicago.

Shimer, Robert. 2005c. "Mismatch." NBER Working Paper No. 11888.

Solow, Robert M. 1960. "Investment and Technical Progress." In K. J. Arrow, S. Karlin, and P. Suppes, eds., *Mathematical Methods in Social Sciences*, 89–104. Stanford, Calif.: Stanford University Press.

Stiglitz, Joseph. 1993. "Endogenous Growth and Cycles." NBER Working Paper No. 4286.

Williamson, Oliver E. 1979. "Transaction-Cost Economics: The Governance of Contractual Relations." *Journal of Law and Economics* 22(2): 233–261.

Williamson, Oliver E. 1985. *The Economic Institutions of Capitalism*. New York: Free Press.

Young, Alwyn. 1992. *A Tale of Two Cities: Factor Accumulation and Technical Change in Hong Kong and Singapore*. Cambridge, Mass.: The MIT Press.

6

Financial Market Specificity and Restructuring

This chapter focuses on the implications of financial frictions for the efficiency of steady-state and cyclical restructuring. At a general level, a financial friction is just an example of the relationship problems discussed in chapter 3—now specifically between entrepreneurs and potential investors. Consequently, many of the dynamic issues highlighted in chapters 4 and 5 apply in this context as well. Aside from highlighting the restructuring consequences of financial frictions per se, this chapter's purpose is to enrich the analytical framework developed in this book along three dimensions: (1) ex ante heterogeneity, (2) a more extensive analysis of privately inefficient separations, and (3) multiple-party relationships.[1]

In terms of substantive results, this chapter provides a quantitative assessment of the costs that arise from the interplay between financial frictions and labor market frictions, and its impact on the level and quality of restructuring. On average, financial frictions increase unemployment and scramble the productivity ranking on the entry and exit margins. Over the course of the business cycle, despite a rise in privately inefficient separations at the start of recessions, the lack of financial resources during the recovery phase is likely to reduce rather than increase restructuring during cyclical downturns. This depressed restructuring adds a significant productivity cost to recessions.

The chapter starts with a static model along the lines of that used in chapter 3 and follows with a (more) quantifiable dynamic model. An analysis of the impact of contractual incompleteness in labor and financial markets on both average and cyclical restructuring patterns, concludes the chapter. In particular, it provides an explanation for the pattern of depressed restructuring that takes place during recessions as illustrated in chapter 2.

6.1   A Static Model

Let us briefly return to the static setup in chapter 3 but extend it to the case of three factors of production: capital, entrepreneurs, and labor. The specificity of capital with respect to entrepreneurs affects financing transactions; its specificity with respect to labor affects employment transactions. All three factors exist in infinitesimal units and derive linear utility from the economy's unique consumption good, which is the numeraire.

As before, factors can work in Joint Production or Autarky modes (see figure 6.1). Autarky for each of the three factors of production is characterized as follows. Capital can be invested in world financial markets at a fixed world interest rate r. Each entrepreneur i has an innate level of skill or "productivity" y_i and starts with net worth a_i. If the entrepreneur does not enter Joint Production, he or she simply invests his or her net worth at the world interest rate. Labor can be employed in the informal

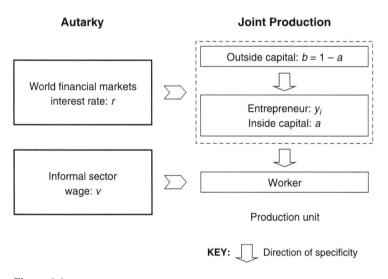

Figure 6.1
Autarky and Joint Production
Source: Caballero and Hammour (2000).

sector at a wage v, with $v'(E) > 0$ and $E = 1 - U$ as in chapter 3 (recall that U represents "employment" in the Autarky sector). Workers possess no wealth or pledgeable income.

In Joint Production, the three factors combine in fixed proportions to form production units. Each production unit is made up of a unit of capital, an entrepreneur i, and a worker.

Capital is partly financed from the entrepreneur's net worth a_i and partly through funds $b_i = 1 - a_i$ provided by external financiers. The team produces y_i units of the consumption good, which is equal to the entrepreneur's productivity. Cooperation in Joint Production gives rise to investment specificity: once committed, capital is fully specific to the entrepreneur and the worker. It has no ex post use outside this specific relationship.

Beginning with preexisting production units as well as a supply of uncommitted factors of production, economic events take place in three consecutive phases: destruction, creation, and production. In the destruction phase, the factors in all preexisting units decide whether to continue to produce jointly or to separate and join uncommitted factors. In the creation phase, uncommitted factors either form new Joint Production units or remain in Autarky. In the final phase production takes place, and factor rewards are distributed and consumed.

Let us assume that the productivities y^o of preexisting units are distributed over the interval $[0, y^{\max}]$, but that the distribution has zero mass so it does not affect equilibrium prices. The supply of uncommitted factors is as follows: the labor force has mass one; the supply of capital is unlimited; and the supply of entrepreneurs with any given productivity $y \in [0, y^{\max}]$ is also unlimited, but not all of them possess positive wealth. There is a finite mass $A > 0$ of entrepreneurs with positive net worth, and they are distributed uniformly over the whole range of productivities $[0, y^{\max}]$. Each of these has sufficient funds to fully finance a production unit $(a_i > 1)$.

6.1.1 Efficient Equilibrium

Without contractual problems, and restricting the analysis to a region where the equilibrium is interior, only entrepreneurs with maximum productivity enter into Joint Production. In this equilibrium, the Autarky wage is

$$v^* = y^{\max} - r. \tag{6.1}$$

Any wage below this value would induce infinite Joint Production labor demand, and any wage above would induce zero demand. Labor supply to Joint Production is

$$E^* = v^{-1}(v^*). \tag{6.2}$$

Equilibrium in the labor market then determines the creation of Joint Production units:

$$E^* = v^{-1}(y^{\max} - r). \tag{6.3}$$

Note that in this efficient equilibrium, Joint Production rewards for capital and labor are equal to their Autarky rewards, and the reward for entrepreneurs is zero because of their unlimited supply. This equilibrium is represented by the intersection of the solid lines in figure 6.2.

Finally, on the destruction side, scrapping (sunk) capital invested in a preexisting unit frees up a unit of labor. Note that capital is fully specific, which means that its opportunity cost is zero. Efficient exit therefore affects all units with productivity:

$$y^o < v^*. \tag{6.4}$$

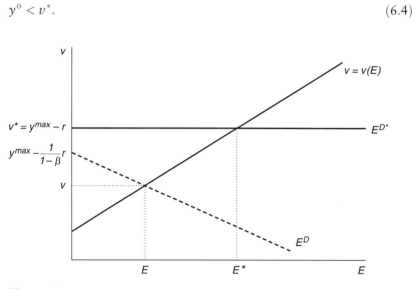

Figure 6.2
Efficient and incomplete-contracts equilibria
Source: Caballero and Hammour (2000).

6.1.2   Incomplete-Contracts Equilibrium

Because of investment specificity, implementing the efficient equilibrium requires a contract that guarantees capital in Joint Production its ex ante opportunity cost r. Let us assume that due to the inalienability of human capital (as in Hart and Moore 1994), both the entrepreneur and the worker can walk away from the relationship after investment is sunk. This ability affects both the employment transaction between labor and capital and the financing transaction between the entrepreneur and external financiers.

Starting with the employment relationship, one could assume that labor is able to distinguish between the capital supplied by the entrepreneur and by the external financier, in which case external liabilities could be used as a device to reduce the rents appropriable by labor (see Bronars and Deere 1991 for a discussion and some empirical evidence on this mechanism). Rather than adopting this strategy, I will simplify the setup and assume that the worker deals with capital as a single entity— one reason could be that the entrepreneur can always disguise internal funds as being external, and vice versa. In this context, if production unit i has productivity y_i, its associated quasi-rent s_i is the difference between the unit's output and its factors' ex post opportunity costs:

$$s_i = y_i - v. \tag{6.5}$$

Assuming that labor receives a share β of quasi-rents yields

$$w_i = v + \beta s_i, \qquad \pi_i = (1 - \beta)s_i, \tag{6.6}$$

where w_i and π_i denote the payments to labor and capital in Joint Production unit i, respectively.

Turning to the financing relationship, the profits π_i are shared by the entrepreneur and the external financiers. Because of the inalienability of human capital, the entrepreneur can threaten to leave the relationship; this threat allows the entrepreneur to capture a share $\alpha \in (0, 1)$ of π_i (the outside options of both the entrepreneur and financier are worthless). The firm's outside liability can therefore never exceed the limit

$$b_i \leq \frac{(1 - \alpha)\pi_i}{r}. \tag{6.7}$$

This financial constraint places a lower bound on the net worth $a_i = 1 - b_i$ the entrepreneur needs to start a project:

$$a_i \geq 1 - \frac{(1-\alpha)(1-\beta)(y_i - v)}{r}.$$

Assume that α is large enough so that this condition requires a positive a_i even for maximum productivity $y^{\max}$. This implies that only entrepreneurs with positive net worth can enter into Joint Production. In this case the entrepreneur fully finances the project, since by our earlier assumption regarding the distribution of internal funds, he or she has sufficient funds to do so.

An entrepreneur able to finance a production unit finds it ex ante profitable to do so if

$$\pi_i \geq r, \tag{6.8}$$

which, given equations (6.5) and (6.6), is equivalent to

$$y_i \geq v + \frac{r}{1-\beta}. \tag{6.9}$$

Because of the rent component in wages, capital behaves as if it faced a world interest rate $1/(1-\beta)$ times as high as r. The Joint Production demand for labor is given by the mass of entrepreneurs whose productivity satisfies equation (6.9) and who can finance a production unit:

$$E^d = A \int_{v+r/(1-\beta)}^{y^{\max}} \frac{1}{y^{\max}} dy$$

$$= \frac{A}{y^{\max}} \left(y^{\max} - v - \frac{r}{1-\beta} \right). \tag{6.10}$$

The supply of labor is given by the equation

$$E^s = v^{-1}(w^m), \tag{6.11}$$

where w^m is the wage offered in the marginal firm.

Together, these equations determine the incomplete-contracts equilibrium level of E. As illustrated in figure 6.2 by the dashed lines, labor demand (6.10) under incomplete contracts falls below its efficient-economy counterpart (6.1). This occurs both because of labor market rents (which shift the curve down vertically) and because of the financial constraint (which rotates the curve clockwise about its vertical-axis intercept). In the incomplete-contracts equilibrium, Joint Production employment and Autarky wages are lower than in the efficient equilibrium:

$$E < E^*, \qquad v < v^*.$$

Turning to destruction, note that a worker who leaves a preexisting production unit finds employment in Joint Production with probability E, and expects to receive a wage

$$w^e = \frac{1}{\left(y^{\max} - v - \frac{r}{1-\beta}\right)} \int_{v+r/(1-\beta)}^{y^{\max}} w(y)\,dy$$

$$= v + \beta \frac{1}{\left(y^{\max} - v - \frac{r}{1-\beta}\right)} \int_{v+r/(1-\beta)}^{y^{\max}} (y - v)\,dy. \qquad (6.12)$$

If entrepreneurs in preexisting units have zero net worth (so they do not want to restart in a new production unit), then the exit condition states that all preexisting firms whose output does not cover labor's opportunity cost are scrapped. That is, exit occurs for all firms with productivity:

$$y^o < Ew^e + (1 - E)v. \qquad (6.13)$$

6.1.3 Equilibrium Characterization

Let us now characterize the equilibrium consequences of incomplete contracting. Since many of these implications are amplified (by the triple-interaction) versions of the mechanisms discussed in chapter 3, I simply list and sketch them here:

1. *Reduced cooperation.* As in earlier chapters, at the purely microeconomic level limited contracting ability hampers cooperation. Positive-value Joint Production projects may not be undertaken because labor or the entrepreneur can capture rents beyond their ex ante opportunity costs.

2. *Underemployment.* Joint Production is characterized by under-employment ($E < E^*$), which is an equilibrium consequence of obstacles to cooperation in the financial and labor markets. In partial equilibrium, rent appropriation reduces the Joint Production return on capital. In order to restore this return to the level r required by world markets, fewer Joint Production units are created, Autarky-sector employment (or partially insured unemployment) rises, and the opportunity-cost component v of wages falls (equation [6.10]).

3. *Market segmentation, low wages, and high profits.* In the incomplete-contracts equilibrium, both the labor and financial markets are segmented. There are workers and entrepreneurs in Autarky who

would strictly prefer to move into Joint Production, but are constrained from doing so. Put another way, these two factors earn rents in Joint Production. It is easy to see that the rent component of Joint Production wages in equation (6.12) is positive and the wage rate is strictly above the Autarky-sector wage. Somewhat paradoxically, however, the presence of rents does *not* entail high wages in equilibrium, but quite the opposite. One can show that Joint Production wages are lower under incomplete contracts than in the efficient economy. To see this for any production unit i, replace $\pi_i = y_i - w_i$ in equation (6.8), and use equation (6.1) to get

$$w_i \leq y_i - r \leq y^{\max} - r = v^* = w^*.$$

As before, the rent component of wages arises through depressed wages in the Autarky sector, not because of high wages in Joint Production. Similarly, from equation (6.9), it is clear that unlike the situation in the efficient equilibrium, an entrepreneur with intramarginal productivity y_i earns a return over and above the rate r by the amount:

$$(1 - \beta)\left(y_i - v - \frac{r}{1 - \beta}\right).$$

Let us now turn to the implications of incomplete contracting in financial and labor markets for the restructuring process.

4. *Depressed creation.* Since creation in this economy is equal to $E < E^*$, it follows that the equilibrium rate of creation is depressed relative to the level found in the efficient economy.

5. *Sclerosis.* The Joint Production structure suffers from sclerosis, in the sense that some production units survive that would be scrapped in an efficient economy. To see this, compare the efficient and incomplete-contracts exit conditions, (6.4) and (6.13). Since $v < v^*$ and $w_i \leq w^*$, it is apparent that cost pressures to scrap units are lower in the incomplete-contracts equilibrium than in the efficient one. Sclerosis is thus a result of the underutilization and low productivity of labor (due, in turn, to the low productivity of entrepreneurs). Sluggish creation and sclerosis can impose a heavy drag on aggregate productivity.

6. *Unbalanced restructuring.* Destruction is excessively high compared to the depressed rate of creation. To see this difference, note that the *private* opportunity cost used in equation (6.13) for exit decisions is higher

Box 6.1
Scrambling in the knitted garment industry in Tirupur, India

Banerjee and Munshi (2004) document *scrambling* in Tirupur's knitted garment industry. This industry (which represents 70 percent of India's knitted garment exports) was dominated by the local Gounders until the early 1990s, but since then migration to Tirupur from the rest of India increased significantly as a response to its success as an export center. Banerjee and Munshi use data from 1991 to 1994 to study whether the performance of these groups—locals (Gounders) and migrants (Outsiders)—differs significantly in a number of dimensions. Their key insight is that these two groups have very different degrees of connections with the local communities and hence face different financing costs. Gounders have better access to local networks and therefore are able to raise more and cheaper capital. They notice that the judicial system is basically defunct in this region suggesting that informal mechanisms of enforcement should be very relevant. For instance, Gounders finance about 64 percent of their investments using what the authors call "network capital," while Outsiders only finance 55 percent of their capital using these private sources.

Their empirical work is careful and controls for numerous obvious selection and endogeneity issues. Their conclusions are consistent with several of the main implications in this chapter. Overall, their evidence points to significant differences in firms' productivity across Gounders and Outsiders:

• The average Gounder firm set up during the period 1991–1994 started with almost three times as much fixed capital as a comparable Outsider firm.

• At all levels of experience (i.e., the number of years since entry as an exporter), the average Gounder firm owns more fixed capital than the average Outsider firm that was started in the same year (though the difference is small for firms that have been exporting for more than six years). The capital intensity of production in an average Gounder firm (measured by the ratio of fixed capital to exports and the ratio of fixed capital to total production) is between 1.5 and 2.5 times that of an average Outsider firm that was started in the same year.

• Output (measured by exports and total production) is initially lower in firms owned by Outsiders compared with firms owned by Gounders started in the same year, but grows faster with experience and outperforms that of the Gounders about five years later.

Thus, the authors conclude that the differences in productivity and use of capital are explained by differences in the shadow price of capital faced by these groups. Outsiders face a higher cost of capital and therefore rely less on capital-intensive technologies. In addition, differences in the cost of capital can also explain the differences in ability of Outsiders and Gounders. On the entry margin, the marginal Gounder that enters the market is less able than the marginal Outsider. On the exit margin, the marginal Outsider exiting the market has higher ability than the marginal Gounder staying in the industry.

than the *social* shadow value v of labor. This is due to the possibility of capturing a rent component in wages, which induces an upward distortion in the private opportunity cost of labor. It may appear paradoxical that the economy exhibits both sclerosis and excessive destruction. In fact, as shown in chapter 3, the former is a comparison with the efficient equilibrium, and the latter is a comparison between private and social values within the incomplete-contracts equilibrium. The unbalanced nature of gross flows is closely related to the presence of rents and market segmentation.

7. *Scrambling*. In the efficient economy only the most productive entrepreneurs with $y = y^{\max}$ are involved in Joint Production. If their number is insufficient, others will be brought in according to a strict productivity ranking. On the creation side, an efficient process should result in the highest productivity projects being implemented. This ranking is scrambled in the incomplete-contracts equilibrium, as the net worth of the entrepreneur affects his or her ability to create a new production unit in this case. This reduces the quality of the churn, in the sense that the same volume of scrapping and reinvestment results in a smaller productivity gain.

8. *Privately inefficient separations*. The possibility of privately inefficient separations, a dimension not incorporated into the basic static model, can also constitute an important consequence of contracting difficulties. As discussed in chapter 3, these can arise if one adds continuation investment to the model, as in this case distortions similar to those that apply to creation decisions also apply to the destruction margin. This issue is analyzed more naturally in a dynamic model, which I turn to next.

6.2   A Dynamic Model

6.2.1   General Structure
Let us now consider an infinite-horizon economy in continuous time, for which the general structure is outlined in figure 6.3.

Production Units   There is a single good (the numeraire) that can either be consumed or invested. Production takes place within infinitesimal production units that combine, in fixed proportions, an entrepreneurial project, a one-time investment of κ units of capital, and a flow input of

(a) New production units

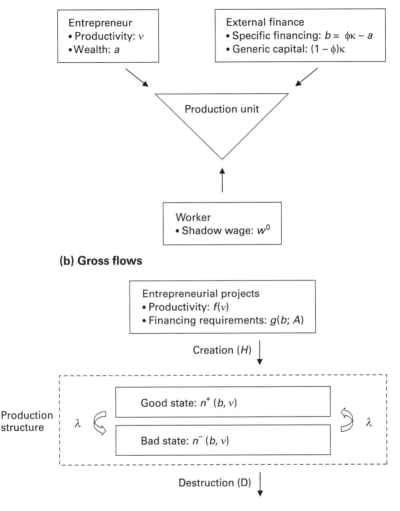

(b) Gross flows

Figure 6.3
General structure of dynamic model economy
Source: Caballero and Hammour (2005).

one unit of labor (see panel [a] of figure 6.3). The output flow of production unit i at time t is made up of three components:

$$\tilde{y}_t + v_i + \tilde{\epsilon}_{it},$$

where $\tilde{y}_t$ is a stochastic *aggregate* component, $v_i \in [-\bar{v}, \bar{v}]$ is a *permanent idiosyncratic* component (the unit's "productivity"), and $\tilde{\epsilon}_{it}$ is a *transitory idiosyncratic* component (the unit's "state"). $\tilde{\epsilon}_{it}$ switches between two states, $\epsilon > 0$ (the "good" state) and $-\epsilon < 0$ (the "bad" state) at hazard rate $\lambda > 0$. Finally, production units fail (and their capital is destroyed) exogenously at hazard rate $\delta > 0$.

Entrepreneurs, Workers, and Financiers   Each production unit forms a nexus for a trilateral relationship among an entrepreneur-manager, a worker, and external financiers. The entrepreneur formulates the project and uses his or her internal funds to finance it; the worker contributes his or her labor; and external financiers provide the unit's financing requirements when the entrepreneur has insufficient funds. Let us characterize each of these three parties, in reverse order.

External finance is intermediated through a non-resource consuming competitive sector. It may be called upon either to finance capital investment at the time a production unit is created or to finance periods of negative cash flow during the lifetime of the unit. As I discuss later, a production unit finances its capital externally through a combination of capital "rental" and external "liabilities," b ($b > 0$ corresponds to a positive external liability and $b < 0$ to positive internal funds).

Workers are infinitely lived agents whose population is represented by a continuum of mass one. Each worker i is endowed with a unit of labor, and maximizes the expected present value of instantaneous utility

$$c_{it} + z(1 - e_{it}), \qquad z \geq 0,$$

with discount rate $\rho > 0$.

Entrepreneurs maximize the expected present value of consumption, also discounted at rate ρ.

All agents are therefore risk neutral, and the market discount rate is ρ. Entrepreneurial projects are held by a continuum of nonactive entrepreneurs indexed by i. Each has a project for a production unit with known productivity v_i, and a certain amount of wealth that translates into a financing requirement b_i—equal to the project's investment requirement minus the entrepreneur's wealth. The distributions of wealth and project productivities are independent in the cross-section. At any time t, the density of project productivities is given by $f(v)$; and the mass density of project financing requirements is given by $g(b; A_t)$, where A_t is an index of the aggregate wealth of nonactive entrepreneurs.

By fixing the distributions of project productivities and financing requirements, one avoids having to model the complex details of the population dynamics of potential entrepreneurs. Implicitly, the assumption is that the process by which potential entrepreneurs invent or discard project ideas is such that it results in the assumed distributions.

Relationship-Specificity   The employment and financing relationships within production units suffer from contracting obstacles. A fraction $\phi \in (0, 1]$ of a production unit's capital is specific, in the sense that its productive value disappears if either the worker or the manager leaves the unit. The nonspecific component of capital, $(1 - \phi)\kappa$, has full collateral value and gives rise to no contracting difficulties. At any time its owner can withdraw the nonspecific component of capital from the relationship and use it elsewhere with no loss of value. Thus, let us consider that this part of capital is always rented at a cost $r > 0$, which covers the cost of capital and depreciation.

Production Structure Dynamics   At any time t the distribution of production units is given by the density $n_t^+(b, v)$ of units that operate in the good state with external liability b and permanent productivity v and the equivalent density $n_t^-(b, v)$ of units in the bad state. These densities can be integrated to yield the total number of units in the good and bad states, and therefore total employment, N_t. Let us normalize labor supply to one, in which case aggregate unemployment—voluntary or involuntary—is given by

$$U_t = 1 - \int_{-\bar{v}}^{\bar{v}} \int_{-\infty}^{+\infty} (n_t^+(b, v) + n_t^-(b, v))\, db\, dv. \tag{6.14}$$

Aggregate output is

$$Y_t \equiv \int_{-\bar{v}}^{\bar{v}} \int_{-\infty}^{+\infty} [(\tilde{y}_t + v + \epsilon)n_t^+(b, v) + (\tilde{y}_t + v - \epsilon)n_t^-(b, v)]\, db\, dv.$$

Four factors drive the distributional dynamics of production units (see panel [b] of figure 6.3): (1) units are continuously created, (2) units are also continuously destroyed, (3) units decumulate or accumulate b, depending on whether they experience positive or negative cash flows, and (4) units switch between the good and the bad idiosyncratic states with hazard rate λ. The effect of distributional dynamics on aggregate employment is captured by the aggregate gross rates of creation and destruction of production units—denoted by H_t and D_t respectively.

The creation of new production units requires two conditions derived later in section 6.2.3: the project must be profitable, and it must find financing. At any point in time, all projects that satisfy both conditions are undertaken. The entrepreneur hires a worker, makes a specific investment of $\phi\kappa$, and rents $(1 - \phi)\kappa$ units of generic capital. If the entrepreneur's wealth is a_i, the initial level of external liabilities is $b_i = \phi\kappa - a_i$. All new production units start in the good state.

There are two distinct types of destruction. It may occur either because the production unit experiences an exogenous failure (at the above-mentioned rate δ) or due to a separation decision within a functioning production unit. In both cases, specific capital loses all value once factors separate. An endogenous separation decision takes place during periods of negative cash flows when the entrepreneur stops making the investment that is necessary to cover negative cash flows and continue operations.

Let us restrict the model's range of parameters such that in the good state operating cash flows are always positive and allow production units to reduce their liabilities and accumulate internal funds, and such that in the bad state operating cash flows are always negative. Section 6.5 describes the conditions that have to be met for these two properties to hold. Once a production unit finds itself in the adverse cash-flow position that characterizes the bad state, it must decide whether to interrupt operations or to fund negative cash flows with the hope of reverting to the profitable good state. Similarly to creation-investment, this continuation-investment decision requires two conditions that are also derived in section 6.2.3: the entrepreneur must find it profitable to cover the unit's negative cash flow, and he or she must find financing for it. Destruction takes place when one of these two conditions fails to be satisfied. Failure of the profitability condition results in privately efficient separation between factors. Failure of the financing condition results in privately inefficient separation.

6.2.2   Contracting Failures in the Labor and Financial Markets

Let us now turn to the determination of factor rewards when a fraction ϕ of capital is specific with respect to labor and to the entrepreneur-manager.

The Employment Relationship   Assume, as in the basic static model, that labor and capital (held by the entrepreneur and external financiers) transact as two monolithic partners. Because of the contracting problem, specific quasi-rents must be divided ex post after investment is sunk. The division is governed by continuous-time Nash bargaining. In addition to its outside opportunity cost labor obtains a share $\beta \in (0, 1)$ of the present value S of the unit's specific quasi-rents, s_{it}, and capital obtains a share $(1 - \beta)$ of S.

The specific quasi-rents in production unit i are

$$s_{it} = (\tilde{y}_t + v_i + \tilde{\epsilon}_{it} - r(1 - \phi)\kappa) - w_t^o,$$

which is equal to output net of the rental cost of generic capital minus labor's flow opportunity cost w_t^o of participating in a production unit. In order to give the worker the amount βS in present value at any point in time the wage path for each production unit i must be equal to

$$w_{it} = w_t^o + \beta s_{it}. \tag{6.15}$$

Profits are equal to

$$\pi_{it} \equiv (\tilde{y}_t + v_i + \tilde{\epsilon}_{it} - r(1 - \phi)\kappa) - w_{it} = (1 - \beta)s_{it}. \tag{6.16}$$

Finally, labor's opportunity cost is given by

$$w_t^o = z + \frac{H_t}{U_t}\beta E_v[S_t^+]. \tag{6.17}$$

As is standard in equilibrium bargaining models, labor's opportunity cost is equal to the marginal utility of leisure plus the product of the rate H_t/U_t at which an unemployed worker expects to find employment and the share he or she expects to obtain of the surplus from a new job, $\beta E_v[S_t]$. The expected surplus $E_v[S_t]$ depends on the distribution of external liabilities and permanent idiosyncratic productivities in new production units. A precise formula will be given later in equation (6.28), and a more detailed discussion of the division of specific quasi-rents through continuous-time Nash bargaining is provided in section 6.6.

Before turning to the discussion of equilibrium, it is useful to consider the behavior of the economy as β goes to zero, that is, as the employment friction vanishes. In this limiting case the wage equals the opportunity cost of labor. As long as new projects are sufficiently profitable and well-financed, this limit economy features full employment. The wage rate in the economy exceeds the marginal utility of leisure in order to clear the labor market.

Expression (6.16) allows us to define profit functions $\pi_{it} = \pi^+(v_i)$ in the good idiosyncratic state and $\pi_{it} = \pi^-(v_i)$ in the bad state, where

$$\pi^+(v) = (1 - \beta)[(\tilde{y}_t + v + \epsilon - r(1 - \phi)\kappa) - w_t^o] \qquad (6.18)$$

and

$$\pi^-(v) = (1 - \beta)[(\tilde{y}_t + v - \epsilon - r(1 - \phi)\kappa) - w_t^o]. \qquad (6.19)$$

If the unit has external liabilities b_{it} and productivity v_i, the expected present discounted value of profit flows is a function $\Pi_t^+(b_{it}, v_i)$ when the unit is in the good state and $\Pi_t^-(b_{it}, v_i)$ when it is in the bad state. These functions are (weakly) decreasing in b_{it} because a higher b_{it} generally increases the probability of privately inefficient liquidation.

The Financing Relationship   The financing relationship is restricted to noncollateralizable investments because the collateralizable share of capital $(1 - \phi)\kappa$ is unproblematic and can be rented. Specificity with respect to the entrepreneur-manager gives rise to contracting problems similar to those that arise in the employment relationship. The entrepreneur-manager can always threaten ex post to withhold his or her human capital from the production unit, and he or she attempts to renegotiate with the financier on that basis. Let us assume that Nash bargaining would give a share $\alpha \in (0, 1)$ of the present value Π of profits to the manager and a share $(1 - \alpha)$ to the financier. Therefore, any external claim for the financier above $(1 - \alpha)\Pi$ is renegotiated down. This puts an upper bound on the external claims a production unit can support.

The inability to obtain financing may prevent an entrepreneur from undertaking an otherwise profitable project, or may force him or her to liquidate a highly productive unit that encounters a period of negative cash flows (see section 6.2.3). In this context, an optimal policy for the entrepreneur that minimizes the risk of inefficient liquidation is not to consume dividends until the production unit fails or is liquidated. This implies, in particular, that loan repayments are effectively made at the fastest possible rate.

A contract that minimizes the impact of the financial constraint must satisfy the following properties: (1) the financier expects to get his money back in present value, (2) the above-mentioned renegotiation constraint is not violated, and (3) the entrepreneur does not consume from the project's cash flow before the financier's claim has been fully paid. For the financier to be paid back in expectation, the entrepreneur can only stop repaying the financier when the latter's claim b_{it} reaches zero. Beyond these requirements, the model does not distinguish between different institutional arrangements—debt-like or equity-like—as long as they result in the same investment decisions and net transfers between the two parties.

6.2.3 Creation and Continuation

Let us now derive the conditions under which creation and continuation investments are undertaken. The first type of investment consists of the specific investment $\phi\kappa$ required to create a production unit. The second type consists of the investments made to cover periods of negative cash flows in order to keep the unit's specific assets intact. By its very nature, continuation investment is fully specific and subject to contracting obstacles. Both types of investments are subject to a profitability and a financial constraint. They will only be undertaken if neither constraint is binding.

Creation Investment   Suppose an entrepreneur with wealth a has a project for a production unit with productivity v. As stated before, a project is always started in the good idiosyncratic state. To create the unit, the entrepreneur needs to incur a liability $b = \phi\kappa - a$. The two conditions for undertaking the project are as follows. First, the project must be profitable ex ante (at the time of creation):

$$\phi\kappa \leq \Pi_t^+(b, v). \tag{6.20}$$

Second, the entrepreneur must be able to attract the required financing, which we have seen is limited to the maximum liability:

$$b \leq (1 - \alpha)\Pi_t^+(b, v). \tag{6.21}$$

Since $\Pi_t^+(b, v)$ is decreasing in b, constraints (6.20) and (6.21) can be rewritten as

$$\phi\kappa - a \leq \min\{\bar{b}_t^{p+}(v), \bar{b}_t^{f+}(v)\}, \tag{6.22}$$

where $\bar{b}_t^{p+}$ is defined implicitly by taking the *profitability constraint* with equality, and $\bar{b}_t^{f+}$ is defined by taking the *financial constraint* with equality (either variable can take value $+\infty$ when the constraint is not binding):

$$\phi\kappa = \Pi_t^+(\bar{b}_t^{p+}(v), v), \tag{6.23}$$

$$\bar{b}_t^{f+}(v) = (1 - \alpha)\Pi_t^+(\bar{b}_t^{f+}(v), v). \tag{6.24}$$

One can show that for projects with sufficiently low productivity it is the profitability constraint that is binding, while for projects with high productivity it is the financial constraint that binds. Figure 6.4 illustrates the operation of the two constraints on the creation of projects with productivities v_1 and v_2, where $v_1 < v_2$. For projects with productivity v_1, it

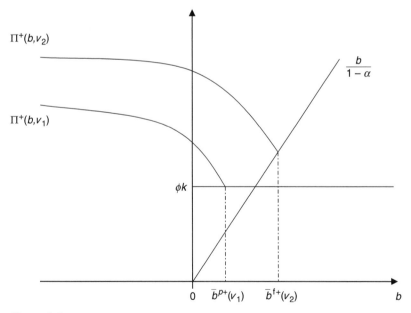

Figure 6.4
Operation of profitability and financing constraints
Source: Caballero and Hammour (1999).

is the profitability constraint $b \leq \bar{b}^{p+}(v_1)$ that is binding, while for projects with productivity v_2, it is the financial constraint $b \leq \bar{b}^{f+}(v_2)$.

Continuation Investment   Given the assumed restriction to parameters such that cash flows are positive in the good state and negative in the bad state—that is, $\pi_t^+(v) > 0$ and $\pi_t^-(v) < 0$—continuation investment is always required in the bad state. The entrepreneur faces profitability and financial constraints, $\bar{b}_t^{p-}(v)$ and $\bar{b}_t^{f-}(v)$, similar to those that impact upon the investment decisions for new projects.

The *profitability constraint* requires

$\Pi_t^-(b, v) \geq 0.$

In other words, continuation of funding in a unit with productivity v is profitable if $b \leq \bar{b}_t^{p-}(v)$, such that

$$0 = \Pi_t^-(\bar{b}_t^{p-}(v), v). \tag{6.25}$$

Section 6.7 shows that, in steady state, $\bar{b}^{p-}(v) \in \{-\infty, 0\}$. That is, for a large enough v all firms with negative b are profitable, whereas for a low v no firms are profitable, regardless of their level of assets.

The *financial constraint* may affect a unit in the bad state with no internal funds to cover its negative cash flow ($b \geq 0$). This can be illustrated most easily in a steady-state setting where aggregate conditions are invariant. In the absence of financing constraints (i.e., taking the limit $b \to -\infty$), one can show that the value of the option to cover negative cash flows in the bad state is

$$\frac{\pi^-(v) + \lambda \Pi^+(-\infty, v)}{\rho + \delta + \lambda}. \tag{6.26}$$

However, because the manager would renegotiate the debt down to $\bar{b}^{f+}(v)$ once in the good state one can show that the value to the financier of the option to finance negative cash flows is no greater than

$$\frac{\pi^-(v) + \lambda(1 - \alpha)\Pi^+(\bar{b}^{f+}(v), v)}{\rho + \delta + \lambda},$$

which is obviously smaller than the private value (6.26) of continuation, since

$$\lambda \bar{b}^{f+}(v) = \lambda(1 - \alpha)\Pi^+(\bar{b}^{f+}(v), v) < \lambda(1 - \alpha)\Pi^+(-\infty, v) < \lambda \Pi^+(-\infty, v).$$

It is therefore possible for *privately inefficient liquidation* to take place, where continuation has positive present value but cannot be financed externally.

One can show that if the entrepreneur is able to attract external financing for continuation purposes, he or she will be able to do so irrespective of the current level of $b \geq 0$. To see this, consider two non-negative levels of external liability, $b_{\text{high}} > b_{\text{low}} \geq 0$. If the outside investor is willing to finance continuation at b_{low}, he or she has all the more reason to finance it at b_{high}, since his or her return in that case can only be greater. Conversely, if continuation is financed at b_{high}, the entrepreneur can always find an interest rate path that will attract finance at b_{low}. One such path is to increase the liability instantly to b_{high}, at which level we know that external finance can be induced. This path is preferable for the entrepreneur to inefficient liquidation, although he or she generally has more favorable alternatives.

In other words, for any productivity level v, the maximum liability $\bar{b}^{f-}(v)$ for continuation financing to be feasible can take only two values: zero or $+\infty$. The interesting case is when continuation in the bad state cannot be financed. Let us therefore restrict the parameters to the region where cash flows in the bad state are sufficiently negative that the finance constraint on continuation is *always binding*:

$$\bar{b}_t^{f-}(v) = 0, \qquad v \in [-\bar{v}, \bar{v}], \ t \geq 0.$$

That is, no unit can obtain external financing for continuation in the bad state.

Finally, one must examine two possible mechanisms to avoid the privately inefficient liquidation problem: (1) an insurance contract with the financier, and (2) the possibility of financing by the worker. Let us look at these in turn.

Conceivably, the financier may offer the entrepreneur an "insurance" arrangement through which he or she commits to finance negative cash flows in the bad state in exchange for the entrepreneur paying an insurance premium in the good state. With large enough cash flows in the good state, the financier may be able to break even. However, if the financier cannot observe or verify the production unit's idiosyncratic state, the insurance scheme becomes infeasible, as the entrepreneur need only claim to be in the bad state to collect the insurance. As is well known, the informational problem is less severe under a simple liability arrangement, where the entrepreneur must liquidate his production unit if he or she is to discontinue payments to the financier.

When a privately inefficient separation takes place, both the entrepreneur and worker lose their share of the production unit's surplus $S_t^-(b, v)$. Could labor come to the rescue by taking a wage cut? One can show that the manager-owner is also subject to a financing constraint with respect to the worker similar to that with respect to an external financier. Let us constrain the parameter space so that this worker financing constraint is always binding. To see that such a situation is feasible, consider the continuous-time Nash bargaining solution behind wage equation (6.15), where labor and the entrepreneur get their shares—β and $(1 - \beta)$, respectively—of the flow surplus s_t. If the entrepreneur runs out of internal funds in the bad state and is unable to finance his share of the negative surplus, the Nash bargaining problem becomes constrained and the solution involving worker's financing breaks down. It may make sense for the worker, in that case, to finance the whole of $s_t^-(v)$ in the bad state in order to retain his share $\beta S_t^+(b, v)$ in the good state. The steady-state condition for this to happen is

$$s_t^-(v) + \lambda \beta S_t^+(-\infty, v) > 0.$$

On the other hand, the condition for continuation to be privately efficient is

$$s_t^-(v) + \lambda S_t^+(-\infty, v) > 0.$$

It is therefore clear that as long as $\beta < 1$, financing may not be worthwhile for labor even when continuation is privately efficient.

6.2.4 Aggregate Dynamics and Equilibrium

Let us conclude our discussion of the model by describing the dynamics that govern the distribution of production units, the aggregate gross rates of creation and destruction of production units, and the wealth dynamics that determine new projects' financing requirements.

Distributional Dynamics Section 6.8 provides the system (equations 6.44–6.45) of stochastic partial differential equations that governs the dynamics of the distributions $n_t^+(b, v)$ and $n_t^-(b, v)$ of production units in the good and bad states. These dynamics are determined by flows on the creation and destruction margins as well as by the dynamics of external liabilities. The latter are determined by the required risk-adjusted return. A production unit's external liabilities, b, evolve according to

$$\dot{b}_t = R(b_t)b_t - \pi_t, \qquad \text{where } R(b) \equiv \begin{cases} \rho + \delta + \lambda, & b > 0; \\ \rho, & b \leq 0. \end{cases}$$

Recall that the analysis is restricted to the case in which negative cash flows cannot be financed externally in the bad state. With positive external liabilities $(b_t > 0)$—which, by assumption, only occur in the good state—the external financier requires a return $\rho + \delta + \lambda$, to cover the opportunity cost ρ of capital as well as the hazard rate $\delta + \lambda$ of failure or liquidation in the bad state. With positive internal funds $(b_t < 0)$, the entrepreneur earns the interest rate ρ (which is equal to $r - \delta$).

From the flows on the creation and destruction margins and from the dynamics of b one obtains the system (equations 6.46–6.48) of stochastic partial differential equations that governs the distribution of production unit values $\Pi_t^+(b, v)$ and $\Pi_t^-(b, v)$ in the good and bad states. These are reported in section 6.8.

Gross Creation   For each productivity v, the creation constraints (6.22) imply that a minimum level of entrepreneur wealth is needed for creation to occur. The entrepreneur's minimum wealth translates into an upper bound $b \leq \min\{\bar{b}_t^{p+}(v), \bar{b}_t^{f+}(v)\}$ on initial external liabilities. This allows us to write total gross creation as

$$H_t = \int_{-\bar{v}}^{\bar{v}} \int_{-\infty}^{\min\{\bar{b}_t^{p+}(v), \bar{b}_t^{f+}(v)\}} g(b; A_t)f(v)\, db\, dv. \tag{6.27}$$

With this expression in hand, we can go back to labor's flow opportunity cost (6.17) and write an explicit expression for the quasi-rents a worker expects to capture in a new job:

$$E_v[S_t] = \frac{1}{1-\beta} \int_{-\bar{v}}^{\bar{v}} \int_{-\infty}^{\min\{\bar{b}_t^{p+}(v), \bar{b}_t^{f+}(v)\}} \Pi_t^+(b, v) \frac{g(b; A_t)f(v)}{H_t}\, db\, dv. \tag{6.28}$$

Gross Destruction   The number D_t of production units destroyed at any point in time has three components:

$$D_t = D_t^\delta + D_t^s + D_t^f,$$

where

$$D_t^\delta = \delta(1 - U_t), \tag{6.29}$$

$$D_t^s = \lambda \int_{-\tilde{v}}^{\bar{v}_t^d} \int_{-\infty}^{\phi\kappa} n_t^+(b, v)\, db\, dv + \max\{\dot{\tilde{v}}_t^d, 0\} \int_{-\infty}^0 n_t^-(b, v_t^d)\, db, \tag{6.30}$$

$$D_t^f = \lambda \int_{\bar{v}_t^d}^{\bar{v}} \int_0^{\phi\kappa} n_t^+(b, v)\, db\, dv + \int_{-\tilde{v}}^{\bar{v}} n_t^-(0, v)\dot{b}_t\big|_{(b,\tilde{\epsilon})=(0,-\epsilon)}\, dv. \tag{6.31}$$

The three terms correspond to three types of destruction: (1) The first term D_t^δ captures the flow of units that fail for *exogenous* reasons. (2) "Privately efficient" (or "Schumpeterian") destruction D_t^s captures units destroyed because on continuation they hit a *profitability* constraint. Define $\bar{v}_t^d$ as the productivity level at which a unit with infinite internal funds would be indifferent about whether to continue operating in the bad state. The first term in D_t^s captures units that become unprofitable because they enter the bad state with productivity $v \leq \bar{v}_t^d$; the second, units that turn unprofitable because they cross that threshold while in the bad state due to deteriorating aggregate conditions. This type of destruction is a form of Schumpeterian destruction, by which unproductive components of the economy's productive structure are purged from the system. (3) "Privately inefficient" (or "spurious") destruction, D_t^f, measures destruction due to *financial* constraints. The first term in D_t^f captures the flow of units that turn bad and must be liquidated because of insufficient capitalization; the second term captures the flow of units in the bad state that run out of internal funds. All else being equal, the lower a unit's productivity, the more likely it is to be liquidated due to financial constraints. This "selectivity" of spurious destruction makes the difference relative to Schumpeterian destruction less stark than may appear at first glance.

Initial Wealth Dynamics   Recall that the mass density $g(b; A_t)$ of new projects' financing requirements is a function of an index A_t, which represents the aggregate wealth of non-active entrepreneurs. In order to allow for aggregate conditions $\tilde{y}_t$ to affect available funding—as emphasized, for example, by Bernanke and Gertler (1989) and Kiyotaki and Moore (1997)—let us assume that A_t follows the process

$$\dot{A}_t = \psi(\tilde{y}_t, A_t), \qquad \psi_1 \geq 0,\ \psi_2 \leq 0. \tag{6.32}$$

The model tracks the internal funds dynamics of production units in operation, but not the population and wealth dynamics of potential entrepreneurs. Although it would be methodologically more sound to track the details of the distribution of potential entrepreneurs' wealth, doing so would add another dimension of complexity. The specification given here uses an ad hoc shortcut designed to capture the observed pro-cyclicality and persistence of available funds.

Equilibrium Conditions   Given a stochastic process $\{\tilde{y}_t\}$ for $t \geq 0$ and initial conditions A_0 and $\{(n_0^+(b, v), n_0^-(b, v))\}$ for $b \in \Re$ and $v \in [-\bar{v}, \bar{v}]$, an equilibrium for this economy is a stochastic sequence $\{(n_t^+(b, v),$ $n_t^-(b, v),\ \Pi_t^+(b, v),\ \Pi_t^-(b, v),\ \pi_t^+(v),\ \pi_t^-(v),\ w_t^o, H_t,\ U_t, \bar{b}_t^{f+}(v),\ \bar{b}_t^{p+}(v),$ $\bar{b}_t^{p-}(v))\}$ for $t \geq 0$, $b \in \Re$, $v \in [-\bar{v}, \bar{v}]$, and $\tilde{\epsilon} \in \{\epsilon, -\epsilon\}$ that satisfies equations (6.14), (6.17)–(6.19), (6.23)–(6.25), (6.27)–(6.28), (6.32), and (6.44)–(6.48).

6.3   Inefficient Restructuring

Let us now use this dynamic model to analyze and gauge the quantitative implications of incomplete contracting in labor and financial markets, and to examine how this combined inefficiency influences the average and cyclical aspects of economic restructuring.

6.3.1   Parameter Choice

Let us engage in the always imprecise game of matching parameters in order to gain some sense on the order of magnitude of the effects discussed in this chapter.

Six parameters characterize technological aspects of production units: κ, ϵ, λ, δ, ϕ, r; two characterize institutional aspects of rent sharing: α and β; and two characterize preferences: ρ and z. One also needs to specify functional forms with associated parameters. Let us assume that (1) the joint distribution of project productivities v and financing requirements b is uniform in v on the interval $[-\bar{v}, \bar{v}]$ and uniform in b on $[0, b^{\max}]$, with total mass A_t at time t; (2) the dynamic process $\psi(y, A)$ that governs internal funds available for creation is linear and stationary; and (3) "business-cycle" dynamics for the aggregate component $\tilde{y}_t$ of firm output follows an Ornstein-Uhlenbeck process:

$$d\tilde{y}_t = -\gamma(\tilde{y}_t - \bar{y})\, dt + \sigma\, d\mathrm{W}_t, \qquad \gamma, \sigma \geq 0,$$

where W_t is a standard Brownian motion. Strictly speaking, some realizations of an Ornstein-Uhlenbeck process will violate two assumptions we have made in section 6.2.3—namely, that the following properties always hold: (1) $\pi_t^+(v) > 0$ and $\pi_t^-(v) < 0$, and (2) $\bar{b}_t^{f-}(v) = 0$. One therefore needs to assume that the process for $\tilde{y}_t$ satisfies these two assumptions, and check that these are always satisfied in the simulations.

Another relatively minor issue is that the expression (6.30) for D_t^s is not compatible with the infinite variation in the process $\tilde{y}_t$, because the term $\dot{\tilde{v}}_t^d$ is not well-defined in this case. However, ignoring this issue simplifies the exposition and has no practical relevance in the simulations, which are based on a discretized version of the model.

Table 6.1 summarizes the values for the model parameters, chosen to match several observed features of the U.S. economy. Section 6.9 provides a detailed description of how the steady-state features of the model were calibrated based on evidence concerning (1) general features of the economy, (2) factor market rents, and (3) the level of unemployment and gross flows. The calibration of the parameters that drive the economy's cyclical dynamics is motivated by the dynamics of employment and gross flows documented in chapter 2, and on proxies for available investment funds. Parameters γ and σ from the process for $\tilde{y}_t$ are set to values that result in unemployment dynamics similar in volatility and persistence to the dynamics documented in chapter 2. This resulting process implies an annual autoregressive coefficient for $\tilde{y}_t$ of about 0.4. In section 6.3.3, I

Table 6.1
Model parameters

Parameter	Value	Parameter	Value
κ	1.940	z	0.000
ϵ	0.283	$\bar{v}$	0.106
λ	0.205	$b^{\max}$	0.394
δ	0.060	ψ_0	−0.009
ϕ	0.329	ψ_1	0.558
r	0.135	ψ_2	−1.940
α	0.700	$\bar{y}$	0.899
β	0.333	γ	0.410
ρ	0.060	σ	0.180

Source: Caballero and Hammour (2005).

examine how the decline in restructuring following recessions is potentially related to the creation margin via the funds available for creation (equation [6.32]). Replacing the process for $\tilde{y}_t$ into the latter, and using a discrete time approximation (with $dt = 1/4$), yields an AR(2) process for A_t:

$$A_{t+dt} = [(1 + \psi_2\, dt) + (1 - \gamma\, dt)]A_t - (1 + \psi_2\, dt)(1 - \gamma\, dt)A_{t-dt}$$
$$+ \psi_1 \sigma\, dW_t.$$

Using as proxies the detrended series for business loans and deposits in the United States during our sample period it can be shown that an AR(2) characterizes these processes well (the series are detrended with an HP filter with $\lambda = 1600$; data source: Federal Reserve Economic Data [FRED]). The autoregressive coefficients are 1.54 and -0.65 for loans, and 1.27 and -0.39 for deposits. The choice of ψ_2 corresponds to an autoregressive coefficient near the middle of the range that is spanned by these estimates (1.41 and -0.46, respectively). Finally, ψ_1 is calibrated to match the relative volatility of the gross flows documented in chapter 2.

The constant term ψ_0 in $\psi(y, A)$ bears little relation to the economy's cyclical features. It effectively determines the steady-state mass A of potential entrants, which can be calibrated based on the steady-state creation rate H^* that an "efficient" economy—namely, one with no contracting impediments—would display. This can be easily seen by considering the experiment of adding mass to the $g(b; A)$ distribution at the right of $b^{\max}$, in such a way as to increase the efficient creation rate without affecting the inefficient economy. In the absence of an observable counterpart for H^*, let us choose a rather arbitrary value for A in the middle of its admissible range that generates an efficient creation rate $H^* = 0.185$.

6.3.2   Structural Unemployment, Sclerosis, and Scrambling

Suppose the economy is in steady state with a constant $\tilde{y}_t \equiv \bar{y}$. In order to sort out the effect of labor and financial market rents, let us describe four different economic environments: the "efficient" economy that suffers from no contracting problems; the α-economy that adds only the financial constraint to the efficient economy ($\alpha > 0, \beta = 0$); the β-economy that adds only the labor market problem ($\alpha = 0, \beta > 0$); and

Table 6.2
Steady-state equilibrium

	Efficient economy	α-economy	β-economy	$\alpha\beta$-economy
$\Delta \mathcal{W}$	—	−0.007	−0.060	−0.077
U	—	—	0.049	0.060
Y^s/N	0.960	0.947	0.886	0.884
H	0.185	0.177	0.094	0.104
D^s	0.125	0.101	0.037	0.024
D^f	—	0.015	—	0.023
w^o	0.745	0.737	0.725	0.697

Source: Caballero and Hammour (2005).

the $\alpha\beta$-economy $(\alpha, \beta > 0)$ that adds both problems. The calibration exercise refers to the $\alpha\beta$-economy.

The economy's aggregate performance is summarized by net output (flow welfare, for short)

$$\mathcal{W} = Y^s - \phi\kappa H, \tag{6.33}$$

where $Y^s \equiv Y - r(1 - \phi)\kappa N - zN$ measures aggregate output net of the return on generic capital and the foregone utility of leisure. Table 6.2 reports the welfare loss in each of the inefficient economies ($\Delta \mathcal{W} \equiv \mathcal{W} - \mathcal{W}^*$), as well as the three basic determinants of the flow welfare term: unemployment, average labor productivity, and creation. It also reports measures of gross flows and the shadow wage. Note that because gross aggregate output is normalized to one in the calibration, measures of aggregate welfare can be interpreted as a percentage of GDP in the $\alpha\beta$-economy.

The annual steady-state welfare cost of contracting impediments in the $\alpha\beta$-economy corresponds to nearly 8 percent of GDP. This cost is accounted for by several factors. In contrast to the efficient economy's zero unemployment, the $\alpha\beta$-economy suffers from a 6 percent *structural unemployment* rate. Moreover, its average productivity is 9 percent lower owing to two factors already highlighted in the static model: *sclerosis* in the productive structure and a *scrambling* of the productivity ranking along which creation and destruction decisions are made. Costs are partly alleviated by a reduction in job creation costs, given the economy's substantially lower restructuring rate.

Structural Unemployment   In steady state, "structural" unemployment is intimately tied to a restructuring process that faces labor market impediments. In the absence of both restructuring motives (when $\delta = \lambda = 0$) and labor market impediments (for $\beta = 0$), steady-state unemployment would be zero. As in section 6.2.2, new projects are sufficiently productive and well-financed such that the economy with $\beta = 0$ exhibits full employment. It is easy to make this assumption precise for the steady state of the economy. For a given value of the wage w^o one can use equation (6.27) to compute steady-state creation $H(w^o)$. Using the distributional dynamics given in equations (6.44)–(6.45) together with the formulae for gross destruction provided by equations (6.29)–(6.31), one can compute the steady-state level of employment $L^d(w^o)$ induced by a wage w^o. If $L^d(0) \leq 1$, then the wage is $w^o = z = 0$ in equilibrium. Instead, if $L^d(0) > 1$ in the region of interest, then the steady-state wage must exceed the marginal utility of leisure in order to clear the labor market.

Financial constraints exacerbate the unemployment problem caused by labor market inefficiencies. Unemployment rises to 4.9 percent due to the introduction of the labor market problem and to 6.0 percent when one adds financial constraints.

Compared to an efficient steady state with full employment, contracting impediments in the labor market give rise to wage rents, which break the efficient free-entry condition on the creation margin. Lower creation and higher unemployment are the economic system's endogenous response. They lead to higher unemployment duration U/H, which reduces labor's outside opportunity cost v (see equation [6.17]). This in turn offsets rent appropriation and helps guarantee the rate of return required by capital markets. Note, however, that although the shadow wage rate v falls with labor market frictions, this is not necessarily true of actual wages inclusive of the rent component (see Caballero and Hammour 1998a).

As mentioned earlier, table 6.2 shows that financial constraints compound labor market constraints to increase the structural rate of unemployment even further. This happens because financial constraints reduce the steady-state demand for labor, both because of the financial restrictions on creation and because the profitability of hiring is reduced by the risk of inefficient liquidation.

Box 6.2
More on depressed restructuring during recessions

Barlevy (2003) presents a model and evidence that further supports the view that the quality of the restructuring process worsens during recessions. He argues that reallocation during recessions may redirect resources from more to less efficient uses if the former face tighter credit constraints. There is reason to suspect that the latter condition holds, since more productive uses of resources typically require more borrowing in equilibrium, which makes these firms more vulnerable to aggregate downturns.

Based on a panel of U.S. firms operating in nondurable manufacturing for the period from 1984 to 1994, Barlevy presents evidence supporting his mechanism. Essentially, he regresses output per worker on new borrowing, controlling for lagged net worth and a set of industry-year dummy variables. The results show that, controlling for initial net worth, firms with higher output per worker tend to borrow more. This effect is larger and more significant for smaller firms. All in all, this evidence suggests that more productive (and relatively small) firms tend to depend more on borrowing, which suggests they should be more affected by recessionary shocks.

Sclerosis and Scrambling   In addition to unemployment, the economy suffers from distortions in the restructuring process. The inefficiency of this process is characterized by a combination of "sclerosis" and "scrambling": respectively, a slower and less effective restructuring. Both labor market and financial market problems create *sclerosis*—the survival of production units that otherwise would be liquidated in an efficient equilibrium. As illustrated in table 6.2, sclerosis arises through the low shadow wage v associated with loose labor market conditions (low H/U). This reduces the pressure to scrap low productivity units in the bad state, which reduces the threshold productivity $\bar{v}_t^d$ at which this is done. The result is a substantial reduction in the Schumpeterian destruction rate D_t^s. The β-economy exhibits a pure sclerosis effect, in which the Schumpeterian destruction rate is about one-third of the efficient-economy rate, while average labor productivity Y^s/N falls by 8 percent. Sclerosis is costly because it leads to an inefficiently low rate of restructuring.

Adding financial constraints to the β-economy worsens the quality of the restructuring process. The $\alpha\beta$-economy has a higher active destruction rate $D^s + D^f$, but slightly lower average productivity Y^s/N. This is

Box 6.3
Financial liberalizations and TFP growth in developing countries

Jeong and Townsend's (2005) case study of Thailand confirms that financial liberalization can be a driving force behind TFP growth in developing countries. Using a structural approach, they argue that the increase in financial system participation, from approximately 6 percent of the population in 1976 to 26 percent in 1996, had a profound impact on resource allocation.

In their model, households that have access to the credit market invest in projects as a function of entrepreneurial talent—capital flows to the entrepreneurs with the highest marginal return—and not of entrepreneurial wealth. Among those households that have no access to credit, on the other hand, investment in projects is determined by entrepreneurial wealth. High-wealth individuals invest their assets in their own businesses if they do not have access to bank savings accounts that pay interest. Putting these households in an intermediated sector generates gains on several margins: unproductive households abandon enterprise as they save and their wealth is put to better use, and talented households with low wealth are able to borrow bank funds to start a business or to expand its scale. Although financial deepening does not necessarily promote entrepreneurship for the entire economy (because unproductive households drop out of business), it improves the allocation of capital. At fixed factor prices, the better allocation of capital to entrepreneurial talent generates higher profits.

Over time, financial deepening raises employment in the more productive businesses and thereby fosters wage growth. The wage growth is common to credit and noncredit sectors, but the response to the wage growth is different between the two sectors. In the noncredit sector, wage growth helps wealth accumulation of workers and may encourage them to become entrepreneurs, improving allocative efficiency. In the credit sector, occupational choice is already efficient and the rise in wages reduces profits and entrepreneurial activity. This will dampen overall productivity growth.

Jeong and Townsend calibrate a model of the Thai economy by choosing the underlying productivity parameters and savings rate to match the actual time series of growth, the labor share and aggregate saving. Using this calibrated model, they calculate that explicit consideration of occupational choice and financial deepening explains about three-quarters of the Solow residual.

due to a *scrambling* phenomenon on the creation and destruction margins, which reduces the effectiveness of the overall restructuring process. In the absence of financial constraints, creation and destruction decisions are based on a strict productivity ranking of individual production units. When internal funds become a factor in those decisions, some units that are financed have lower productivity than others that are not financed (see Barlevy 1999 and the summary in box 6.3 for a related mechanism and supporting evidence). Given the creation rate H, this lowers the productivity of the average unit that is created. It also increases the productivity of the average unit that is destroyed by shifting the composition of destruction from the Schumpeterian component D^s to the spurious component D^f.

6.3.3   Depressed Restructuring following Recessions

Chapter 2 offered evidence from the U.S. economy that suggests that, contrary to conventional wisdom, a recessionary shock reduces aggregate restructuring. It turns out that the model presented here can account for this phenomenon. Let us turn to this issue next.

It is useful to develop the argument in two steps. In the first stage, let us assume that there are no financial constraints and look at the cyclical properties of the β-economy. Although this economy exhibits neither the financial constraints on creation nor the privately inefficient separations discussed in the calibration exercise, analyzing it helps to isolate a specific mechanism for the reduced restructuring based on *productivity selection*. Reintroducing financial constraints in the second stage (the $\alpha\beta$-economy) we see that the productivity-based mechanism is weakened and replaced by a much costlier fall in restructuring based on a *financial* mechanism (the business-cycle simulation method is described in section 6.10).

Figures 6.5 and 6.6 depict the impulse response functions for recessionary shocks in the β-economy and in the $\alpha\beta$-economy, respectively. For the sake of comparability, the size of the shock is such that it yields the same cumulative unemployment in the $\alpha\beta$-economy as a two-standard-deviation shock in the VAR estimated in chapter 2. Panels (a) and (b) depict the response of unemployment and job flows. Panel (c) depicts the cumulative response of creation and destruction, $\int_0^t \hat{H}_s \, ds$

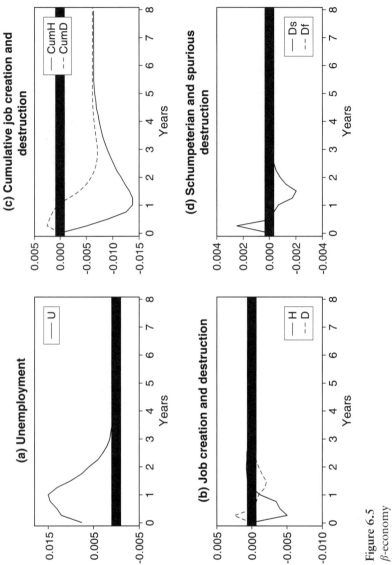

Figure 6.5

β-economy

Source: Caballero and Hammour (2005).

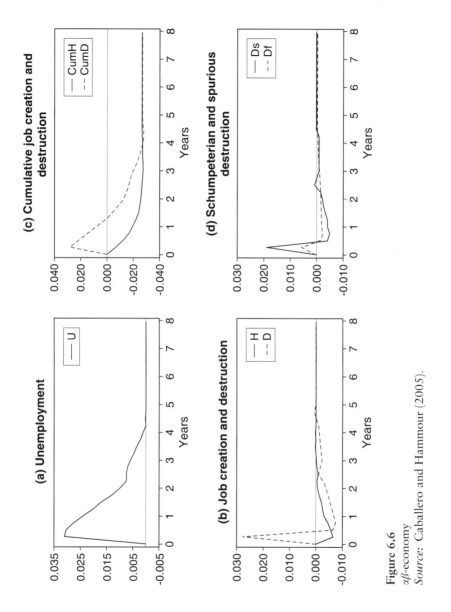

Figure 6.6

$\alpha\beta$-economy

Source: Caballero and Hammour (2005).

and $\int_0^t \hat{D}_s \, ds$. Panel (d) depicts the privately efficient and inefficient components of destruction.

The β-economy: Productivity-Based Mechanism   The β-economy in figure 6.5 exhibits a positive unemployment response to the recessionary shock, and the response dissipates over time so that the economy returns to the steady-state unemployment rate. The unemployment response is due to the wage "rigidity" brought about by workers' rent-seeking behavior ($\beta > 0$). In the absence of rents ($\beta = 0$), one can show that in an interior solution the shadow wage v_t absorbs all fluctuations in $\tilde{y}_t$ with no concomitant quantity response. When $\beta > 0$, a central determinant of the shadow wage is the job finding hazard H/U (see equation [6.17]). In that case, a quantity response in the form of increased unemployment or reduced hiring is required to induce a fall in the shadow wage in response to a contraction in $\tilde{y}_t$.

In terms of gross flows, the recession materializes through an increase in destruction and a decrease in creation. What determines which of these two margins' response dominates? As in chapter 5, the key to this question lies in the "insulating" mechanism by which a fall in creation reduces v and dampens the response of destruction to aggregate shocks. If a response that occurs exclusively on the creation margin is not costly, the economy will respond on the creation margin only and destruction will be fully insulated. In fact, it can be shown that this is what would happen if all projects in the economy had the same productivity v. Heterogeneous productivities within the pool of potential entrants makes it costly to concentrate all adjustment on the creation side. In this case, the average productivity of the entrant pool rises when the rate of creation falls, which makes further reductions in creation increasingly costly. The optimal response then shifts part of the burden of adjustment to destruction.

The recession's effect on cumulative flows depends not only on the response of gross flows at impact, but on the manner in which the economy recovers. As can be seen in panel (c), the economy experiences an increase in destruction at impact, but ultimately ends up with a decrease in cumulative destruction. The reason is that the recovery takes place essentially through a lower-than-normal destruction rate, while creation simply converges back to its normal level without much overshooting. Cumulative destruction is lower because employment is lower along the path. Quantitatively more important is the selectivity of creation with respect to project productivity. Those units that are not created during the recession are precisely units that have relatively low productivity, and therefore a high destruction rate. Their absence reduces destruction in the ensuing recovery. Overall, there is less restructuring throughout the cyclical episode.

The αβ-economy: Finance-Based Mechanism   Compared to the β-economy, the αβ-economy in figure 6.6 experiences more volatile unemployment, responds much more on the destruction rather than on the creation margin, and exhibits a more significant decline in restructuring. Overall, the αβ-economy is able to match the empirical impulse response functions of employment, gross flows, and the cumulative restructuring presented in chapter 2.

As an aside, note that the αβ-economy exhibits interesting nonlinearities as well. Although destruction is nearly four times more responsive to a large negative shock than is creation, the ratio of the overall standard deviations of destruction to creation is only 1.5—approximately the same as in the U.S. manufacturing sector. This is essentially due to a substantial difference in the economy's response to negative versus positive shocks. Relative to creation, destruction responds much more to a negative than to a positive shock. This feature has been documented for U.S. manufacturing gross flows (e.g., Caballero and Hammour 1994; Davis and Haltiwanger 1999). As a result, unemployment in this economy responds more to a negative than to a positive shock. This asymmetry in net employment fluctuations is reminiscent of features documented for the U.S. economy (see, e.g., Sichel 1989) and arises out of a fully symmetric shock process.

Returning to our main themes:

1. The introduction of financial constraints induces a significant shift in the economy's cyclical responsiveness from the creation to the destruction margin. Since the entry decision for many projects is now determined by the ability of entrepreneurs to finance them, there are financial rents on the creation margin. Those rents allow many projects to absorb negative profitability shocks, which shifts more of the response to the destruction margin. This dampening effect of financial rents on creation investment goes against the common conclusion that financial

constraints increase the volatility of investment (an exception is Carl-strom and Fuerst 1997). The conclusion of increased volatility relies on internal fund dynamics (Bernanke and Gertler 1989) or cyclical fluctuations in the value of collateral assets (Kiyotaki and Moore 1997), which are present in the model in reduced form through the dynamics of funds available for creation (see equation [6.32]). As a result of this cyclical financial mechanism, the creation margin regains part of its volatility.

2. The fact that financial constraints dampen creation investment does not mean that they dampen the *net* employment response. On the contrary, employment becomes more volatile as the economy's cyclical response shifts to the destruction margin. This margin is more sensitive to current conditions because of a shorter expected survival horizon.

3. The decline in restructuring following the recession is of a rather different nature than the productivity-based decline in the β-economy. The quantitative significance of the selection mechanism behind the productivity-based decline is now greatly reduced, as creation becomes much less responsive and the productivity ranking for entry decisions is scrambled by financial constraints. At the core of the decline in restructuring are the dynamics of the financial resources available for creation. The procyclical and persistent nature of fund dynamics leads to cyclical shifts in the creation margin. While the reduction in financial resources can accentuate the fall in creation during the recession, it will constrain the recovery from taking place along that margin until resources recover. The result is a shift from the creation to the destruction margin in the recovery phase—that is, a shift from more creation to less destruction—which results in significantly reduced cumulative restructuring.

4. On the destruction side, the decline in the importance of the productivity mechanism also implies that the fall in restructuring is not accommodated as much by a (cumulative) decline in Schumpeterian destruction as by the decline in privately inefficient separations (see section 6.3.4).

6.3.4   Decomposing Depressed Restructuring and Its Costs

In addition to the direct cost associated with unemployment, recessions in the model result in reduced cumulative restructuring. In an economy that suffers from structural sclerosis, there are positive gains from increased restructuring, and therefore the presumption is that the decline in restructuring adds yet another cost to recessions. However, there are at least two important caveats to this observation. On the one hand, if the decline in restructuring is primarily productivity-based, the losses arising from depressed restructuring are relatively small: the fall in creation selectively affects projects with low productivity. On the other hand, a financially driven decline in restructuring could in principle be beneficial since it reduces the number of privately inefficient separations. It turns out that the $\alpha\beta$-economy model calibration suggests that the fall in restructuring represents a cost of recessions, perhaps of the same order of magnitude as the unemployment costs.

Assume that the economy starts out in stochastic steady state, and experiences a negative aggregate shock to $\tilde{y}_t$ at time $t = 0$. If this shock affects "real" productivity, an obvious *direct* social loss results from lower productivity of all units. In order to separate the costs of inefficient restructuring from this direct cost let us assume that the shock to $\tilde{y}_t$ is due to an "aggregate distortion"—for example, due to a distortionary tax on gross output that is redistributed lump-sum. To compare the recession path of any variable X_t with stochastic steady-state value $\bar{X}$ in the absence of the new shock, define $\hat{X}_t \equiv X_t - \bar{X}$ and the resulting present-value operator

$$\mathscr{L}_X \equiv \int_0^\infty \hat{X}_t e^{-\rho t}\, dt.$$

Let us also define, for any two variables X_t and Y_t, the interaction operator

$$\mathscr{X}_{X,Y} \equiv \int_0^\infty \hat{X}_t \hat{Y}_t e^{-\rho t}\, dt.$$

One can now measure the social-welfare (net output) effect of a recession as the present value $\mathscr{L}_\mathscr{W}$ of the shock's effect on flow welfare $\mathscr{W}$, as defined in equation (6.33). The welfare effect can be decomposed into a component $\mathscr{L}_U$ that captures the unemployment effect, and a component that captures the productivity effects related to the restructuring process:

$$
\begin{aligned}
\mathscr{L}_\mathscr{W} = {} & -(\rho + \delta)(\bar{V}^b - \phi\kappa)\mathscr{L}_U \\
& + (\bar{V}^b - \bar{V}^{ds} - \phi\kappa)\mathscr{L}_{D^s + D^f} \\
& - (\bar{V}^{df} - \bar{V}^{ds})\mathscr{L}_{D^f} \\
& + (\bar{H}\mathscr{L}_{V^b} - \bar{D}^s \mathscr{L}_{V^{ds}} - \bar{D}^f \mathscr{L}_{V^{df}}) \\
& + \mathscr{X}.
\end{aligned}
\tag{6.34}
$$

The term V_t^b measures the average social value of creating a production unit, V_t^{ds} and V_t^{df} measure the average social loss from privately efficient and privately inefficient destruction, and $\mathcal{X}$ is an interaction term.

Formally, define

$$V_t^b \equiv \frac{\bar{y}^s + v_t^b}{\rho + \delta} + \frac{\epsilon}{\rho + \delta + 2\lambda},$$

$$V_t^{ds} \equiv \frac{\bar{y}^s + v_t^{ds}}{\rho + \delta} - \frac{\epsilon}{\rho + \delta + 2\lambda},$$

$$V_t^{df} \equiv \frac{\bar{y}^s + v_t^{df}}{\rho + \delta} - \frac{\epsilon}{\rho + \delta + 2\lambda},$$

where

$$v^x \equiv \int_{-\bar{v}}^{\bar{v}} \frac{x(v)}{X} v \, dv, \qquad X \in \{H, D^s, D^f\},$$

and

$$\mathcal{X} \equiv \mathcal{X}_{H, V^b} - \mathcal{X}_{D^s, V^{ds}} - \mathcal{X}_{D^f, V^{df}}.$$

The "unemployment" effect, which corresponds to the first line in equation (6.34), captures the direct social cost of unemployment adjusted for the passive response of δ-destruction. Formally, it is equal to the cumulative employment effect of the recession, $-\mathcal{L}_U$, multiplied by the flow social value $(\rho + \delta)(\bar{V}^b - \phi\kappa)$ of a production unit.

The "productivity" effect, captured in the next four lines, reflects the potential cost of maladjustment in addition to the unemployment cost. Lines two to five of equation (6.34) capture, respectively, the following terms:

• $\mathcal{L}_{D^s+D^f}$, which is the present value of the response of active destruction to the recessionary shock, as well as the response of the composition of gross flows over time.

• The welfare effect of changes in the amount of restructuring activity, assuming that it affects all productivities in equal proportions and that all destruction is privately efficient (the "restructuring" effect). We value a unit increase in cumulative reallocation at $(\bar{V}^b - \bar{V}^{ds}) - \phi\kappa$. It is equal to the *private* value increase from updating a production unit minus the reinvestment cost. Because of private rents on the creation margin, this social value is positive.

• By how much that welfare effect should be adjusted to account for the fact that some destruction is privately inefficient (the "spurious de-

Table 6.3
Response to a recessionary shock

	β-economy	$\alpha\beta$-economy
$\mathscr{L}_U$	0.022	0.046
$\mathscr{L}_H$	−0.008	−0.024
$\mathscr{L}_{D^s}$	−0.006	−0.003
$\mathscr{L}_{D^f}$	—	−0.015

Source: Caballero and Hammour (2005).

Table 6.4
Welfare (net output) effect of a recession

	β-economy	$\alpha\beta$-economy
Unemployment	−0.017	−0.035
Restructuring	−0.003	−0.015
Spurious destruction	—	0.007
Selection	0.002	−0.002
Interaction	−0.001	−0.001
Productivity	−0.002	−0.011
Total	−0.019	−0.046

Source: Caballero and Hammour (2005).

struction" effect). From the first term one must subtract the private loss $\bar{V}^{df} - \bar{V}^{ds}$, which applies to privately inefficient separations.

• By how much the effect should be adjusted to account for the fact that some productivities are affected more than others by changes in restructuring (the "selection" effect).

• An interaction term, which captures the fact that the previous effects are not independent of each other.

Tables 6.3 and 6.4 report the cumulative responses and the social welfare decompositions that correspond to the impulse response functions in Figures 6.5 and 6.6 for the β-economy and the $\alpha\beta$-economy. As explained in section 6.3.2, social costs can again be interpreted as a percentage of steady-state annual GDP in the $\alpha\beta$-economy.

The social cost of a two-standard-deviation recession in the β-economy is 1.9 percent of one year's GDP. It is essentially attributable to the unemployment cost of 1.7 percent. Productivity reduction adds only another 0.2 percent to this cost. Although a lower cumulative restructuring is harmful in an economy that suffers from sclerosis, it is less detrimental

Box 6.4
Pre-Keynesian "liquidationism"

Governments' unwillingness to use fiscal or monetary policy to counteract the 1929–1933 slide into the Great Depression may appear extraordinarily puzzling from today's perspective, but it was motivated by a conscious determination not to hinder the process of liquidation and reallocation of factors of production. As Herbert Hoover (1952, 3:30) bitterly recalls: "The 'leave-it-alone liquidationists' headed by Secretary of the Treasury Mellon felt that government must keep its hands off and let the slump liquidate itself. Mr. Mellon had only one formula: 'Liquidate labor, liquidate stocks, liquidate the farmers, liquidate real estate.' He held that even panic was not altogether a bad thing. He said: 'It will purge the rottenness out of the system'" (qtd. in De Long 1990, 5).

This "liquidationist" view found strong support among some of the most eminent economists of the day, such as Lionel Robbins, Joseph Schumpeter, and Friedrich von Hayek. Robbins (1934, 62) summarizes their argument as follows: "In ... a boom many bad business commitments are undertaken. ... [Goods] are produced which it is impossible to sell at a profit. Loans are made which it is impossible to recover. ... [W]hen the boom breaks, these ... commitments are revealed. Nobody wishes ... bankruptcies. Nobody likes liquidation as such. ... [But] when the extent of mal-investment and over-indebtedness has passed a certain limit, measures which postpone liquidation only make matters worse" (qtd. in De Long 1990, 7).

Based on this, Schumpeter (1934) viewed "depressions [as] not simply evils, which we might attempt to suppress, but ... forms of something which has to be done, namely, adjustment to ... change" (16). This led him to "believe that recovery is sound only if it does come of itself. For any revival which is merely due to artificial stimulus leaves part of the work of depressions undone and adds, to an undigested remnant of maladjustment, new maladjustment of its own which has to be liquidated in turn, thus threatening business with another [worse] crisis ahead" (20).

Von Hayek (1931a) concurred with this rejection of expansionary policy: "[T]he great expectations attached to ... public works in times of depression [are] ... fallacious," for public works also "bring about all those evil effects which ... arise when [the] money [supply] is increased" (qtd. in De Long 1990, 8).

once one considers that units created in a recession have high productivity (and therefore the option of restructuring is less valuable). This is why the selection term slashes the social cost of reduced restructuring by almost one-half.

Relative to the β-economy, the $\alpha\beta$-economy exhibits a larger employment response, and the depressed restructuring is more detrimental to welfare. The unemployment cost rises to 3.5 percent, and the depressed restructuring cost adds another 1.5 percent. The recessionary fall in creation is mostly financially driven, and hence is less selective across productivities than in the β-economy. Since it is not offset by a selection effect, the finance-based fall in the pace of restructuring is more costly.

Much of the fall in restructuring is due to a lower level of privately inefficient separations—which means the welfare cost of depressed restructuring is lower (see the positive welfare contribution of the decline in spurious destruction in table 6.4). Nevertheless, this is not nearly enough to overcome the restructuring cost that arises from the gap between the average *social* value of a newly created unit and that of a unit destroyed, privately efficient or not.

6.4 Conclusion

Opportunism in financial relationships compounds the macroeconomic problems identified in previous chapters, such as underemployment, market segmentation, depressed restructuring, sclerosis, and unbalanced restructuring. To these, one must add privately inefficient separations and scrambling, that is, the breakdown in the strict productivity (or profitability) ranking of entry and exit.

Over the business cycle, financial factors have the potential to exacerbate the productivity losses concomitant with sclerosis and scrambling during recessions. This observation leads to the main substantive contribution of this chapter. A common presumption exists among macroeconomists that a recession increases restructuring activity, but there is controversy about whether this is socially costly or beneficial. A tradition that goes back to the pre-Keynesian "liquidationist" school views increased liquidations as healthy; another view holds that liquidations are often privately inefficient and wasteful. As chapter 2 documents, the evidence from U.S. manufacturing contradicts the common presumption and seems to indicate that recessions *reduce* rather than increase the cumulative amount of restructuring in the economy.

Building upon this observation, the premise of this chapter is that a systematic treatment of contracting problems—of which privately inefficient liquidations are only one manifestation—is required to make an assessment of the costs associated with depressed restructuring.

For a reasonable parametrization of the model presented in this chapter, the conclusion is that depressed restructuring adds a significant *cost* to recessions.

6.5   Appendix: Parameter Restrictions

For the operating cash flows to be positive in the good state and negative in the bad state, it must be true that $\pi^+(v) > 0$ and $\pi^-(v) < 0$ for all v types and for all states of nature.

$\pi^+(v) > 0$ is hardest to satisfy for low types, thus it is sufficient to verify that it holds for them:

$$\pi^+(\underline{v}) = (1 - \beta)[(y + \underline{v} + \epsilon - r(1 - \phi)\kappa) - w^o] > 0$$

for all states of nature.

For this to be true, it has to hold in the most unfavorable state of nature:

$$\min(y - w^o) + \underline{v} + \epsilon - r(1 - \phi)\kappa > 0.$$

Likewise, $\pi^-(v) < 0$ is hardest to satisfy for high types, thus it is sufficient to verify that it holds for them:

$$\pi^-(\bar{v}) = (1 - \beta)[(y + \bar{v} - \epsilon - r(1 - \phi)\kappa) - w^o] < 0$$

for all states of nature.

In the most favorable state of nature, this corresponds to

$$\max(y - w^o) + \bar{v} - \epsilon - r(1 - \phi)\kappa < 0.$$

Both conditions are met for a high enough ϵ:

$$\epsilon > \max[\max(y - w^o) + \bar{v} - r(1 - \phi)\kappa, r(1 - \phi)\kappa - \min(y - w^o) - \underline{v}].$$

6.6   Appendix: Division of Specific Quasi-Rents

The arbitrage equation for the present value of profits of a unit in state $s \in \{+, -\}$ is

$$\rho\Pi_t^s(b, v) = [\tilde{y}_t + v + \epsilon^s - r(1 - \phi)\kappa - w_t^s(b, v)] + \lambda[\Pi_t^{\neg s}(b, v) - \Pi_t^s(b, v)]$$

$$- \delta\Pi_t^s(b, v) + \frac{\partial\Pi_t^s}{\partial b}(b, v)\dot{b}_t^+(b, v) + \frac{E[d\Pi_t^s(b, v)]}{dt}. \tag{6.35}$$

The term in square brackets captures flow profits. The remaining four terms reflect the capital gains associated respectively with transition to the other state $\neg s$, exogenous destruction, accumulation of external liabilities and changes in aggregate productivity. The corresponding arbitrage equation for the human wealth of an employed worker is

$$\rho W_t^{e,s}(b, v) = w_t^s(b, v) + \lambda[W_t^{e,\neg s}(b, v) - W_t^{e,s}(b, v)]$$

$$+ \delta[W_t^u - W_t^{e,s}(b, v)] + \frac{\partial W_t^{e,s}}{\partial b}(b, v)\dot{b}_t^+(b, v)$$

$$+ \frac{E[dW_t^{e,s}(b, v)]}{dt}. \tag{6.36}$$

The human wealth of an unemployed worker satisfies the arbitrage equation

$$\rho W_t^u = z + \frac{H_t}{U_t}E_v[W_t^{e,+} - W_t^u] + \frac{E[dW_t^u]}{dt}. \tag{6.37}$$

In addition to the marginal utility of leisure there are two capital-gain terms appearing on the right-hand side. The worker finds employment at rate $\frac{H_t}{U_t}$. The expected capital gain from a new job is $E_v[W_t^{e,+} - W_t^u]$. Changes in aggregate productivity give rise to the second capital-gain term. The present value of the unit's specific quasi-rents is defined as

$$S_t^s(b, v) \equiv \Pi_t^s(b, v) + W_t^{e,s}(b, v) - W_t^u. \tag{6.38}$$

Using the arbitrage equations (6.35)–(6.37) produces the following arbitrage equation for the present value of specific quasi-rents:

$$\rho S_t^+(b, v) = [\tilde{y}_t + v + \epsilon - r(1 - \phi)\kappa - w_t^o] + \lambda[S_t^-(b, v) - S_t^+(b, v)]$$

$$- \delta S_t^+(b, v) + \frac{\partial S_t^+}{\partial b}(b, v)\dot{b}_t^+(b, v) + \frac{E[dS_t^+(b, v)]}{dt}, \tag{6.39}$$

where labor's flow opportunity cost w_t^o is defined as

$$w_t^o \equiv z + \frac{H_t}{U_t}E_v[W_t^{e,+} - W_t^u]. \tag{6.40}$$

Specific quasi-rents are divided according to continuous-time Nash bargaining:

$$W_t^{e,s}(b,v) = W_t^u + \beta S_t^s(b,v), \tag{6.41}$$

$$\Pi_t^s(b,v) = (1-\beta)S_t^s(b,v). \tag{6.42}$$

Multiplying equation (6.39) by $(1-\beta)$, using equation (6.42) and subtracting from equation (6.35) yields the wage path

$$w_t^s(b,v) = w_t^o + \beta[\tilde{y}_t + v + \varepsilon^s - r(1-\phi)\kappa - w_t^o]. \tag{6.43}$$

Combining equations (6.40) and (6.41) produces the formula for labor's flow opportunity cost given in equation (6.17) in the main text.

6.7 Appendix: Exit Profitability Condition (Steady State)

In steady state, one can show that $\bar{b}^{p-}(v) \in \{-\infty, 0\}$. Let $\bar{v}^d$ be the level of productivity at which a unit with infinite funds ($b = -\infty$) is indifferent between continuing or liquidating in the bad state, namely, $\pi^-(\bar{v}^d) + \lambda\Pi^+(-\infty, \bar{v}^d) = 0$.

When $v = \bar{v}^d$, the value $\Pi^-(b,v)$ of a unit in the bad state is zero, irrespective of its level of b (a lower b cannot improve $\Pi^-(b,v)$ and $\Pi^-(b,v) \geq 0$), which implies that its value $\Pi^+(b,v)$ in the good state is also independent of b (dependence on b is exclusively the result of what happens in the bad state). Thus, any unit in the bad state will also find that $\pi^-(\bar{v}^d) + \lambda\Pi^+(b, \bar{v}^d) = 0$ irrespective of b and will be indifferent between continuation and liquidation.

When $v < \bar{v}^d$, it is clear that continuation is undesirable for any unit in the bad state, irrespective of the level of b.

When $v > \bar{v}^d$, continuation is strictly desirable irrespective of b for any unit in the bad state because it must be strictly more desirable than in the case $v = \bar{v}^d$.

From these statements, one concludes that, generically, $\bar{b}^{p-}(v)$ takes either value $-\infty$ (when $v < \bar{v}^d$) or 0 (when $v > \bar{v}^d$).

6.8 Appendix: Distributional Dynamics

This section provides the systems of stochastic partial differential equations that govern the dynamics of the distributions of production units and of production unit values in the good and bad states.

The equations that define $n_t^+(b, v)$ and $n_t^-(b, v)$ are

$$
\begin{cases}
\dot{n}_t^+(b, v) = g(b; A_t)f(v) + \lambda n_t^-(b, v) - (\delta + \lambda + R(b))n_t^+(b, v) \\
\qquad\qquad - \frac{\partial n_t^+(b, v)}{\partial b}(R(b)b - \pi_t^+(v)), \qquad b \neq 0; \\
\lim_{b \nearrow 0} n_t^+(b, v) = \lim_{b \searrow 0} n_t^+(b, v);
\end{cases} \tag{6.44}
$$

and

$$
\begin{cases}
\dot{n}_t^-(b, v) = \lambda n_t^+(b, v) - (\delta + \lambda + R(b))n_t^-(b, v) \\
\qquad\qquad - \frac{\partial n_t^-(b, v)}{\partial b}(R(b)b - \pi_t^+(v)), \qquad b < 0 \text{ and } v > \bar{v}_t^d; \\
n_t^-(b, v) = 0, \qquad\qquad\qquad\qquad\qquad \text{otherwise,}
\end{cases} \tag{6.45}
$$

together with the initial values of $\{n_0^+(b, v), n_0^-(b, v)\}_{b \in \Re, v \in [-\bar{v}, \bar{v}]}$.

The equations that determine $\Pi_t^+(b, v)$ and $\Pi_t^-(b, v)$ are

$$
\begin{cases}
(\rho + \delta + \lambda)\Pi_t^+(b, v) = \pi_t^+(v) + \lambda \Pi_t^-(b, v) \\
\qquad\qquad + \frac{\partial \Pi_t^+(b, v)}{\partial b}(R(b)b - \pi_t^+(v)) \\
\qquad\qquad + \frac{E[d\Pi_t^+(b, v)]}{dt}, \qquad b < \bar{b}_t^{p+}(v); \\
\Pi_t^+(b, v) = 0, \qquad\qquad b > \bar{b}_t^{p+}(v); \\
\lim_{b \nearrow 0} \Pi^+(b, v) = \lim_{b \searrow 0} \Pi_t^+(b, v);
\end{cases} \tag{6.46}
$$

and

$$
\begin{cases}
(\rho + \delta + \lambda)\Pi_t^-(b, v) = \pi_t^-(v) + \lambda \Pi_t^+(b, v) \\
\qquad\qquad + \frac{\partial \Pi_t^-(b, v)}{\partial b}(R(b)b - \pi_t^-(v)) \\
\qquad\qquad + \frac{E[d\Pi_t^-(b, v)]}{dt}, \qquad b < 0 \text{ and } v \geq \bar{v}_t^d; \\
\Pi_t^-(b, v) = 0, \qquad\qquad \text{otherwise;} \\
\lim_{b \nearrow 0} \Pi^-(b, v) = \lim_{b \searrow 0} \Pi_t^-(b, v);
\end{cases} \tag{6.47}
$$

together with the transversality conditions

$$
\lim_{t \to \infty} \Pi_t^+(b, v)e^{-(\rho+\delta)t} = \lim_{t \to \infty} \Pi_t^-(b, v)e^{-(\rho+\delta)t} = 0. \tag{6.48}
$$

6.9   Appendix: Model Calibration and Simulation Method

This section details the parameter choice procedure behind table 6.1, which was used to calibrate steady-state features of the economy. A number of parameters were calibrated to match quantities that arise endogenously within our model to the economic data. Although this amounts to a simultaneous equations exercise, it will be intuitive to think of it in terms of the assignment of one parameter for each matched quantity.

6.9.1   General Features of the Economy

Let us start with noninstitutional parameters. (1) The discount rate was set to $\rho = 0.06$. (2) The gross rental cost of generic capital was set to $r = 0.135$. Given the discount rate, this means a depreciation rate of 7.5 percent, which falls between the rates of depreciation of structures and equipment (*source*: BEA). (3) The aggregate component $\bar{y}_t$ of production-unit output was chosen in such a way as to normalize aggregate output to one. (4) The capital requirement of a production unit was set to $\kappa = 1.94$, which is the value needed to match the observed capital-output ratio (equal to 1.9 for the U.S. business sector in 1995; *source*: OECD). One must distinguish between the amount of capital actually utilized in production units and capital as measured using national-accounting, perpetual-inventory procedures. Since the separation rate is higher than the depreciation rate of generic capital, the stock of capital in production units is less than the version using the perpetual inventory procedure. The calibrations are aimed at matching measured capital. (5) The entrepreneurs' share parameter α determines the return premium on internal funds and hence the economy's profit rate. Let us set it to the value $\alpha = 0.7$ that yields a profit rate of 15 percent. (6) For the dispersion of project productivities, we set $\bar{v} = 0.106$ near the maximum value compatible with the model's constraint on bad-state financing. This corresponds to ± 10 percent of average productivity.

6.9.2   Factor Market Rents

The model exhibits private rents to labor and firms on the creation and spurious-destruction margins. (1) Abowd and Lemieux (1993) estimate the equivalent of labor's share β of rents to fall in the range $[0.23, 0.39]$.

See Oswald (1996) for a survey of the related literature. Using a value of $\beta = 1/3$ for labor's bargaining share means that the average rent component of wages is equal to 8 percent of the average wage. Expressions for private rents on the creation and spurious-destruction margins can be found in Caballero and Hammour (1998c). (2) Alderson and Betker (1995) estimate the liquidation value of a firm to be about two-thirds of firm assets. This leads us to set the capital specificity parameter ϕ to about one-third, which results in an average flow rent on the firm's side equivalent to 6 percent of the average wage.

(3) On the destruction side, privately inefficient separations can cause rent losses to labor and to the firm. The literature includes a wide range of estimates for the cost of job loss, which range from less than two weeks of wages to substantially more than a year's worth. See, for example, Ruhm (1987), Topel (1990), Farber (1993), Jacobson, LaLonde, and Sullivan (1993), and Whelan (1997). Using unemployment insurance data, Anderson and Meyer (1994) estimate an average worker loss of fourteen weeks of wages. Although this is an estimated average over all permanent separations—including privately efficient ones—let's apply it conservatively to the privately inefficient component of separations D^f. In fact, the median loss is of only about one week of wages, while about 9 percent of workers suffer a loss of more than a year. The literature on the firm side is much less developed. Hamermesh (1993) surveys various estimates, again with a wide range that goes from three weeks to two and a half years of a worker's wage depending on characteristics of the firm. Let us use the estimate of twenty weeks of wages from one of the more careful studies (Button 1990). The total loss of thirty-four weeks for the whole production unit is obtained by choosing a value $\epsilon = 0.283$, which determines the output gap between the good and the bad state.

6.9.3 Unemployment and Gross Flows

Let us now anchor the following quantities: U, H, and the different types of destruction. (1) The variable z can be used to calibrate the unemployment rate to $U = 0.06$, which yields $z = 0$. (2) By choosing the appropriate width $b^{\max}$ for the distribution of financing requirements one can fit the annual restructuring rate $H/(1 - U) = 0.11$. This gross restructuring rate is an average value between a sectoral measure of flows in U.S. manufacturing and an economy-wide measure of flows limited to the state of

Pennsylvania (Davis, Haltiwanger, and Schuh 1998). (3) On the destruction side, the restructuring rate translates into three types of destruction: $H = \delta(1 - U) + D^f + D^s$. Let us set the failure rate of production units to $\delta = 0.06$ to determine the first type, chosen in the lower range of values compatible with the parameter restrictions we impose in the main text. (4) The annual rate of privately inefficient separations D^f is about 2.5 percent of employment, which corresponds to the annualized rate of "displacements" as reported by the Displaced Workers Survey for the period 1991–1993 (Hall 1995, table 1). This survey was conducted in 1994 and asked whether the respondent had lost a job during the 1991–1993 period as a result of a plant closing, an abolished shift, insufficient work, or similar reasons. Hall points out that a separation is "more likely to be considered a displacement in a retrospective survey if it has larger personal consequences" (235). The Poisson parameter λ is used to calibrate this concept.

6.10   Appendix: Detailed Iterative Procedure

This section describes the method used to simulate the equilibrium dynamics defined in section 6.2.4 and simulated in section 6.3.2. The simulation is based on a discrete-time version of the model and a discretized (b, v) state space. Section 6.8 describes the systems of partial differential equations that govern the basic distributions of the model: the distributions $n_t^+(b, v)$ and $n_t^-(b, v)$ of production units, and the distributions $\Pi_t^+(b, v)$ and $\Pi_t^-(b, v)$ of production-unit values. The evolution of the former is mechanical and can be computed forward based on the economy's current state. Computation of the latter is more intricate, as it requires forward-looking expectations. In what follows, we describe the method we use to compute the functions $\Pi_t^+(b, v)$ and $\Pi_t^-(b, v)$. Although our simulation is in discrete time, we present our method in continuous time in order to keep the notation concise.

The only manner in which profits are affected by a production unit's environment is through the aggregate component of profit margins, $p_t \equiv \tilde{y}_t - w_t^o$. Thus, production unit values $\Pi_t^+(b, v)$ and $\Pi_t^-(b, v)$ must, in principle, be computed as a function of a state space that contains all variables known at time t that are relevant for forming expectations of the future path of $\{p_s\}_{s>t}$. In principle, this state space is infinite since it contains the distributions $n_t^+(b,v)$ and $n_t^-(b,v)$. However, the detailed shape of these distributions is unlikely to be important for the present value of profits over an extended horizon. It is plausible that p_t can be forecast reasonably well using only aggregate variables. Following this lead, the expectations of p_t were obtained from an AR(1) model, which ex post captures most of the predictive power of more general ARMA models. With this, one can approximate the value distributions by $\Pi_t^+(b,v) \simeq \Pi^+(b,v;p_t)$ and $\Pi_t^-(b,v) \simeq \Pi^-(b,v;p_t)$ using the following iterative procedure:

1. *Initialization.* Solve for the steady-state functions $\Pi^{+*}(b,v;p^*)$ and $\Pi^{-*}(b,v;p^*)$ assuming $\tilde{y}_t = \bar{y}$, for all t. Set $\Pi^{+\langle 0\rangle}(b,v;p) = \Pi^{+*}(b,v;p^*)$ and $\Pi^{-\langle 0\rangle}(b,v;p) = \Pi^{-*}(b,v;p^*)$. Set i equal to 1.

2. *Iteration i.*
   a. Assuming $\Pi^+(b,v;p) = \Pi^{+\langle i-1\rangle}(b,v;p)$ and $\Pi^-(b,v;p) = \Pi^{-\langle i-1\rangle}(b,v;p)$, simulate a long sample path for the economy and recover the sequence $\{(dp_t, p_t\,dt)\}_t$.
   b. Estimate the conditional Normal density $\phi^{\langle i\rangle}(dp\,|\,p)$ for the distribution of dp. To do so, run the regression $dp_t = (\alpha_0^{\langle i\rangle} + \alpha_1^{\langle i\rangle} p_t)\,dt + \varepsilon_t$ and recover the mean $\mu^{\langle i\rangle}(p,\Omega) = (\hat{\alpha}_0^{\langle i\rangle} + \hat{\alpha}_1^{\langle i\rangle} p)\,dt$ and standard deviation $\sigma_p^{\langle i\rangle} = \sigma_\varepsilon^{\langle i\rangle}\,dt^{1/2}$ of this distribution.
   c. Construct new functions $\Pi^{+\langle i\rangle}(b,v;p)$ and $\Pi^{-\langle i\rangle}(b,v;p)$. To do so, solve the system of partial differential equations (6.46)–(6.48) with $\Pi_t^+(b,v) = \Pi^{+\langle i\rangle}(b,v;p_t)$, $\Pi_t^-(b,v) = \Pi^{+\langle i\rangle}(b,v;p_t)$ and $p_t = p$ using

$$\frac{E[d\Pi_t^+(b,v)]}{dt}$$
$$= \frac{E[\Pi^{+\langle i\rangle}(b,v;p_t + dp_t) - \Pi^{+\langle i\rangle}(b,v;p_t)]}{dt}$$
$$= \frac{\int_{\Delta p} \Pi^{+\langle i\rangle}(b,v;p_t + \Delta p_t)\phi^{\langle i\rangle}(\Delta p_t\,|\,p_t)d(\Delta p_t) - \Pi^{+\langle i\rangle}(b,v;p_t)}{dt}$$

and

$$\frac{E[d\Pi_t^-(b,v)]}{dt}$$
$$= \frac{\int_{\Delta p_t} \Pi^{-\langle i\rangle}(b,v;p_t + \Delta p_t)\phi^{\langle i\rangle}(\Delta p_t\,|\,p_t)d(\Delta p_t) - \Pi^{-\langle i\rangle}(b,v;p_t)}{dt}.$$

d. Check for convergence in terms of $|U_t^{\langle i\rangle} - U_t^{\langle i-1\rangle}|$, $|H_t^{\langle i\rangle} - H_t^{\langle i-1\rangle}|$ and $|w_t^{o\langle i\rangle} - w_t^{o\langle i-1\rangle}|$. If the procedure has not converged, increment i by 1 and repeat this iteration. If the procedure has converged, use the current functions $\Pi^+(b,v;p)$ and $\Pi^-(b,v;p)$ to simulate the model.

Note

1. This chapter is based on Caballero and Hammour (2001, 2005).

References and Suggested Readings

Abowd, John M., and Thomas Lemieux. 1993. "The Effects of Product Market Competition on Collective Bargaining Agreements: The Case of Foreign Competition in Canada." *Quarterly Journal of Economics* 108(4): 983–1014.

Aghion, Philippe, and Gilles Saint-Paul. 1998. "Virtues of Bad Times." *Macroeconomic Dynamics* 2(3): 322–344.

Alderson, Michael J., and Brian L. Betker. 1995. "Liquidation Costs and Capital Structure." *Journal of Financial Economics* 39(1): 45–69.

Anderson, Patricia M., and Bruce D. Meyer. 1994. "The Extent and Consequences of Job Turnover." *Brookings Papers on Economic Activity: Microeconomics* 1994: 177–248.

Banerjee, Abhijit, and Kaivan Munshi. 2004. "How Efficiently Is Capital Allocated? Evidence from the Knitted Garment Industry in Tirupur." *Review of Economic Studies* 71(1): 19–42.

Barlevy, Gadi. 1999. "Credit Market Frictions and the Reallocation Process." Mimeo., Northwestern University.

Barlevy, Gadi. 2002. "The Sullying Effect of Recessions." *Review of Economic Studies* 69(1): 65–96.

Barlevy, Gadi. 2003. "Credit Market Frictions and the Allocation of Resources over the Business Cycle." *Journal of Monetary Economics* 50(8): 1795–1818.

Beaudry, Paul, and Frank Portier. 2004. "An Exploration into Pigou's Theory of Cycles." *Journal of Monetary Economics* 51(6): 1183–1216.

Bernanke, Ben, and Mark Gertler. 1989. "Agency Costs, Net Worth, and Business Fluctuations." *American Economic Review* 79(1): 14–31.

Blanchard, Olivier J., and Peter A. Diamond. 1990. "The Cyclical Behavior of the Gross Flows of U.S. Workers." *Brookings Papers on Economic Activity*, no. 2: 85–143.

Bronars, Stephen G., and Donald R. Deere. 1991. "The Threat of Unionization, the Use of Debt, and the Preservation of Shareholder Wealth." *Quarterly Journal of Economics* 106(1): 231–254.

Bureau of Economic Analysis, United States Department of Commerce. http://www.bea.gov/bea/dnl.htm.

Button, Peter. 1990. "The Cost of Labour Turnover: An Accounting Perspective." *Labour Economics and Productivity* 2: 146–160.

Caballero, Ricardo J., and Mohamad L. Hammour. 1994. "The Cleansing Effect of Recessions." *American Economic Review* 84(5): 1350–1368.

Caballero, Ricardo J., and Mohamad L. Hammour. 1996. "On the Timing and Efficiency of Creative Destruction." *Quarterly Journal of Economics* 111(3): 805–852.

Caballero, Ricardo J., and Mohamad L. Hammour. 1998a. "Jobless Growth: Appropriability, Factor Substitution, and Unemployment." *Carnegie-Rochester Conference Series on Public Policy* 48: 51–94.

Caballero, Ricardo J., and Mohamad L. Hammour. 1998b. "The Macroeconomics of Specificity." *Journal of Political Economy* 106(4): 724–767.

Caballero, Ricardo J., and Mohamad L. Hammour. 1998c. "Improper Churn: Social Costs and Macroeconomic Consequences." NBER Working Paper No. 6717.

Caballero, Ricardo J., and Mohamad L. Hammour. 1999. "The Cost of Recessions Revisited: A Reverse-Liquidationist View." NBER Working Paper No. 7355.

Caballero, Ricardo J., and Mohamad L. Hammour. 2000. "Creative Destruction and Development: Institutions, Crises and Restructuring." Paper presented at the Annual World Bank Conference on Development Economics, Washington, D.C.

Caballero, Ricardo J., and Mohamad L. Hammour. 2001. "Institutions, Restructuring, and Macroeconomic Performance." In J. Dreze, ed., *Advances in Economic Theory*, 171–193. New York: Palgrave.

Caballero, Ricardo J., and Mohamad L. Hammour. 2005. "The Cost of Recessions Revisited: A Reverse-Liquidationist View." *Review of Economic Studies* 72: 313–341.

Campbell, Jeff, and Jonas Fisher. 2000. "Aggregate Employment Fluctuations with Microeconomic Asymmetries." *American Economic Review* 90(5): 1323–1345.

Carlstrom, Charles, and Timothy Fuerst. 1997. "Agency Costs, Net Worth and Business Fluctuations: A Computable General Equilibrium Analysis." *American Economic Review* 87(5): 893–910.

Davis, Steven J., and John C. Haltiwanger. 1992. "Gross Job Creation, Gross Job Destruction and Employment Reallocation." *Quarterly Journal of Economics* 107(3): 819–864.

Davis, Steven J., and John C. Haltiwanger. 1999. "On the Driving Forces Behind Cyclical Movements in Employment and Job Reallocation." *American Economic Review* 89(5): 1234–1258.

Davis, Steven J., and John C. Haltiwanger. 2001. "Sectoral Job Creation and Destruction Responses to Oil Shocks." *Journal of Monetary Economics* 48(3): 465–512.

Davis, Steven J., John C. Haltiwanger, and Scott Schuh. 1998. *Job Creation and Destruction*. Cambridge, Mass.: The MIT Press.

De Long, J. Bradford. 1990. "Liquidation Cycles: Old-Fashioned Real Business Cycle Theory and the Great Depression." NBER Working Paper No. 3546.

Farber, Henry S. 1993. "The Incidence and Costs of Job Loss: 1982–91." *Brookings Papers on Economic Activity: Microeconomics* 1993(1): 73–119.

Hall, Robert E. 1995. "Lost Jobs." *Brookings Papers on Economic Activity*, no. 1: 221–256.

Hamermesh, Daniel S. 1993. *Labor Demand*. Princeton, N.J.: Princeton University Press.

Hart, Oliver. 1995. *Firms, Contracts and Financial Structure: Clarendon Lectures in Economics*. Oxford: Oxford University Press.

Hart, Oliver, and John Moore. 1994. "A Theory of Debt Based on the Inalienability of Human Capital." *Quarterly Journal of Economics* 109(4): 841–880.

Hoover, Herbert. 1952. *The Memoirs of Herbert Hoover*, 3 vols. New York: Macmillan.

Jacobson, Louis S., Robert J. LaLonde, and Daniel G. Sullivan. 1993. "Earnings Losses of Displaced Workers." *American Economic Review* 83(4): 685–709.

Jeong, Hyeok, and Robert M. Townsend. 2005. "Sources of TFP Growth: Occupational Choice and Financial Deepening." IEPR Working Paper Series No. 05.19.

Kiyotaki, Nobuhiro, and John Moore. 1997. "Credit Cycles." *Journal of Political Economy* 105(2): 211–248.

Klein, Benjamin, Robert G. Crawford, and Armen A. Alchian. 1978. "Vertical Integration, Appropriable Rents, and the Competitive Contracting Process." *Journal of Law and Economics* 21(2): 297–326.

Organization for Economic Cooperation and Development (OECD). *Statistical Compendium*, OECD. http://sourceoecd.org/.

Oswald, Andrew. 1996. "Rent-Sharing in the Labor Market." Mimeo., University of Warwick.

Ramey, Garey, and Joel Watson. 1997. "Contractual Fragility, Job Destruction and Business Cycles." *Quarterly Journal of Economics* 112(3): 873–911.

Robbins, Lionel. 1934. *The Great Depression*. London: Macmillan.

Ruhm, Christopher. 1987. "The Economic Consequences of Labor Mobility." *Industrial and Labor Relations Review* 41(1): 30–41.

Schumpeter, Joseph A. 1934. "Depressions." In Douglas V. Brown et al., eds., *Economics of the Recovery Program*, 3–21. New York: McGraw-Hill.

Sichel, Daniel E. 1989. "Business Cycle Asymmetry: A Deeper Look." Economic Activity Working Paper No. 93, Board of Governors of the Federal Reserve System.

Topel, Robert. 1990. "Specific Capital and Unemployment: Measuring the Costs and Consequences of Worker Displacement." *Carnegie-Rochester Series on Public Policy* 33: 181–214.

von Hayek, F. A. 1931a. "The 'Paradox' of Saving." *Economica*, no. 32: 125–169.

von Hayek, F. A. 1931b. *Prices and Production*. London: George Routledge and Sons.

Whelan, Karl. 1997. "The Welfare Cost of Worker Displacement: A New Approach." Mimeo., Federal Reserve Board.

7

Application: Structural Adjustment

Let us conclude part III of the book by applying several of the insights developed thus far to situations requiring large structural adjustments. For simplicity, I will limit the incomplete contracting problem to the labor market, but, as highlighted in chapter 6, it should be apparent that in reality the interaction of labor and financial frictions compounds the ills of restructuring.[1]

The need to restructure the economy's productive system and to reallocate factors is common to a variety of experiences in the developing world, as these countries face changing external opportunities or attempt to liberalize their economic systems. Such adjustment episodes are often times of crisis. These crises have important financial and political dimensions, but, at a more fundamental level, these extreme situations can be symptomatic of a failure of restructuring to take place in an orderly and efficient manner.

Adjustment crises are generally characterized by an existing productive structure that bears the full burden of the shock and faces extensive destruction, while the pace of creation and investment in the new structure remains excessively timid. For countries subject to adverse external shocks, sharp contractions in nontradable goods production are typically followed by slow growth in the tradables sector, giving rise to an acute unemployment problem. Rapid trade liberalization, it is often feared, may also lead to such an economic crisis, with an immediate contractionary effect on importables output that in the short run is hardly offset by the gradual growth in export production. For the reforming economies in Eastern Europe, the immediate collapse of the old state sector during the 1990s was typically accompanied by a sluggish emergence of the new private sector ultimately intended to replace it.

As a consequence of the gap between sharp immediate destruction and sluggish creation, an employment problem develops. Many workers who lose their jobs in the contracting sectors find themselves either in a state of overt unemployment or of being forced to take up much less attractive work in the informal sector. When the state sector is involved, the employment crisis often leads to an upsurge in idle public sector jobs.

This chapter develops a model with appropriability problems designed to shed light on the dynamics of liberalization reforms and the speed at which these should be implemented. In such restructuring episodes, the appropriability problem is prevalent, applying to much more than simply job-specific human capital. There are a number of levels at which capital and labor interact—the individual worker-firm level, the union level, the aggregate political level—each level imprinting its own form of specificity on investments.

7.1 Appropriability in a Simple Model of Adjustment

To focus our attention on a concrete real-world setup, let us take the example of trade reform as a paradigmatic case of adjustment. I start the section with a linear model. This yields nice closed-form solutions but results in some unrealistic features, such as instantaneous reallocation in the efficient economy, as well as degenerate destruction more generally. However, the main results do not hinge on linearity, which is relaxed in sections 7.2 and 7.3.

7.1.1 A Simple Linear Model of Adjustment
The economy has two goods, X ("exportables") and M ("importables"). Importables are used as the numeraire. The representative infinitely lived household at time t has linear utility:

$$\int_t^\infty [C_x(s) + C_m(s)]e^{-r(s-t)} \, ds. \tag{7.1}$$

Household labor supply is perfectly inelastic, with a labor force equal to one. Both goods are produced with similar Leontief technologies. For each good, one unit of sector-specific capital and one worker combine in fixed proportions to form a production unit and produce one unit of the good.

Initial Conditions   Before liberalization the economy is closed to international trade and begins in the relevant long-run full-employment equilibrium. Since consumers are indifferent with respect to X and M, both goods have preliberalization prices equal to one and the initial allocation of factors is arbitrary. Let E_m^- and E_x^- stand for employment in the M and X sectors respectively, where a minus-sign superscript denotes preliberalization quantities.

Liberalization   Let the international relative price of X with respect to M be $\theta^* > 1$, which is given for the country. An unanticipated full trade liberalization takes place at $t = 0$. It amounts to exposing domestic consumers and producers to X's international relative price. Let us assume that the capital account is open and the world interest rate is r, the same as the domestic discount rate. Since consumers are indifferent between the two goods, they specialize in good M. Producers, on the other hand, would like to specialize in good X. The cost of setting up a new production unit is c_0, which is a generic investment cost that stands for physical capital as well as organizational and training costs. Creation $H(t)$ takes place in the X sector, with all workers being hired from the unemployment pool $U(t)$.

Appropriability   The parameter $\phi \in (0, 1]$ measures the share of investment which is specific to the productive relationship, as defined in chapter 3. Let $S(t)$ denote the surplus over which a firm and a worker who meet at time t must bargain. Bargaining takes place according to the continuous-time generalized Nash solution. A share $\beta \in (0, 1)$ of the surplus goes to the worker and $(1 - \beta)$ goes to the firm.

The surplus $S(t)$ is equal to the value that the match creates above what the worker and the firm can effectively claim as their best alternative. Because of the appropriability problem, the firm can only recover $(1 - \phi)c_0$ of its investment if it drops out of the match. The worker's best alternative in the calculation of the match surplus is the *shadow wage* $v(t)$, equal to the worker's opportunity cost of remaining on the job rather than becoming unemployed and searching for another job. Thus, the match surplus is equal to the present value of the future revenue θ^* from production minus the worker's shadow wage v, after subtracting the protected part of the creation cost c_0:

$$S(t) = \int_t^\infty [\theta^* - v(s)]e^{-r(s-t)}\, ds - (1 - \phi)c_0, \qquad t \geq 0. \tag{7.2}$$

The opportunity cost $v(s)$ for the worker of holding the job is equal to the instantaneous probability $H(t)/U(t)$ of finding another match times the part $\beta S(t)$ of the match surplus he or she would obtain in the job:

$$v(t) = \frac{H(t)}{U(t)} \beta S(t). \tag{7.3}$$

Equilibrium Conditions   There is free entry for new production units. This means that in an interior solution the cost of creating a production unit is equal to the entrant's share of the match surplus plus the part of investment that can be protected. Formally, the free-entry condition is

$$c_0 = (1 - \beta)S(t) + (1 - \phi)c_0.$$

Rearranging this condition yields

$$\phi c_0 = (1 - \beta)S(t). \tag{7.4}$$

The firm's share of the match surplus must compensate it exactly for the unprotected investments it is called upon to make. This shows clearly that, under free entry, a positive match surplus is created if and only if there is an appropriability problem. Otherwise, if $\phi = 0$, the free-entry condition becomes $S(t) = 0$, which by equation (7.2) is the standard condition that equates c_0 to the present value of profits.

Solving for $S(t)$, equations (7.3) and (7.4) imply the following equilibrium conditions for all $t \geq 0$:

$$\tilde{c}(t) = \int_t^\infty [\theta^* - v(s)]e^{-r(s-t)}\, ds, \tag{7.5}$$

$$\begin{cases} E_m(t) = E_m^-, & \text{if } v(t) < 1; \\ 0 \leq E_m(t) \leq E_m^-, & \text{if } v(t) = 1; \\ E_m(t) = 0, & \text{if } v(t) > 1, \end{cases} \tag{7.6}$$

$$U(t) = 1 - E_x(t) - E_m(t), \tag{7.7}$$

$$H(t) = dE_x(t)/dt, \tag{7.8}$$

where

$$\tilde{c}(t) = (1 + b)c_0, \tag{7.9}$$

$$v(t) = \frac{H(t)}{U(t)} bc_0, \tag{7.10}$$

and

$$b \equiv \frac{\beta}{1 - \beta} \phi. \tag{7.11}$$

The first equation governs free entry in the economy, where the "effective" creation cost $\tilde{c}(t)$ is equal to the cost of investment distorted by a factor b (with $(1 + b)c_0 < \theta^*/r$ so creation is positive). This distortion is due to the problem of appropriability. In equilibrium, the portion of investment whose quasi-rents are appropriated by workers is bc_0. The "appropriation" parameter b given by expression (7.11) is increasing in the degree of appropriability ϕ and in the bargaining power of workers β. The second equation is the exit condition. It states that production units in the M sector are scrapped or preserved depending on whether their associated quasi-rents are negative or positive, which in turn depends on whether the shadow wage $v(t)$ is greater or smaller than one (the productivity in that sector). The shadow wage rate is given by equation (7.10), which follows from equations (7.3) and (7.4). The third and fourth equations are accounting equations that define unemployment and hiring.

As we already know from previous chapters, an attractive feature of the decentralized-bargaining equilibrium in this economy is that it converges to the efficient competitive outcome as the appropriation parameter b goes to zero. In the limit, the effective creation cost in equation (7.9) becomes undistorted, and the shadow wage in equation (7.10) becomes whatever is needed to clear the labor market and bring unemployment down to zero. Note that equation (7.10) turns into the full-employment equation once we multiply both sides by $U(t)$ and set $b = 0$.

The Nature of Unemployment   The free-entry condition (7.5) can be solved for the constant shadow wage rate that guarantees the required return on investment. Expression (7.10) can then be used to calculate, for a given level of hiring, the level of unemployment needed to yield the required shadow wage in equilibrium. We get

$$v(t) = \theta^* - r(1 + b)c_0, \tag{7.12}$$

$$U(t) = \frac{bc_0}{\theta^* - r(1 + b)c_0} H(t). \tag{7.13}$$

It is clear that in an economy with an important need to restructure and hire workers in new sectors, unemployment is the result of the positive match surpluses that result from appropriability. If unemployment were zero, workers would find it infinitely easy to capture the positive surplus of an alternative job. This outside alternative would make their shadow wage rate infinite (equation [7.10]), which would render job creation prohibitively expensive and generate unemployment. Thus, unemployment is an equilibrium response of the economic system, and it serves to restrain the bargaining position of workers in the presence of appropriability. This preserves the profitability of investment. As equation (7.13) makes clear, periods of adjustment and intense gross hiring require high transitional unemployment to prevent surges in shadow wages. Unemployment keeps shadow wages at a level that makes job creation pay off.

7.1.2   Sclerosis and Unbalanced Restructuring

Sclerosis   Let us now solve for the evolution of this economy. Solution (7.12) for the shadow wage, together with the exit condition (7.6), defines an *inaction range* in the parameter space, in which sector M remains profitable and no adjustment takes place following structural reform. The inaction range is given by $\theta^* < 1 + r(1 + b)c_0$, which clearly indicates that it is not enough for the world relative price θ^* of exportables versus importables to be greater than one for restructuring to occur. θ^* must be sufficiently larger than one to justify spending the additional creation costs.

Note that there is a segment $\theta^* \in (1 + rc_0, 1 + r(1 + b)c_0]$ of the inaction range where the inefficient economy does not adjust, despite adjustment being the efficient response. The greater the appropriation parameter b, the larger this segment of the inaction range. Thus, appropriability can prevent adjustment from taking place altogether in cases when it is efficient to adjust. This is *sclerosis*.

Sclerosis arises in the economy whenever the productive structure does not adjust sufficiently in response to new conditions—where adjustment may take the form of changing the sectoral composition of output, of adopting new techniques, of changing the capital-labor ratio, and so on. In this particular case, appropriability can cause the productive structure to be locked into its inherited form: the structure may not adjust in response to the trade opening, despite the efficiency of doing so. As in earlier chapters, the reason for sclerosis is the high effective creation costs induced by appropriability (equation [7.9]), which reduce the incentives for creation as well as the hiring pressures on wages and destruction (equation [7.12]).

The fact that sclerosis takes the extreme form of fully aborting restructuring is due to the degenerate initial distribution in the M sector. More generally, sclerosis leads to incomplete—rather than fully aborted—restructuring, as is the case in the heterogeneous technology model analyzed in section 7.1.4, or when the M-sector exhibits diminishing returns to labor.

Unbalanced Restructuring   Outside the inaction range, the M sector is instantly scrapped, and dynamics are governed by equations (7.7) and (7.8) with $E_m(t) = 0$:

$$dU(t)/dt = -H(t) \qquad \text{with} \qquad U(0) = E_m^-. \tag{7.14}$$

Taking (7.13) into account, the solution to this equation is, for $t \geq 0$:

$$U(t) = E_m^- e^{-((\theta^* - r(1+b)c_0)/bc_0)t}, \tag{7.15}$$

$$E_x(t) = 1 - U(t),$$

$$E_m(t) = 0.$$

The whole M sector is scrapped instantly following reform, leading to a jump in unemployment. However, creation in the X sector is gradual and can only absorb the unemployed progressively over time. Asymptotically, the economy adjusts fully and reaches full employment.

In the efficient competitive outcome, which corresponds to the limit when b goes to zero, adjustment is instantaneous and complete at time $t = 0$. In contrast, an economy subject to appropriability problems exhibits sluggish creation. This means that creation and destruction are out of balance and lead to transitional unemployment costs. The convex creation costs model of section 7.2 shows that the desynchronizing effect of appropriability on creation and destruction cannot be eliminated simply by slowing down adjustment. More generally, at the outset of reforms, appropriability leads to *insufficient creation* and *excessive destruction* relative to the efficient outcome. The fact that destruction is

Box 7.1
Disorganization

Blanchard and Kremer (1997) illustrate the potential importance of specificity problems in the context of transition economies. They argue that under central planning, many firms relied upon single suppliers for inputs and many firms had or only knew of one buyer. In this context, the main instrument to enforce production and delivery of goods was the coercive power of the central planner; thus bargaining inefficiencies should not have been significant. In contrast, transition economies eliminated the central planner and instituted decentralized bargaining between suppliers and buyers. Therefore, the economic system lost the main instrument used to limit the adverse effects of specificity and opportunism under the previous regime. Transition economies lack key mechanisms to deal with bargaining inefficiencies: new buyers and sellers cannot be created right away; the role of contracts is minimal (due to nonenforceability) when many firms are close to bankruptcy; and many state firms are expected to disappear or change suppliers, thus shortening horizons and reducing the scope for long-term relations to mitigate the adverse effects of specificity. This reasoning can explain a sharp reduction in total output after central planning was eliminated.

Blanchard and Kremer (1997) report anecdotal evidence supporting their view:

• Trade between the republics of the former Soviet Union fell by far more than seems consistent with efficient reallocation.
• Despite price liberalization, many firms reported shortages of inputs and raw materials.
• Firms lost crucial workers/managers, who may have been their only hope for restructuring and survival.
• Cannibalization of machines was widespread, even when it appeared that machines could be more productive in their original use.

The main empirical support for their view comes from a differences-in-differences exercise: they compare the decline in production during transition for goods with more and less complex production processes. The specificity/incomplete-contracts view predicts a bigger decline for goods with more complex production processes. To implement this idea, they measure complexity using the 1990 "100-sector" input-output table for Russia. Complexity is defined to be one minus the Herfindahl index of input concentration for different economic sectors (all goods produced in a sector have the same complexity index).

Using production data on 159 goods for nine countries (Moldova, FYR Macedonia, Kyrgyzstan, Georgia, Belarus, Azerbaijan, Armenia, Albania, and Russia) from 1992 to 1994 (1991–1994 for Russia), they construct output growth for each country/good observation (the choice of starting date reflects the fact that these economies were liberalized substantially in

Box 7.1
(continued)

1992). Next, they regress output growth on a set of country dummies, the index of complexity, and controls for the durability of goods, the ratio of world-to-domestic prices of goods in 1990 (to proxy for preexisting subsidization), and the growth rate of the factor cost index for each sector. Their results indicate that the index of complexity is highly significant, with and without controlling for the other variables. That is, production of goods with more complex production processes (i.e., using a larger number of inputs and, therefore, needing more bargaining processes) fall by more in transition economies, as expected when incomplete contracts create room for inefficient bargaining.

---

equal to its efficient level in the present case is only due to the maximal instantaneous rate at which destruction takes place (see box 7.1 for an amplification mechanism where a central component of the transition is a *worsening* of ϕ).

7.1.3   Covert Wage Rigidity Revisited

Although this model exhibits the transitional unemployment usually associated with fixed-wage models (e.g., Lapan 1976; Neary 1982; Edwards and van Wijnbergen 1989), here real wages may appear quite flexible. In fact, in the special linear case, wages are the *same* as what they would be in an efficient economy. To see this result, denote by w_x the actual wage paid by exporting firms (the only firms surviving after liberalization). Note that w_x is not equal to the opportunity cost of labor, v, for we need to add the part of the match surplus that goes to the worker, which in flow terms amounts to rbc_0:

$$w_x = v + rbc_0 = \theta^* - rc_0.$$

This expression is independent of b and is therefore exactly equal to the wage paid in an efficient economy where $b = 0$.

   Although the wage rate behaves as in the efficient outcome, the *quantity* adjustments are inefficient. Unbalanced restructuring and high transitional unemployment are needed in order to restrain the wage from surging beyond that level during times of intense hiring (see equation [7.10]). In other words, the wage rate appears adequately flexible, but actually harbors a hidden form of rigidity that manifests itself entirely in the equilibrium quantities that support it. This is a situation of *covert rigidity*, as discussed in chapter 5. As we will see in the convex creation costs model of section 7.2, observed wages more generally exhibit a mixture of "overt" and "covert" rigidity. The result is both that wages are above the efficient level and that quantity adjustments are required to prevent them from being even higher.

The variability of wages is consistent with the empirical evidence on wage rates, which generally exhibit a high degree of responsiveness in case studies of adjustment (Fallon and Riveros 1989; Horton, Kanbur, and Mazumdar 1994). However, the preceding analysis raises an important caveat for the interpretation of those findings, from which some authors have concluded that adjustment crises are not due to malfunctioning labor markets. In their World Bank study of the role of labor markets in the process of adjustment, for example, Horton, Kanbur and Mazumdar (1994, 1: 19–20) conclude:

[T]here are three possible explanations as to why unemployment may persist during stabilization. The first is that the labor market is not working well because of real wage rigidity. The evidence presented by the case studies certainly does not favor the view that real wages were rigid, and therefore led to unemployment. Even for Chile, where unemployment was highest and persisted the longest, real wages fell dramatically. . . . [T]his leaves the other two explanations: aggregate demand feedback from declining real wages to output and output market imperfections.

The model presented here clearly shows that looking at the path of real wages in isolation to assess the extent of labor market rigidity—which comes from the practice of modeling wages as exogenously fixed—can be quite misleading. Variable real wages do not necessarily imply that the labor market functions adequately. Other forms of empirical evidence are needed to assess the workings of the labor market. Looking at the degree of segmentation in labor markets—which is preponderant in the developing world (see, e.g., Lopez and Riveros 1989; Fallon and Riveros 1989)—may constitute a better test. Another class of evidence can be gleaned from the institutional features of labor markets that characterize the more "visible" aspects of appropriability. Cox-Edwards (1993) gives a careful account of the predominant institutional distortions in Latin American labor markets. These include employment protection laws, payroll taxes and antagonistic labor-management relations that encourage confrontation and costly settlement procedures. Consistent with

Box 7.2
Labor market distortions in Latin America and their effects on appropriability

Latin American economies exhibit a number of institutional distortions in their labor markets. Most labor codes follow the civil law tradition and incorporate detailed regulations related to labor contracts (including aspects such as type, duration, and conditions for termination of contracts). Cox-Edwards (1993, 1997) provides a detailed review of these regulations in Latin America in the mid-1990s. She classifies the distortions into three broad categories: job security laws, dispute resolution systems, and payroll taxes. The first two groups are directly relevant for the issues of appropriability highlighted in this book. The first group includes regulations such as severance payments (amount and reason for severance), advance notice of dismissal, as well as restrictions on temporary contracts (including probation period). Regulations in the second category define the rights of workers (i.e., to strike, to receive wage replacement during strikes, and to renounce union membership and go back to work during a strike), rights of employers (to lock out, to temporarily replace workers), maximum duration of strike, and the judicial body in charge of resolving conflicts. She documents that Latin America exhibits a pattern of relatively high job security, including elements such as a general absence of economic or technical reasons as "just" causes for dismissal, a bias against temporary contracts, and high severance payments.

These conclusions have been reinforced by the recent work of Heckman and Pagés (2000, 2003), Djankov et al. (2003), and Botero et al. (2004), who produced indices summarized in table B7.1. The index of Heckman and Pagés includes legal provisions that have a direct impact on the costs of dismissal. They compute the expected cost (at hiring) of future dismissal. The index includes both the costs of advance notice legislation and firing costs, and is measured in units of monthly wages. The first index in the table from Djankov et ai. has been described in section 2.5.1.

Dispute resolution systems affect the relative bargaining power of workers and therefore should play a role in creation and destruction decisions, as highlighted by equation (7.11). The "appropriation" parameter b is increasing in the bargaining power of workers β. Cox-Edwards (1993, 1997) presents evidence suggesting that workers have disproportionate power in comparison to employers. For instance, rights to lock out or replace workers during strikes do not exist in most countries. Djankov et al. (2003) also present indices of the protection of workers during collective disputes. Their index is the average of each of the following components (measured in 1997), which takes on values between 0 and 1: (1) legal strikes, (2) procedural restrictions to strikes, (3) employer defenses, (4) compulsory third-party arbitration during a labor dispute, and (5) right to industrial action in the constitution. Clearly, workers in Latin American countries have more bargaining power than workers in OECD countries.

Box 7.2
(continued)

Table B7.1
Empirical measures of labor market regulations in Latin America

	Job security index		Protection of workers during strikes
	Heckman and Pagés	Djankov et al.	Botero et al.
Argentina	2.98	0.44	0.72
Bolivia	4.76	0.57	0.67
Brazil	1.79	0.69	0.55
Chile	3.38	0.31	0.40
Colombia	3.49	0.62	0.70
Costa Rica	3.12	—	—
Dominican Republic	2.81	0.33	0.38
Ecuador	4.04	0.67	0.83
El Salvador	3.13		
Honduras	3.53		
Mexico	3.13	0.71	0.72
Nicaragua	2.56		
Panama	2.72	0.67	0.80
Paraguay	2.17		
Peru	3.80	0.70	0.82
Uruguay	2.23	0.03	0.47
Venezuela	2.96	0.46	0.50
Average Latin American countries	**3.09**	**0.52**	**0.63**
Median Latin American countries	**3.12**	**0.60**	**0.69**
Average high-income OECD countries	**1.41**	**0.27**	**0.44**
Median high-income OECD countries	**1.20**	**0.24**	**0.46**

Sources: Heckman and Pagés (2000); Djankov et al. (2003); Botero et al. (2004).

the authors cited earlier, she concludes that minimum wages are not on the list of the most pressing labor market issues in Latin America. All in all, the findings in this empirical literature are consistent with a richer characterization of labor (and financial) market frictions, where rigidity stems from widespread appropriability problems rather than from some exogenously high real wage.

7.1.4 Productivity Cleansing during Adjustment

Let us now introduce heterogeneous technologies to study the productive "cleansing" that accompanies restructuring episodes. For this, assume that the initial distribution of production units in the X and M sectors is heterogeneous with regard to the technologies in use. For each production unit, let a be an index for the outdatedness of the technique in use and assume a productivity of $1 - a$. Technology that is available in both sectors today corresponds to $a = 0$.

The distribution of production units across techniques is given by the history of technology adoption (as in chapter 4) and by government intervention. For each sector, there is a non-degenerate initial distribution over the range $a \in [0, \bar{a}^-]$, where the scrapping margin $\bar{a}^-$ is determined by the zero-profit condition

$$1 - \bar{a}^- = v^-,$$

and the shadow wage rate

$$v^- = 1 - r(1 + b)c_0$$

is determined in the same way as in equation (7.12). Note that the shadow wage rate is determined by the free-entry condition, even though the economy at time $t = 0$ is in long-run equilibrium with zero entry. This is because the threat point of a worker is still to find a potential entrant, even if such a threat is not realized in equilibrium.

Consider next what happens after liberalization. The interesting phenomena here arise inside the old inaction range $(\theta^* < 1 + r(1 + b)c_0)$; otherwise, there is still a complete and instantaneous scrapping of the M sector. In this old inaction range, liberalization is followed by instant scrapping of all production units that do not satisfy the new zero-profit condition, which is now different for the two sectors because of the change in their relative prices. The new scrapping margins for sectors M and X, respectively, are given by

$$1 - \bar{a}_m = v \qquad (7.16)$$

and

$$\theta^*(1 - \bar{a}_x) = v, \qquad (7.17)$$

where v is still given by the free-entry condition in the X sector (equation [7.12]). Dynamics after the initial scrapping are as before. The workers who become unemployed after the initial shock of liberalization are hired gradually into the expanding X sector, while production units in both sectors that were not initially scrapped survive in the long run.

Following liberalization, the scrapping margins (7.16) and (7.17) tighten in both sectors by the amount of increase in the product wage. This phenomenon of "cleansing" the productive structure following reform, resulting in an improvement in average productivity, finds empirical support in the literature (see, e.g., Liu's 1993 study of Chilean manufacturing plants during the 1979–1986 period). It is also immediate from equations (7.16) and (7.17) that the scrapping margin tightens more markedly for the M sector than for the X sector $(\bar{a}_m < \bar{a}_x)$. This implies that productivity cleansing following reform is likely to be more extensive in importables than in exportables. This prediction also has empirical support (see, e.g., Tybout, de Melo, and Corbo 1991; Corbo and Sanchez 1992; Marshall 1992).

With heterogeneous technologies, the problem of sclerosis discussed in section 7.1.2 gains a technological dimension. One can see from equations (7.12) and (7.16) that a greater degree of appropriation b lowers the shadow wage and raises the scrapping margin $\bar{a}_m$ in the M sector. All production units with $a \in [rc_0 - (\theta^* - 1), r(1 + b)c_0 - (\theta^* - 1)]$ survive despite the fact that these would be scrapped in an efficient world. Sclerosis is now not just a problem of producing the wrong goods, but also one of producing all goods with outmoded technology.

7.1.5 Unemployment, the Informal Sector, and Segmented Labor Markets

In developing countries, where unemployment benefits are sparse at best, unemployment is typically "hidden" in the form of participation in low-productivity, informal-sector activities. Instead of a surge in open unemployment, the transitional employment problem may take the form of a surge in informal-sector employment.

The segmentation of labor markets between the formal and informal sectors arises naturally in our context if informal-sector technology requires lower asset specificity or allows workers to avoid entering into a bilateral transaction with capital owners. (For an analysis of some of the consequences of labor market segmentation in small open economies see, e.g., Agenor and Aizenman 1994). The simplest case in which this happens is when the informal-sector technology requires no capital. Let us modify our model and assume that in the informal sector, workers can become self-employed in an activity that requires no capital and yields a (possibly quite low) productivity $\varepsilon < 1$. To stay as close as possible to the above model, let us denote total informal-sector employment by U and assume that all workers hired in the formal sector come from the informal one.

The only modification to equilibrium conditions (7.5) through (7.11) comes from the fact that we must add the productivity of informal-sector activity to the opportunity cost of labor in equation (7.10):

$$v(t) = \frac{H(t)}{U(t)}bc_0 + \varepsilon.$$

This means that the level of informal-sector employment $U(t)$ needed for a given level of hiring is now higher than in equation (7.13) and equal to

$$U(t) = \frac{bc_0}{(\theta^* - \varepsilon) - r(1+b)c_0}H(t).$$

The possibility of engaging in informal-sector activity strengthens the workers' threat point, which must therefore be offset by an even higher level of $U(t)$ to maintain firm profitability. The dynamic equation (7.15) characterizing $U(t)$ becomes

$$U(t) = E_m^- e^{-(((\theta^* - \varepsilon) - r(1+b)c_0)/bc_0)t}.$$

A more productive informal sector further slows down the adjustment process (note that exactly the same effect would arise from the introduction of unemployment benefits).

The divide between the formal and informal sectors is only one aspect of the labor market segmentation that can arise in the presence of appropriable investment. Naturally, as mentioned earlier, any sectoral differences in the degree of asset specificity can cause segmentation. Moreover, many determinants of profitability that arise *after* some investment is sunk can interact with appropriability and lead to wage differentials—as is the case, for example, in the model with heterogeneous technologies developed earlier in section 7.1.4 (also see section 7.5).

7.2   Gradualism

Appropriability induces two distortions in the transition process: depressed creation and excessive destruction. The wedge between the two gives rise to an employment crisis. Much of the popularity of gradualist policy prescriptions—that is, of gradual rather than cold-turkey trade and market liberalization—derives from the idea that the policies can relieve the transitional employment crisis by slowing down destruction, presumably under the incorrect implicit assumption that creation is little affected. Slowing down the transition is also likely to further depress creation. The net efficiency effect of slowing down *both* creation and destruction—and of delaying the net benefits of adjustment in the process—is ambiguous and likely to depend on the specific situation under consideration.

To illustrate the tension between the effects of gradualism on the creation and destruction margins, let us analyze two extreme cases. The first extreme highlights the distortion in the creation margin and corresponds to the simple linear model presented earlier. Because destruction in this model is instantaneous in both the efficient and inefficient cases, the only problem with transitional dynamics is sluggish creation. Since gradualism can only slow down creation further, its efficiency effect is unambiguously negative. In that case, what would be required instead is "accelerationism."

The other extreme case highlights the distortion on the destruction margin. It consists of the same simple model analyzed previously, but now with a special form of *convex* creation costs. Convex creation costs lead to nondegenerate destruction dynamics, and for the particular specification adopted the dominant distortion is always on the destruction side. In this case, gradualism is always beneficial.

These two extreme cases reveal the limitations of gradualism when the goal is to simultaneously slow down destruction and to accelerate creation. Because it slows down both margins simultaneously, gradualism is unlikely to be an effective "synchronizer" of creation and destruction. Its main effect is to spread out transitional underemployment costs over time, but it is unlikely to reduce them effectively. In a more general setting, the economic transition process is a mixture of the two extremes, with phases of adjustment when gradualism is beneficial and phases where accelerationism is preferable. This switching between gradualism and its opposite, depending on whether distortions dominate on the creation margin or destruction margin, shows more generally the limitation of using a single policy instrument to address distortions on the two margins. Policy analysis should go beyond the gradualism-versus-cold-turkey dichotomy to the design of managed adjustment programs with multiple policy instruments, along the lines of the policy discussion in chapter 5.

Let us model a gradualist reform as the temporary introduction of a path of tariffs $\{\tau(t)\}_{t \geq 0}$ following reform to protect the importables sector. These tariffs are small enough so the domestic relative price of exportables $\theta(t)$ remains above one:

$$\theta(t) = \frac{\theta^*}{1 + \tau(t)} \geq 1, \qquad t \geq 0.$$

In order to reduce technical complications in the analysis, let us assume from here on that the capital account is closed and that the interest rate r is given by the subjective discount rate in the utility function (7.1) (otherwise, a constant interest rate abroad does not yield a constant domestic interest rate as long as $\theta(t)$ is changing). The rest of the parameters are such that the balance of payments constraint is not binding (i.e., desired domestic investment does not exceed desired domestic saving).

7.2.1 Gradualism with Sluggish Creation

In the simple linear model of section 7.1.1, it is easy to see how equations (7.5)–(7.14) remain the same when a tariff is introduced at time $t = 0$, except that the world relative price θ^* must now be replaced by the distorted domestic price $\theta(t)$. In particular, the shadow wage rate is now given by

$$v(t) = \theta(t) - r(1 + b)c_0. \tag{7.18}$$

Assuming model parameters are such that even with gradualism the economy does not fall inside the inaction range (i.e., that $\theta(t) > 1 + r(1 + b)c_0$ for all $t \geq 0$), the path of unemployment is now given by

$$U(t) = E_m^- e^{-\int_0^t ((\theta(s) - r(1+b)c_0)/bc_0)\, ds}, \qquad t \geq 0. \tag{7.19}$$

Let us define two paths of reform. The *gradualist* path $\{\theta^g(t)\}_{t=0}^{\infty}$ is characterized by an increasing $\theta^g(t)$ that reaches θ^* asymptotically. The *cold-turkey* path $\{\theta^c(t)\}_{t=0}^{\infty}$ is simply given by $\theta^c(t) = \theta^*$ for all $t \geq 0$. It is clear from equations (7.18) and (7.19) that the gradualist path is characterized by lower shadow wages, higher unemployment, more sluggish creation, and a smaller X sector. Since by assumption the economy remains outside the inaction range, destruction is the same in both scenarios. Gradualism in this case has one effect, which is to reduce the relative price incentives to create in the exportables sector. This policy leads to reduced creation and, given complete destruction in importables, to higher unemployment.

Let us analyze *welfare* in this economy from the perspective of allocative efficiency and define it as the present value of aggregate domestic income net of investment expenses:

$$W(t) = \int_t^{\infty} [\theta^* E_x(s) + E_m(s) - c_0 H(s)] e^{-r(s-t)}\, ds. \tag{7.20}$$

Section 7.6 calculates welfare for three scenarios: cold-turkey adjustment (W^c), gradualist adjustment (W^g), and no adjustment (W^n, which corresponds to keeping the old productive structure intact). We can show that, notwithstanding the disruptions due to appropriability problems, if cold-turkey adjustment is desirable from the point of view of private incentives, it will also be desirable from the social point of view:

$$W^c(0) - W^n(0) = \frac{1}{r}[(\theta^* - 1) - r(1 + b)c_0]E_m^-,$$

which is clearly positive outside the inaction range. The reason for this is that outside the inaction range the private distortion bc_0 to creation costs exceeds the social cost of the additional unemployment that results from creating an additional unit (equal to $U/H = bc_0/v$ by equation [7.10], and this is less than bc_0 outside the inaction range), while the private value of a new unit created in the X sector is less than its social value (because the private shadow wage rate exceeds the social shadow wage of zero in the presence of unemployment). Thus, a private decision to create is both cheaper and yields greater value from a social welfare perspective.

Turning to gradual adjustment, one can show that

$$W^g(0) - W^c(0) = -\int_0^\infty [\theta^* - \theta^g(t)] U^g(t) e^{-rt}\, dt,$$

where $U^g(t)$ designates unemployment along the gradualist path. It is clear that this expression is negative when $\theta^g(t)$ stays below θ^*, and that gradualism is inferior to cold-turkey adjustment.

In this extreme linear case, gradualist adjustment can only affect the creation margin. It slows down an already depressed creation rate, and results in increased unemployment as well as a delay in the net benefits of adjustment.

7.2.2 Gradualism with Excessive Destruction

The reason why gradualism fails to have any beneficial effect in the linear model is that destruction is degenerate and happens instantaneously. The linear model gives no chance to the gradualist argument, which hinges precisely on the idea that, by slowing down the destruction of the old structure, a gradualist approach can give more time for creation to build up the new one and thus reduce transitional underemployment.

To capture the gradualist mechanism, let us drop the assumption of linear creation costs and assume instead that fast creation is costly. The shadow wage rate no longer jumps to its long-run value following reform, precipitating all destruction at that point, but converges over time to its long-run value and brings about a progressive destruction of the M sector.

In order to highlight the beneficial effects of gradualism on destruction in as simple a setting as possible, let us make special assumptions—on the form of creation costs and on the initial distribution of production units—that greatly simplify the analysis and imply that the destruction margin distortion always dominates. In this extreme case, gradualism is always a beneficial—albeit far from optimal—policy response.

The Model There are many reasons why an economy cannot instantly create a new productive structure: time to build, slow learning and sluggish technology adoption, limited savings, uncertainty, and so forth. To capture some of these effects, let us modify the model in section 7.1.1 and assume that the unit creation cost is increasing with the rate of creation

$H(t)$. This can be due to standard convex capital installation and learning costs. It can also be due to a nondegenerate distribution of potential entrants (see, e.g., chapter 6). For the reasons explained earlier, let us adopt a marginal creation cost function of the form $c_1 H(t)$, $c_1 > 0$.

Equilibrium conditions (7.5)–(7.11) (with θ^* replaced by the distorted price $\theta(t)$) must be modified. The change in the specification of creation costs means that the shadow price signals (7.9) and (7.10) are now given by

$$\tilde{c}(t) = (1 + b)c_1 H(t) \tag{7.21}$$

and

$$v(t) = \frac{H(t)}{U(t)} bc_1 H(t). \tag{7.22}$$

Let us first characterize adjustment in this economy without government intervention. We can show that as long as θ^* is not too large, the transition ends in finite time $\bar{T}$—that is, creation, destruction, and unemployment are positive before $\bar{T}$ and zero afterward.

Ongoing destruction requires that wages rise to exactly eliminate all quasi-rents in sector M. By exit condition (7.6), the shadow wage has to be one for $t < \bar{T}$, and θ^* afterward to prevent further creation.

$$v(t) = \begin{cases} 1, & 0 \leq t < \bar{T}; \\ \theta^*, & t \geq \bar{T}. \end{cases} \tag{7.23}$$

Note that, in contrast to the linear model, the shadow wage initially *falls* in terms of exportables (it drops from one to $1/\theta^*$). The same holds for the actual product wage w_x/θ^* in the X sector, which must fall below one to encourage intense job creation. Section 7.7 shows that, for $t < \bar{T}$,

$$\frac{w_x}{\theta^*} = 1 - \frac{(\theta^* - 1)}{(1 + b)\theta^*}.$$

Thus, although the product wage falls in the transition, it falls by less— and exhibits more "overt" rigidity—the greater is the appropriability parameter b.

Now we can use equations (7.5), (7.21), and (7.23) to solve for the creation rate

$$H(t) = \begin{cases} \frac{\theta^* - 1}{r(1 + b)c_1} [1 - e^{-r(\bar{T} - t)}], & 0 \leq t < \bar{T}; \\ 0, & t \geq \bar{T}. \end{cases} \tag{7.24}$$

This can be used to integrate the dynamic equation (7.8) using the boundary condition $E_x(0) = E_x^-$:

$$E_x(t) = \begin{cases} E_x^- + \frac{\theta^*-1}{r(1+b)c_1}\left[t - \frac{e^{-r\bar{T}}}{r}(e^{rt} - 1)\right], & 0 \le t < \bar{T}; \\ 1, & t \ge \bar{T}. \end{cases} \tag{7.25}$$

The unemployment rate along this path can be obtained from equations (7.23) and (7.22), taking equation (7.24) into account:

$$U(t) = \begin{cases} bc_1 H(t)^2, & 0 \le t < \bar{T}; \\ 0, & t \ge \bar{T}, \end{cases} \tag{7.26}$$

with the destruction margin adjusting to generate the required unemployment rate. Assuming that the technical condition $(\theta^* - 1) < \frac{1+b}{2b}$ holds, M-sector employment $E_m(t) = 1 - E_x(t) - U(t)$ initially drops by $U(0)$ and then falls monotonically to reach zero at time $\bar{T}$.

To see this, we need to check that $dE_m(t)/dt < 0$ for $t < \bar{T}$. Using equations (7.8), (7.24), and (7.26) to differentiate $E_m(t) = 1 - E_x(t) - U(t)$, we get

$$\frac{dE_m(t)}{dt} = -H(t)\left[1 - \frac{2b}{1+b}(\theta^* - 1)e^{-r(\bar{T}-t)}\right],$$

which is strictly negative for all $t < \bar{T}$ if and only if the aforementioned technical condition holds.

Finally, the length $\bar{T}$ of the transition is determined from equation (7.25) by the requirement that the transition be completed at $\bar{T}$, namely, $E_x(\bar{T}) = 1$. It is implicitly determined by the following equation:

$$\bar{T} - \frac{1 - e^{-r\bar{T}}}{r} = \frac{r(1+b)c_1}{\theta^* - 1}(1 - E_x^-). \tag{7.27}$$

This model with progressive destruction adds realism and insight, and allows us to generalize to a convex setting the conclusions concerning unbalanced restructuring and sclerosis in the presence of appropriability. The path of adjustment in this economy and the disruptive effect of appropriability problems are illustrated in figure 7.1. The dashed lines correspond to an economy that suffers from appropriability problems ($b = 1$), while the solid lines correspond to an efficient economy (the limit as $b \to 0$). The values of parameters used in the calibrations below can be found in section 7.9.

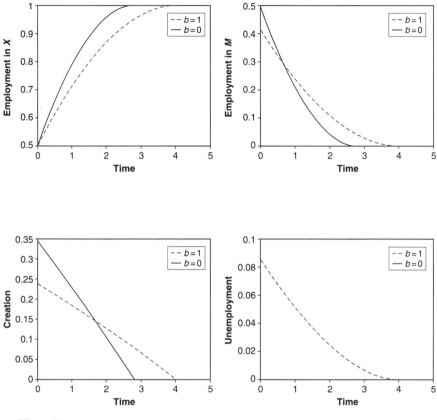

Figure 7.1
Adjustment in a convex economy

To characterize adjustment in an efficient economy, we set $b = 0$ in equations (7.23)–(7.27). Because fast creation is costly, creation and destruction in this economy are gradual. More important, they go hand in hand and therefore generate no unemployment in the process (equation [7.26]).

Turning to the inefficient economy with $b > 0$, section 7.8 derives the following results: (1) $\bar{T} > \bar{T}^e$ (where the superscript "e" refers to the efficient-economy benchmark), namely, the transition, as measured by $\bar{T}$, takes longer than is efficient. (2) $E_x(t) < E_x^e(t)$ for all $t \in (0, \bar{T}^e]$, which means that creation in the X sector is slower than efficient, because of the high effective creation costs induced by appropriability. (3) Sector

M suffers excessive destruction at the outset of reform. This is followed by a more progressive destruction that further depletes that sector over time. The gap created between slow creation and excessive destruction gives rise to a wasteful surge in unemployment during the economic transition and corresponds to the *decoupling* of flows highlighted in chapter 5.

Gradualism   This model with nondegenerate destruction dynamics adds a new dimension to the welfare analysis of gradualism. The inefficient economy exhibits sluggish creation and excessive destruction. Although gradualism will slow down creation even further, it may also help by reducing destruction. Are there times when slower creation combined with reduced destruction has a positive net effect and justify gradualism?

To address this question, let us write the aggregate welfare in this economy as

$$W(0) = \frac{E_m^- + \theta^* E_x^-}{r}$$

$$+ \int_0^\infty \left[(\theta^* - 1)(E_x(t) - E_x^-) - U(t) - \frac{1}{2} c_1 H(t)^2 \right] e^{-rt}\, dt.$$

The first term corresponds to welfare if no adjustment takes place. The second term is equal to the improvement in welfare due to adjustment: the increase in the output of units that are reallocated from the M to the X sector minus the loss of M sector output due to transitional unemployment minus total creation costs.

The loss of output due to unemployment can be considered an "unemployment cost" of creation. That is because, by equation (7.26), lost output per unit flow of creation is given by

$$\frac{U(t)}{H(t)} = bc_1 H(t), \qquad t < \bar{T}. \tag{7.28}$$

Note that this average unit cost is exactly equal to the distortion to marginal creation costs introduced by appropriability. In other words, the appropriability distortion gives an adequate private signal of the unemployment cost of creation that appears at the social level, up to one caveat: the left-hand side of equation (7.28) is an average cost, whereas the right-hand side is a marginal cost. Because of this subtle difference, private signals do not reflect the full social costs of creation.

To explore the desirability of a gradualist path $\{\theta(t)\}$, let us look for the path $\{\theta^o(t)\}$ that maximizes aggregate welfare. The first-order condition for the problem of finding the optimal creation path $\{H^o(t)\}$ as driven by the optimal policy $\{\theta^o(t)\}$ is

$$\tilde{c}(t) + bc_1 H(t) = \int_t^{\bar{T}^o} [\theta^* - 1]e^{-r(s-t)}\,ds, \qquad t < \bar{T}^o.$$

Compared with the decentralized free-entry condition (7.5), the social effective marginal creation cost exceeds the private cost by a term $bc_1 H(t)$ that precisely reflects the difference between marginal and average costs discussed previously.

The fact that the social effective cost of creation is higher than the private one implies that slowing down creation can be beneficial. One can show that the optimal gradualist path is

$$\theta^o(t) = \begin{cases} \theta^* - \dfrac{b}{1+2b}(\theta^* - 1), & 0 \le t < \bar{T}^o; \\ \theta^*, & t \ge \bar{T}^o, \end{cases}$$

which is clearly less than θ^* during the adjustment period.

In this specific model, gradualism helps because it can reduce the unemployment cost of creation along the best feasible path through a subtle difference between average and marginal costs. But gradualism by itself cannot eliminate unemployment altogether. In other words, it is not an effective synchronizer because it involves reducing creation in order to reduce destruction. One would wish to reduce destruction in order to reduce unemployment, but at the same time the optimal policy on the creation margin would be to *accelerate* creation up to the efficient rate.

In more general models, with creation costs $(c_0 + c_1 H)$ and a nongeneric initial productivity distribution in the M sector, one can show that adjustment will be a mixture of the two extremes analyzed in this section. There will be some phases in the transition process when gradualism is beneficial and others when "accelerationism" is preferable. This highlights the limitation of using a single policy tool to address distortions on two margins and points to the need for the dual policy tools approach discussed in the next section.

7.3   Managed Adjustment

Even if it is the case that gradualism can be of some use in restoring efficiency, this does not mean that other forms of managed adjustment cannot be more effective. Let us consider a model with search costs and turn
to the problem of constructing a set of policies that can restore efficiency
to the adjustment process.

7.3.1   Introducing Frictional Unemployment

Up to now the model has envisioned no useful role for unemployment in
the *efficient* economy's transition, mostly in order to sharpen the focus
on the disruptions that result from appropriability problems. This simpli-
fication is inconvenient when designing optimal policies, since the limit
of zero unemployment can be achieved in an inefficient economy only by
means of infinite subsidies and taxes. Therefore let us start by introducing some efficiency role for frictional unemployment by assuming that it
facilitates factor reallocation during the transition.

Let us modify our basic model by introducing a search cost $c_2(H/U)$
that firms have to pay per production unit created in addition to an
investment cost $(c_0 + c_1 H)$. Such a search cost can be derived from a
standard constant-returns, Cobb-Douglas matching function with equal
elasticities for unemployment and vacancies together with a constant
vacancy-posting cost, as explained in chapter 4.

Since our concern is with inefficiencies that result from appropriability
rather than externalities in the search process, let us assume the standard
efficiency condition that the worker's bargaining share parameter β is
equal to the unemployment elasticity of the matching function, which is
set to one-half.

What appropriation parameter should we apply to the search
cost component of creation costs? Note that since search costs are incurred *before* bargaining, they are fully appropriable. From equation
(7.11), this entails an appropriation parameter equal to $\beta/(1-\beta) =
0.5/(1-0.5) = 1$. The shadow prices in equilibrium conditions (7.5)–
(7.11) are now given by

$$v(t) = \frac{H(t)}{U(t)} \left[b(c_0 + c_1 H(t)) + c_2 \frac{H(t)}{U(t)} \right] \qquad (7.29)$$

and

$$\tilde{c}(t) = (1+b)(c_0 + c_1 H(t)) + 2c_2 \frac{H(t)}{U(t)}. \tag{7.30}$$

It is clear from equation (7.29) that even in the efficient case where $b = 0$, the presence of search costs gives rise to positive unemployment as long as creation $H(t)$ is positive.

7.3.2 Distorted Margins and Policy

The distortions that result from appropriability problems in this economy are reflected in the two shadow price signals, equations (7.29) and (7.30). Their social counterparts, the social shadow cost of creation and social shadow wage rate, correspond to the limiting case when b goes to zero:

$$v^*(t) \equiv c_2 \left(\frac{H(t)}{U(t)}\right)^2, \tag{7.31}$$

$$\tilde{c}^*(t) \equiv c_0 + c_1 H(t) + 2c_2 \frac{H(t)}{U(t)}. \tag{7.32}$$

The social shadow wage is given by the social value of an unemployed worker, which is positive because unemployment reduces search costs. What is the direction of distortion in these two signals? It is easy to see that both are inflated in the presence of appropriability:

$$v(t) > v^*(t) \quad \text{and} \quad \tilde{c}(t) > \tilde{c}^*(t), \qquad \text{for } b > 0.$$

It is not surprising, then, that the inefficient economy exhibits sluggish creation and excessive destruction following economic reforms.

What policies can offset the distortions on each of the destruction and creation margins and improve allocative efficiency in this economy? Along the destruction margin, since the private shadow wage rate is excessively high and the economy is inefficiently shedding labor, job protection measures in sector M may help. In particular, let $i_p(t)$ denote a production or employment subsidy to sector M so that the effective shadow wage in exit condition (7.6) becomes $v(t) - i_p(t)$. It is clear from equations (7.29) and (7.31) that by selecting

$$i_p(t) = v(t) - v^*(t) = b(c_0 + c_1 H(t))\frac{H(t)}{U(t)},$$

the efficient exit condition is restored. However, such a measure cannot restore full efficiency to the economy because it depresses creation by raising the opportunity cost of labor employed in sector X (see free-entry condition [7.5]).

Turning to the creation margin, the excessively high effective creation costs can be offset by providing sector X with a creation incentive $i_c(t)$. Therefore, the effective creation costs after the subsidy in the free-entry condition (7.5) become $\tilde{c}(t) - i_c(t)$, where, without loss of generality, I have assumed that $i_c(t)$ is appropriable. If this policy is implemented in isolation (i.e., when $i_p(t) = 0$), it restores the efficient entry condition when

$$i_c(t) = \tilde{c}(t) - \tilde{c}^*(t) = b(c_0 + c_1 H(t)).$$

The drawback of this policy is that by increasing hiring, creation incentives build up additional pressure on the shadow wage rate (7.29), and therefore exacerbate an already high level of job destruction in the contracting sector.

7.3.3 Optimal Policies

It should be clear that a combination of job protection measures i_p in sector M and of creation incentives i_c in sector X is likely to remedy the economy's ills. By replacing these incentives into the entry and exit conditions, it is straightforward to show that efficient and inefficient equilibrium conditions coincide for the following canonical policies:

$$i_p(t) = v(t) - v^*(t)$$

and

$$i_c(t) = \tilde{c}(t) - \tilde{c}^*(t) + \int_t^\infty i_p(s)e^{-r(s-t)}\,ds.$$

The first term in the optimal creation incentive $i_c(t)$ solves the direct appropriability problem, while the second one—only positive while sector M employment is positive and needs to be protected—offsets the increase in labor costs due to the job protection policy in sector M.

As an illustration, figure 7.2 simulates an example of these canonical policies. Policy incentives are at their highest value at transition's beginning when the need for creation and the costs of excessive destruction are highest. These then decline monotonically as reallocation slows down,

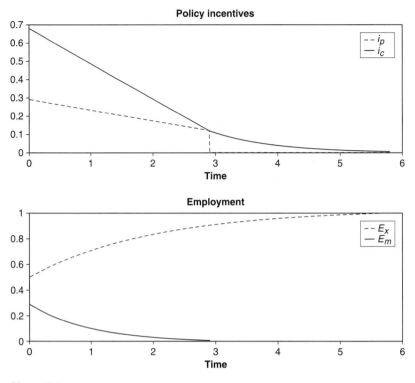

Figure 7.2
Optimal canonical policies

and unemployed workers are incorporated into the new productive structure. Parameter values are described in section 7.9.

The canonical policies $i_p(t)$ and $i_c(t)$ capture the essential elements of the incentive structure that a managed-adjustment program should target. The art of the practitioner is to incorporate such incentives in a program that accounts for institutional and political constraints as well as the existing policy environment. Consideration should be given to the distortionary effects of implementing and financing the program. The choice between encouraging capital investment or job creation, for example, has important implications for the resulting capital-labor ratio. And the existing policy environment may incorporate elements—for example, employment protection legislation, a heavy corporate fiscal burden, or ongoing macroeconomic stabilization—that either reinforce or offset the targeted incentives.

7.4 Conclusion

Transition and developing economies have a mixture of substantial factor reallocation needs and poor institutional infrastructure that naturally gives rise to a severe appropriability problem. Gradual creation that cannot keep up with accelerated destruction, inefficient unemployment and sclerosis are all direct manifestations of that problem. At the outset of these ills a standard policy response is to attempt to slow down the transition. Such a response is incomplete at best and in many instances exacerbates the costs of adjustment by worsening the sclerosis problem.

7.5 Appendix: Wage Differentials

This section computes the wage differentials between workers employed in production units with different profitabilities for the linear model with heterogeneous technologies in section 7.1.

To calculate the actual wage differentials, one needs to make additional assumptions about the out-of-equilibrium uses of the nonappropriable component of capital, including the relationship between those uses and current productivity and location. Let us assume that if a unit with productivity $1 - a$ changes an employee, it loses a percentage ϕ of its value. For this, let us assume that capital and labor are divisible and focus only on the production units that remain.

For the M sector, let $V_m(a_m)$ denote the value (for its owner) of having a production unit of "outdatedness" a_m. Likewise, let $S_m(a_m)$ denote the appropriable surplus of such a unit.

The value for the owner is given by the nonappropriable value of the firm plus the share of rents to which he or she is entitled:

$$V_m(a_m) = (1 - \phi)V_m(a_m) + (1 - \beta)S_m(a_m).$$

This can be written as

$$V_m(a_m) = \frac{1}{\phi}(1 - \beta)S_m(a_m).$$

The appropriable surplus is given by the present value of the firm's profits minus the opportunity cost of labor and the nonappropriable value of the firm:

$$S_m(a_m) = \frac{1 - a_m - v}{r} - (1 - \phi)V_m(a_m).$$

Putting the two conditions together, one finds that

$$V_m(a_m) = \frac{1 - a_m - v}{(1 + b)r},$$

$$S_m(a_m) = \frac{\phi}{1 - \beta + \phi\beta}\frac{1 - a_m - v}{r}.$$

The full wage paid to the worker is given by

$$w_m(a_m) = v + r\beta S_m(a_m)$$

$$= v + \frac{\beta\phi}{1 - \beta + \phi\beta}[1 - a_m - v].$$

Following a similar procedure for the X sector, we find that

$$w_x(a_x) = v + \frac{\beta\phi}{1 - \beta + \phi\beta}[\theta^*(1 - a_x) - v].$$

Thus, workers in units with higher relative profitability earn a higher effective wage since these firms have a larger appropriable surplus.

7.6   Appendix: Welfare Calculations

For the linear model of section 7.1, this section computes the following: (1) the value of welfare $W^n(0)$ if no adjustment takes place, (2) the welfare gain $W^c(0) - W^n(0)$ from cold-turkey adjustment, and (3) the welfare gain $W^g(0) - W^c(0)$ from gradualist over cold-turkey adjustment.

1. The value of $W^n(0)$ follows from the definition of welfare (7.20) assuming that the initial full-employment allocation of labor $1 = E_m^- + E_x^-$ between the M and the X sectors is preserved and no investment takes place:

$$W^n(0) = \frac{E_m^- + \theta^* E_x^-}{r} = \frac{\theta^*}{r} - \frac{\theta^* - 1}{r}E_m^-.$$

2. If adjustment does take place, $E_m(t) = 0$ for all $t \geq 0$, and the flow of welfare becomes $\theta^* E_x(t) - c_0 H(t)$. Since equation (7.7) implies $E_x(t) = 1 - U(t)$, and equation (7.10) implies $H(t) = v(t)U(t)/bc_0$, we can write the present value of this flow as

$$W(0) = \frac{\theta^*}{r} - \int_0^\infty \left(\theta^* + \frac{v(t)}{b} \right) U(t) e^{-rt} \, dt. \tag{7.33}$$

To compute welfare under cold-turkey adjustment, we substitute expressions (7.12) and (7.15) for $v(t)$ and $U(t)$:

$$W^c(0) = \frac{\theta^*}{r} - c_0(1+b)E_m^-.$$

Subtracting $W^n(0)$ from $W^c(0)$ yields the gain from cold-turkey adjustment:

$$W^c(0) - W^n(0) = \frac{1}{r}[(\theta^* - 1) - r(1+b)c_0]E_m^-.$$

3. Turning to welfare gains under gradualism, note that, by equation (7.18), the integrand in expression (7.33) can be written as

$$\left(\theta^* + \frac{v(t)}{b} \right) U(t) e^{-rt} = (\theta^* - \theta(t))U(t)e^{-rt} + \frac{(1+b)}{b}(\theta(t) - rc_0)U(t)e^{-rt}.$$

Replacing this in equation (7.33), we get

$$W^g(0) - W^c(0)$$

$$= -\int_0^\infty (\theta^* - \theta^g(t))U^g(t)e^{-rt} \, dt$$

$$- \frac{(1+b)}{b}\int_0^\infty [(\theta^g(t) - rc_0)U^g(t) - (\theta^* - rc_0)U^c(t)]e^{-rt} \, dt, \tag{7.34}$$

where $U^c(t)$ and $U^g(t)$ denote unemployment under cold-turkey and gradualist adjustment, respectively. One can show that the second term in expression (7.34) is zero by noting that

$$(\theta(t) - rc_0)\frac{U(t)}{b} = v(t)\frac{U(t)}{b} + rc_0 U(t) \quad \text{by (7.18);}$$

$$= c_0(H(t) + rU(t)) \quad \text{by (7.10);}$$

$$= -c_0 e^{rt}\frac{d(U(t)e^{-rt})}{dt} \quad \text{by (7.14).}$$

Multiplying both sides by e^{-rt}, and integrating over time, yields

$$\int_0^\infty (\theta(t) - rc_0)\frac{U(t)}{b}e^{-rt} \, dt = -c_0\int_0^\infty \frac{d(U(t)e^{-rt})}{dt} \, dt = c_0 U(0) = c_0 E_m^-.$$

Since the value of the above expression is constant for both the cold-turkey and gradualist paths of $\theta(t)$, the second term in equation (7.34) is equal to zero. Thus,

$$W^g(0) - W^c(0) = -\int_0^\infty [\theta^* - \theta^g(t)]U^g(t)e^{-rt}\,dt.$$

7.7   Appendix: "Overt" Wage Rigidity

This section computes the actual product wage w_x/θ^* in the X sector for the model of excessive destruction described in section 7.2.

Now that each unit's surplus is no longer constant, the wage paid to workers in the X sector is given by

$$w_x(t) = v(t) + r\beta S(t) - \beta\frac{dS(t)}{dt}, \qquad \text{with } S(t) = \frac{b}{\beta}c_1 H(t).$$

For $t < \bar{T}$, using equation (7.23) we get

$$w_x(t) = 1 + rbc_1 H(t) - bc_1\frac{dH(t)}{dt}.$$

We can now use equation (7.24) to obtain

$$w_x = 1 + \frac{b}{1+b}(\theta^* - 1).$$

Dividing by θ^* and manipulating the equation, we find that

$$\frac{1}{\theta^*} < \frac{w_x}{\theta^*} = 1 - \frac{\theta^* - 1}{(1+b)\theta^*} < 1,$$

which means that the larger the appropriability parameter b, the smaller is the wage rate drop during the transition. This is overt rigidity.

7.8   Appendix: Adjustment in an Inefficient Economy

This section proves the following claims made in section 7.2.2:

1. The transition takes longer than is efficient: namely, $\bar{T} > \bar{T}^e$ (where the superscript "e" refers to the efficient-economy benchmark).

Proof: Let us rewrite equation (7.27) as

$$F = \bar{T} - \frac{1 - e^{-r\bar{T}}}{r} - \frac{r(1+b)c_1}{\theta^* - 1}(1 - E_x^-).$$

Differentiating this expression with respect to $\bar{T}$ and b yields

$$\frac{dF}{d\bar{T}} = 1 - re^{-r\bar{T}} > 0 \qquad \text{since } \bar{T} > 0,$$

$$\frac{dF}{db} = -\frac{rc_1}{\theta^* - 1}(1 - E_x^-) < 0.$$

Using the implicit function theorem, we can find

$$\frac{d\bar{T}}{db} = -\frac{dF/db}{dF/d\bar{T}} > 0,$$

which means that the length of the transition is increasing with respect to the degree of inefficiency in the economy.

2. $E_x(t) < E_x^e(t)$ for all $t \in (0, \bar{T}^e]$, which means that the pace of creation in the X sector is slower than efficient.

Proof: Let us start by showing that $H(0) < H^e(0)$. Differentiating equation (7.24) with respect to time yields

$$\frac{dH(t)}{dt} = -\frac{(\theta^* - 1)}{(1+b)c_1}e^{-r(\bar{T}-t)} = -\frac{(\theta^* - 1)}{(1+b)c_1} + rH(t).$$

Note that the absolute value of $dH(t)/dt$ is decreasing with respect to the degree of inefficiency. This implies that $H(0) < H^e(0)$, otherwise we would have $H(t) > H^e(t)$, but $H(t)$ cannot exceed $H^e(t)$ over the whole interval $[0, \bar{T}^e]$, because that would contradict the fact that $\bar{T} > \bar{T}^e$.

Since $H(t)$ is decreasing, the fact that $H(0) < H^e(0)$ together with $H(\bar{T}^e) > H^e(\bar{T}^e) = 0$ implies that the inefficient path $\{H(t)\}$ crosses the efficient path $\{H^e(t)\}$ from below at a point $t^* \in (0, \bar{T}^e)$. This proves that $E_x(t) < E_x^e(t)$ for all $t^* \in (0, \bar{T}^e]$, for if $E_x(t)$ were to exceed $E_x^e(t)$ at some point, that point would have to be after t^* and then $E_x(t) > E_x^e(t)$ from then on. But that contradicts the fact that $E_x(\bar{T}^e) < E_x^e(\bar{T}^e) = 1$.

3. Sector M suffers excessive destruction at the outset of reform.

Proof: To see this, note that, unlike in the efficient economy, equations (7.24) and (7.26) at $t = 0$ show that a portion of the M sector is destroyed instantly after implementing reform in order to generate the unemployment required to prevent surging wages in response to increased hiring.

7.9   Appendix: Parameters

Figure 7.1 was generated with parameters: $r = 0.06$, $\theta^* = 1.2$, $c_1 = 1.5$, and $E_x^- = E_m^- = 0.5$.

Figure 7.2 was generated with parameters: $r = 0.06$, $\theta^* = 1.2$, $b = 1$, $c_0 = 0$, $c_1 = 1.5$, $c_2 = 1.5$, and $E_x^- = E_m^- = 0.5$.

Note

1. This chapter is based on Caballero and Hammour (1996b).

References and Suggested Readings

Agenor, Pierre-Richard, and Joshua Aizenman. 1994. "Macroeconomic Adjustment with Segmented Labor Markets." NBER Working Paper No. 4769.

Aghion, Philippe, and Olivier J. Blanchard. 1994. "On the Speed of Transition in Central Europe." In Stanley Fischer and Julio Rotemberg, eds., *NBER Macroeconomics Annual 1994*, vol. 9, 283–320. Cambridge, Mass.: The MIT Press.

Amsden, Alice H. 1989. *Asia's Next Giant: South Korea and Late Industrialization*. New York: Oxford University Press.

Atkeson, Andrew, and Patrick J. Kehoe. 1996. "Social Insurance and Transition." *International Economic Review* 37(2): 377–401.

Blanchard, Olivier J., and Michael Kremer. 1997. "Disorganization." *Quarterly Journal of Economics* 112(4): 1091–1126.

Botero, Juan, Simeon Djankov, Rafael La Porta, Florencio Lopez-de-Silanes, and Andrei Shleifer. 2004. "The Regulation of Labor." *Quarterly Journal of Economics* 119(4): 1339–1382.

Caballero, Ricardo J., and Mohamad L. Hammour. 1996a. "On the Timing and Efficiency of Creative Destruction." *Quarterly Journal of Economics* 111(3): 805–852.

Caballero, Ricardo J., and Mohamad L. Hammour. 1996b. "On the Ills of Adjustment." *Journal of Development Economics* 51: 161–192.

Castañeda, Tarsicio, and Funkoo Park. 1992. "Structural Adjustment and the Role of Labor Market." In Vittorio Corbo and Sang-Mok Suh, eds., *Structural Adjustment in a Newly Industrialized Country: The Korean Experience*, 228–255. Baltimore, Md.: Johns Hopkins University Press.

Chadha, Bankim, Fabrizio Coricelli, and Kornelia Krajnyak. 1993. "Economic Restructuring, Unemployment, and Growth in a Transition Economy." *IMF Staff Papers* 40(2): 744–780.

Coase, Ronald. 1937. "The Nature of the Firm." *Economica* 4(4): 386–405.

Corbo, Vittorio, and J. Miguel Sanchez. 1992. "El Ajuste de Las Empresas del Sector Industrial en Chile durante 1974–1982." *Colección Estudios CIEPLAN* 35: 125–152.

Cox-Edwards, Alejandra. 1993. "Labor Market Legislation in Latin America and the Caribbean." Regional Studies Program, Report No. 31, World Bank Latin America and the Caribbean Technical Department.

Cox-Edwards, Alejandra. 1997. "Labor Market Regulation in Latin America: An Overview." In Sebastian Edwards and Nora Claudia Lustig, eds., *Labor Markets in Latin America: Combining Social Protection with Market Flexibility*, 127–150. Washington, D.C.: Brookings Institution.

Diamond, Peter A. 1994. *On Time*. Cambridge, UK: Cambridge University Press.

Djankov, Simeon, Rafael La Porta, Florencio Lopez-de-Silanes, Andrei Shleifer, and Juan Botero. 2003. "The Regulation of Labor." NBER Working Paper No. 9756.

Edwards, Sebastian. 1988. "Terms of Trade, Tariffs, and Labor Market Adjustment in Developing Countries." *World Bank Economic Review* 2: 165–185.

Edwards, Sebastian, and Sweder van Wijnbergen. 1989. "Disequilibrium and Structural Adjustment." In H. Chenery and T. N. Srinivasan, eds., *Handbook of Development Economics*, vol. 2, 1481–1533. Amsterdam: North-Holland.

Fallon, Peter R., and Luis A. Riveros. 1989. "Adjustment and the Labor Market." World Bank Policy, Planning, and Research Working Papers no. 214.

Gavin, Michael. 1993. "Unemployment and the Economics of Gradualist Policy Reform." Mimeo., Columbia University.

Grout, Paul A. 1984. "Investment and Wages in the Absence of Binding Contracts: A Nash Bargaining Approach." *Econometrica* 52(2): 449–460.

Hart, Oliver, and John Moore. 1988. "Incomplete Contracts and Renegotiation." *Econometrica* 56(4): 755–785.

Heckman, James, and Carmen Pagés. 2000. "The Cost of Job Security Regulation: Evidence from Latin American Labor Markets." *Economía* 1(1): 109–144.

Heckman, James, and Carmen Pagés. 2003. "Law and Employment: Lessons from Latin America and the Caribbean." NBER Working Paper No. 10129.

Horton, Susan, Ravi Kanbur, and Dipak Mazumdar, eds. 1994. *Labor Markets in an Era of Adjustment*, 2 vols. Washington, D.C.: The World Bank.

Hosios, Arthur J. 1990. "On the Efficiency of Matching and Related Models of Search and Unemployment." *Review of Economic Studies* 57(2): 279–298.

Klein, Benjamin, Robert G. Crawford, and Armen A. Alchian. 1978. "Vertical Integration, Appropriable Rents, and the Competitive Contracting Process." *Journal of Law and Economics* 21(2): 297–326.

Krueger, Anne O. 1983. *Trade and Employment in Developing Countries*. Chicago, Ill.: University of Chicago Press.

Lapan, Harvey E. 1976. "International Trade, Factor Market Distortions, and the Optimal Dynamic Policy." *American Economic Review* 66(3): 335–346.

Liu, Lili. 1993. "Entry-Exit, Learning, and Productivity Change: Evidence from Chile." *Journal of Development Economics* 42(2): 217–242.

Lopez, Ramon E., and Luis Riveros. 1989. "Macroeconomic Adjustment and the Labor Market in Four Latin American Countries." World Bank Policy, Planning, and Research Working Papers no. 335.

Marshall, Isabel. 1992. "Liberalizacion Comercial en Chile y su Impacto sobre la Eficiencia Tecnica Industrial: 1974–1986." *Colección Estudios CIEPLAN*, vol. 35: 201–246.

Mazumdar, Dipak. 1994. "The Republic of Korea." In Susan Horton, Ravi Kanbur, and Dipak Mazumdar, eds., *Labor Markets in an Era of Adjustment*, vol. 2, 535–583. Washington, D.C.: World Bank.

Mussa, Michael. 1978. "Dynamic Adjustment in the Heckscher-Ohlin-Samuelson Model." *Journal of Political Economy* 86(5): 775–791.

Neary, J. Peter. 1982. "Capital Mobility, Wage Stickiness, and the Case for Adjustment Assistance." In Jagdish Bhagwati, ed., *Import Competition and Response*. Chicago, Ill.: University of Chicago Press.

Roberts, Mark J., and James R. Tybout, eds. 1994. "Producer Heterogeneity and Performance in the Semi-Industrialized Countries." Mimeo., Pennsylvania State University.

Shimer, Robert. 1995. "Microfoundations of the Optimal Speed of Transition." Mimeo., Massachusetts Institute of Technology.

Thomas, Jonathan, and Tim Worrall. 1994. "Foreign Direct Investment and the Risk of Expropriation." *Review of Economic Studies* 61(1): 81–108.

Tybout, James R., Jaime A. P. de Melo, and Vittorio Corbo. 1991. "The Effects of Trade Reforms on Scale and Technical Efficiency: New Evidence from Chile." *Journal of International Economics* 31(3–4): 231–250.

Williamson, Oliver E. 1979. "Transaction-Cost Economics: The Governance of Contractual Relations." *Journal of Law and Economics* 22(2): 233–261.

Williamson, Oliver E. 1985. *The Economic Institutions of Capitalism*. New York: Free Press.

IV

Institutional and Technological Evolution

Institutions, Interest Groups, and the Response of Markets and Technology

This chapter examines the incentives and consequences of coalitions promoting institutions that serve their own special interests. Further, the chapter analyzes the manner in which market forces constrain special-interest politics. Interest groups are constrained by each other as well as by the prospect of market backlash, which may take the form of a breakdown in the market mechanism, resource misallocation, and distorted technological choice.[1]

Individually, capital and labor come together through market transactions; as organized groups, they interact as unions, lobbies, and coalitions that determine the arrangements, contracts, and regulations constituting the market's institutional framework. Institutions perform two functions: efficiency and redistribution. It is naïve to think that markets can generally function properly without an institutional framework that defines property rights, ensures transparent information, guarantees that contracts are legally enforceable, curbs monopolistic power, and so on. For their efficiency role, the basic determining guideline for economic institutions is that each party ought to receive the social return of its contribution to production. It is equally naïve to think that such institutions, in part determined in the political arena, will not also be used as instruments in the politics of redistribution. In such capacity, institutions can be an effective instrument of social insurance, but conflicts of interest are unavoidable when political agents are both judge and party to such redistribution policies.

Since many of the issues that concern us here are long-run ones, it is convenient to ignore the dynamics momentarily and focus on the basic one-period model developed in chapter 3. Recall that the nature of market equilibrium is determined by the sign of capital's net effective specificity $\Delta^{(k)} = \phi_k r - \phi_l v$. If this sign is positive, capital is the appropriated factor and the labor market is segmented. If it is negative, the reverse is true. Over the medium and long term, institutional and technological forces are likely to directly affect net specificity through changes in unitary specificity (the ϕ_i's) and through technological adaptation (as reflected in the capital-labor ratio). The first part of this chapter discusses how capital and labor determine unitary specificity, the ϕ_is, while the second part discusses the impact of such choices on technology selection and economic aggregates.

8.1 The Politics of Capital and Labor

This section tries to account for the incentives of interest groups representing labor or capital to develop institutions that affect their mutual "specificity." Although interest groups may be strongly driven by distributional concerns, market forces are likely to prevent the institutional outcome from drifting too far away from balanced specificity.

8.1.1 Institutional Specificity

Institutional arrangements can reinforce the effective specificity of one factor with respect to another by allocating rights (e.g., the right not to lose one's job "without cause") or by making otherwise feasible contracts unenforceable (e.g., the unenforceability of worker commitment to long-term employment contracts). In order to capture this institutional dimension of specificity, let us think of the ϕ_i's as having an institutional component that is, to a large extent, a political choice variable. What are the different groups' interests in setting or changing this value?

8.1.2 Interest Groups

In order to clarify the incentives of different interest groups, let us denote by W_i the aggregate income for capital and labor:

$$W_k = \pi E + r(1 - E), \tag{8.1}$$

$$W_l = w E + v(1 - E). \tag{8.2}$$

The first term in each of these expressions corresponds to the income of units of each factor engaged in Joint Production, and the second term is the income of units in Autarky. Note that $W_l + W_k$ does not add up to aggregate income because it omits the income of the "shadow" factor implicit in the decreasing returns assumption for labor's Autarky sector. Let us ignore the political incentives of this third "factor."

The interest of factor i *as a group* is to maximize W_i, but there are distributional issues within each group in the presence of market segmentation. The argument for maximizing W_i in the "long run" is that it represents the factor's unconditional expected income. Let us assume that interest groups recognize the *general-equilibrium* impact of their political choices. Although "partial-equilibrium myopia" can undoubtedly play an important role in the political process, this assumption captures the idea that interest groups will partly anticipate and partly adjust to the general-equilibrium consequences of their choices.

8.1.3   A Balancing Act

Given the opportunity, a factor of production picks a combination of ϕ_k and ϕ_l that maximizes its welfare. It turns out that in the simple single-period model used in this chapter, one can reduce this optimization problem to finding a value of Δ that maximizes this welfare.

From the free-entry condition

$$y = r + v(E) + \Delta,$$

we see that the value of E only depends on the value of Δ, not on the identity of the appropriated factor of production. For *given* absolute value Δ, each factor of production would prefer the net specificity of the *other* factor to be positive, so that the latter factor is appropriated. Moreover, when choosing the *level* of Δ, a factor of production will always set this to a strictly positive quantity.

These two claims can be more easily seen by rewriting the welfare expressions (8.1) and (8.2) as

$$W_k = r + (\pi - r)E = r + \max\{\Delta^{(l)}, 0\}E, \tag{8.3}$$

$$W_l = v + (w - v)E = v(E) + \max\{\Delta^{(k)}, 0\}E. \tag{8.4}$$

It is apparent that $W_k = r$ for $\Delta^{(l)} \leq 0$ and $W_k > r$ for $\Delta^{(l)} > 0$. Thus if capital chooses the value of $\Delta^{(l)}$, one only needs to focus on the latter region. The first-order condition for capital in this region follows from differentiating (8.3) with respect to $\Delta^{(l)}$, so that

$$\frac{\partial W_k}{\partial \Delta^{(l)}} = \Delta^{(l)} \frac{\partial E}{\partial \Delta^{(l)}} + E = 0, \tag{8.5}$$

which has $\Delta^{(l)} > 0$ (recall that $\partial E / \partial \Delta^{(l)} < 0$).

Using the symbol $\chi_{E, \Delta^{(l)}}$ to denote the elasticity of the number of Joint Production units with respect to $\Delta^{(l)}$, one can rewrite (8.5) as

$$-\chi_{E, \Delta^{(l)}} = 1, \tag{8.6}$$

which is the familiar solution to a monopolist's problem when the latter has zero marginal cost of changing the number of production units, E.

The problem for labor when choosing the value of $\Delta^{(k)}$ is similar to that for capital, except that the marginal cost of increasing E is negative since the opportunity cost of labor, v, is increasing with respect to E (and hence decreasing with respect to $\Delta^{(k)}$):

$$-\chi_{E, \Delta^{(k)}} = 1 + \frac{v'(E)}{E} \frac{\partial E}{\partial \Delta^{(k)}} < 1. \tag{8.7}$$

It is apparent from these expressions that while the political incentive is to appropriate rents, there are internal limits to such attempts. Moreover, these limits are more severe when there are few Autarky opportunities (i.e., when $v'(E)$ is large).

Inherently, a factor's attempt to capture rents results in own-market segmentation, and it creates winners and losers within the interest group. The winners are "insiders" employed in Joint Production, whose ex post incentive for rent appropriation is unlimited; the losers are "outsiders" who remain in Autarky, and whose ex post incentive is to minimize macroeconomic inefficiency. As appropriation rises, the outsiders increase in number relative to the insiders and have greater influence in the factor's ex ante objective function. It is thus through the internal segmentation of the appropriating factor that macroeconomic efficiency enters its objective function and limits the incentive for rent appropriation.

The degree to which institutions can deviate from balanced specificity is therefore bounded. If in the long run political power lies with ex ante interest groups, the values of $\Delta^{(l)}$ and $\Delta^{(k)}$ in the previous first-order conditions represent upper bounds on labor's and capital's long-run net specificity. Beyond those limits, both factors would attempt to reduce the degree of appropriation in the economy. It is in this sense that one expects institutional forces to perform a "balancing act" and keep the economy from deviating too far away from balanced specificity.

This reasoning is related to that of Becker (1983). He provides another argument as to why a highly inefficient political outcome is unlikely to persist, using an analysis that attempts to unify the view that government favors interest groups with the view that government corrects market failures. Taking an economic approach to political behavior, he argues that in competing for influence, pressure groups benefiting from activities that raise efficiency have an intrinsic advantage over groups harmed by those activities and therefore will lobby more effectively for efficiency.

8.1.4 Institutional Rigidity

It goes without saying that while long-run political forces may shape institutions so that net factor specificity does not deviate too far from the balanced case, in practice there are many short-run obstacles to that convergence. Let us pause briefly to examine the evolution of European labor market institutions in light of the insights contained in this and previous chapters.

Institutions are slow to evolve and adapt, and they often react to crises rather than anticipate them. Even though large and persistent changes in the macroeconomic environment would eventually lead to institutional adjustment, in the intervening period it is the model given in chapter 3 that determines the fortunes of different factors of production. Suppose, for example, that the political outcome leads to a situation of balanced specificity for a certain expected level of y. Recall from chapter 3 that we have balanced specificity if and only if

$$\frac{\phi_k}{\phi_l} = \frac{y-r}{r}.$$

If realized y is less than expected, the ratio ϕ_k/ϕ_l is too high, capital is appropriated, and the labor market becomes segmented. In contrast, if realized y is higher than expected, it is the capital market that becomes segmented.

This mismatch between the frequency at which institutions react and that at which shocks occur, together with our analysis of the incomplete-contracts economy's inefficient response to shocks, naturally accords with accounts of Western European macroeconomic performance in the postwar period. The European experience in the 1950s and 1960s was one where vigorous growth (high y) allowed the development of welfare-state institutions that benefited labor in its relationship with capital (high ϕ_k), without much cost in terms of unemployment or resistance on the part of capital. In fact, Europe exhibited signs of labor shortages during that period, which necessitated a substantial flow of immigrant labor. However, starting in the 1970s, sustained political momentum for labor market regulation clashed with a period of negative aggregate shocks, often contractionary macroeconomic policy, and a productivity slowdown (volatile and low y). Regulation then became a burden on the labor market and gave rise to a serious unemployment problem. Eventually, the institutional framework responded—most notably in the United Kingdom and the Netherlands—although quite slowly, as it faced resistance from secure "insiders." Technology also adjusted with substantial capital-labor substitution, a point that will be developed further in the next section.

In the meantime, the analysis in chapter 3 recommends introducing large job creation incentives, while the requisite "protection subsidies" are probably more than provided for by existing job protection legislation (which, unlike pure subsidies, have the unfortunate additional effect of effectively increasing capital specificity). Note that in an inefficient economy job creation is too low, since in this economy it is true that $y \geq r + v + \Delta$, whereas it would be optimal to create any unit with $y \geq r + v$. By reducing this gap, a creation subsidy can improve welfare.

In contrast, in their early response to the unemployment problem European governments generally favored increasing workers' protection (high ϕ_k), which accentuated the distortion in the economy; later on in the period, they favored "passive" labor market policies, such as increased unemployment benefits (see OECD 1996, table T, 205–212). Increasing unemployment benefits amounts to subsidizing the segmented factor's Autarky sector and exacerbates the appropriability problem. Such policies may actually have *increased* the persistence of unemployment (see, e.g., Blanchard and Jimeno 1995; Ball 1996).

It must be acknowledged that except for very narrowly targeted policies, active labor market policies have also had mixed results. The precise form active policies should take in order to be effective is an important applied research question. Box 8.1 discusses the case of Denmark, which recently seems to have found a successful combination of active policies to reenergize its economy and labor market.

Box 8.1
The Danish model of active labor market policies

Unemployment rates in Denmark have been among the lowest in Europe since the later half of the 1990s. This success has been attributed by various observers to the country's unique "flexicurity" system—a combination of high unemployment benefits (security) and low employment protection (flexibility)—that resulted from an extensive labor market reform beginning in 1994.

One of the key elements of this reform was to make eligibility for unemployment benefits conditional on participation in active labor market programs (ALMPs)—in line with the "rights and obligations" principle. Individual action plans have been introduced to target efforts to the needs of the unemployed and local labor markets (Danish Economic Council, 2002). Benefits entitlements were reduced from nine to seven years in 1994, and since then they have been gradually reduced to four years. By January 2001 the unemployed were effectively forced to participate in an ALMP after one year of unemployment. Moreover, the expiration of the period of unconditional benefits brought with it the obligation to participate in such programs for at least 75 percent of further time spent unemployed. Participation in ALMPs grew from 35 percent of the unemployed at the inception of the reform to 60 percent in 2001. By 2003, expenditure in ALMPs represented about 40 percent of total expenditures on labor market policies (up from 23 percent in 1985 and 30 percent in 1996).

Currently, ALMP training programs can be divided into four main types: private job training, public job training, classroom training, and residual programs. *Private job training* consists of private employers (who receive a subsidy) taking in an unemployed person for job training and paying the participant the negotiated salary of the regularly employed. The duration of this type of training is twenty-two weeks on average. In *public job training*, the participants work in a public institution with a maximum hourly wage rate. This type of training lasts longer, about thirty-nine weeks. In *classroom training* programs, trainees receive compensation equivalent to their unemployment insurance benefits and remain in the program for about twenty-eight weeks (usually only with access to programs with a maximum duration of two years). *Residual programs* are primarily targeted toward the weaker groups of unemployed (those who find it harder to obtain jobs) and consist of individual job training (either public or private), targeted courses, and other programs (see Jespersen, Munch, and Skipper [2004] for a detailed description of these programs).

Jespersen, Munch, and Skipper (2004) assess the social value of the implemented job training programs. Benefits are measured using the discounted earnings impact of participation. The costs of the programs comprise unemployment benefits to participants, subsidies to firms and operational costs. The authors also include indirect costs associated with the deadweight loss of taxation. Private job training programs have the highest

Box 8.1
(continued)

net social return, with a net present discounted value (PDV) of about 37,000 euros for the 1995–2000 period. Public job training programs also exhibit a strong earnings gain for participating workers, but around two-thirds of this is due to the subsidy so the net PDV is around 9,500 euros. Classroom programs have a surplus of 3,000 euros, while residual programs have a negative net PDV of 18,500 euros due to loss of earnings.

The implementation of labor market reforms marked the turning point for the better in Danish unemployment trends, and this accords with the observation that the flexicurity approach is a policy implication of the models outlined in this book. Within the category of active labor market programs, there is substantial evidence from other high-unemployment economies that training programs are the most effective (see, e.g., Kluve and Schmidt 2002; Boone and van Ours 2004), with a "significant positive effect on the employment rate of beneficiaries" (Cahuc and Zylberberg 2004, 685). Essentially, the Danish ALMP framework is a scaled-up and extensive version of these programs.

However, it remains a puzzle as to why Denmark's achievements have not always been successfully replicated in other countries. A major factor in the Danish reforms was the reduction in the role of the judiciary in dismissal procedures. This was part of the package of reforms which curtailed employment protection, but it has not always been implemented in other countries. Another interpretation developed by Algan and Cahuc (2006) posits that social norms affect the optimal design of labor market institutions. In particular, these authors provide evidence that differences in public-spiritedness (i.e., how justifiable it is to claim government benefits to which one is not entitled) can go some way to explain why Denmark has been able to implement ALMPs (and low job security) successfully. If social norms matter greatly for the effectiveness of ALMPs, there is only limited hope that such policies can be implemented on a broad basis around the world.

It is also important to note that the positive returns of training programs in the Danish case contrast with the smaller returns observed for public training programs in the United States (see Heckman and Carneiro 2003 for more details). An investigation into the causes of these differences goes beyond the scope of this book, but it is likely that they are due at least in part to composition effects: for example, participants in Danish programs have higher skill levels than U.S. participants and training appears to be complementary to skills. Other potential explanatory factors may include the strength of the incentives provided by the Danish scheme and, more mechanically, the fact that unemployment benefits are higher in Denmark. Social returns from training programs that increase employment are larger in countries where unemployment benefits are more substantial, because the reduction in unemployment brings with it large reductions in the distortionary taxation that is needed to finance benefit expenditures.

8.2   The Response of Technology

In addition to underemployment and segmentation in the appropriating factor's market, another dimension of the market's response that constrains special interests is in the development of new technologies that help overcome factor specificity. In this respect, a central aspect of technology choice is relative factor intensity. Even though available technologies may allow only limited factor substitution in the short run, over a longer horizon new technologies can be developed that allow a broader menu of factor intensities. This section asks the question, How will technology choice respond to the appropriability problem, and how in turn will that response affect macroeconomic equilibrium? This analysis can also be used to shed light on the consequences of allowing some degree of factor substitution in the short run.

8.2.1   Technological Menu

From a long-run perspective, let us assume a menu of available technologies for the Joint Production sector that is characterized by a constant-returns function $y(k, l)$, increasing and concave in each argument, that determines output as a function of factor inputs. Let us normalize a production unit to contain one unit of labor and κ units of capital, so that each level of the capital-labor ratio corresponds to a different technology, and denote $\tilde{y}(\kappa) \equiv y(\kappa, 1)$. The technological menu is thus characterized by the function $\tilde{y}(\kappa)$, $\tilde{y}' > 0$, $\tilde{y}'' < 0$, that determines the output of a production unit.

Technology selection is likely to influence the bargaining problem between capital and labor. On the one hand, it may affect relative factor bargaining strength. On the other hand, it may affect the degree of net specificity of factors of production; I focus in this chapter on the latter channel.

Each available technology is associated with a different degree of relationship specificity. Let us assume that a technology's specificity is determined by constant-returns functions $F_k(k, l)$ and $F_l(k, l)$, weakly increasing in both arguments. These functions determine the total amount of factors k and l, respectively, that becomes specific to the Joint Production relationship. By constant returns, we can write the following:

$$F_l(k, l) = F_l(k/l, 1)l = \phi_l f_l(k/l)l$$

and

$$F_k(k,l) = F_k(1, l/k)k = \phi_k f_k(k/l)k,$$

where $\phi_l f_l(\kappa) \equiv F_l(\kappa, 1)$ and $\phi_k f_k(\kappa) \equiv F_k(1, 1/\kappa)$ are, respectively, weakly increasing and weakly decreasing functions in the argument κ.

Examples:
1. Consider that workers must be given specific training in order to create a new Joint Production unit. In the event of a breakup, the training cost cannot be recouped. If the cost of training a worker is x_t, unitary specificity (the specificity of one unit of capital) is given by $f_k(\kappa) \equiv x_t/\kappa$.
2. Now consider an institutionally driven example of capital specificity that derives from legislated severance pay. If severance pay is fixed in monetary terms at a level x_f, then unitary specificity is given by $f_k(\kappa) \equiv x_f/\kappa$.

   In both cases, $f_k(\kappa)$ is a decreasing function of κ.

8.2.2 Technology Selection in the Inefficient Economy

The efficient economy ignores the specificity aspects of technology and sets its capital-labor ratio, κ^*, to satisfy

$$\tilde{y}'(\kappa^*) = r. \tag{8.8}$$

In the incomplete-contracts environment, the question arises of how technology is selected. Should it be determined by capital, labor, or both? While in practice there are many factors behind control delegation, our framework offers an answer to this question. Equilibrium with technological choice is characterized by balanced specificity for some parameter configurations; and by net appropriation with factor market segmentation for other configurations. In the balanced-specificity case, equilibrium technology is determined by the joint *free-entry* conditions of the two factors. In the segmented market case, however, technology is determined by the *first-order* condition of the optimization problem faced by the *appropriated* factor. This result is akin to the idea in the property rights literature that control rights are often optimally deposited with the agent who must make the largest specific investment (see, e.g., Grossman and Hart 1986; Dow 1993). However, it is different from this microeconomic explanation in that it is an equilibrium outcome and not the result of optimal contract design.

For concreteness, let us discuss this issue from the perspective of capital; but, of course, there is a nearly symmetric discussion from the point of view of labor. Capital's technology selection problem is

$$\max_{\kappa} \tilde{y}(\kappa) - r\kappa - w(\kappa, E) \tag{8.9}$$

subject to

$$w(\kappa, E) = v(E) + \max\{0, \Delta^{(k)}\} \geq v(E), \tag{8.10}$$

$$\Delta^{(k)}(\kappa, E) \geq 0. \tag{8.11}$$

The first constraint incorporates the expression for the wage rate. The second constraint embodies the conclusion of the previous discussion that the optimization problem is only meaningful either when capital is the appropriated factor of production or when specificity is balanced, namely, $\Delta^{(k)} \geq 0$.

Note that the net specificity of capital and labor can be written as a function of aggregate employment, E, and the production unit's capital-labor ratio, κ:

$$\Delta^{(k)}(\kappa, E) = \phi_k f_k(\kappa) r\kappa - \phi_l f_l(\kappa) v(E) = -\Delta^{(l)}(\kappa, E). \tag{8.12}$$

The weak inequality of constraint (8.10) holds by construction, and since the net specificity of capital is always nonnegative one can rewrite the wage expression to obtain the simpler optimization problem:

$$\max_{\kappa}\{\tilde{y}(\kappa) - r\kappa - v(E) - \Delta^{(k)}(\kappa, E) \text{ s.t. } \Delta^{(k)}(\kappa, E) \geq 0\}. \tag{8.13}$$

The Lagrangean expression of this problem is

$$L = \tilde{y}(\kappa) - r\kappa - v(E) + (\lambda - 1)\Delta^{(k)}(\kappa, E),$$

with first-order conditions

$$\tilde{y}'(\kappa) = r + (1 - \lambda)\frac{d\Delta^{(k)}}{d\kappa},$$

$$0 = \lambda \Delta^{(k)}(\kappa, E),$$

$$\lambda \geq 0 \quad \text{and} \quad \Delta^{(k)}(\kappa, E) \geq 0, \tag{8.14}$$

where the last two conditions hold with complementary slackness.

In contrast, when capital is the appropriating factor ($\Delta^{(k)} < 0$), the market for labor clears with $w(\kappa, E) = v(E)$. Considering that labor's technology-choice problem yields a maximum value $w(\kappa, E) = v(E)$ for labor compensation, no other choice of technology can yield a higher

$w(\kappa, E)$. In other words, constraint $w(\kappa, E) \geq v(E)$ of the optimization problem for capital, expression (8.9), cannot be satisfied with strict inequality for any value of κ. Technically, this means that the *constraint qualification* fails to be satisfied for capital's optimization problem, so the first-order condition is not necessary. Intuitively, since its free-entry condition holds with equality, the appropriated factor, labor, breaks even with the equilibrium technology and could not do better with any other technology. The appropriating factor, capital, therefore has no choice but to accept the equilibrium technology (this assumes that there is a single technology produced in equilibrium; otherwise, when the constraint qualification is not satisfied, the disgruntled factor could still work in Joint Production by itself if there are enough substitution possibilities).

8.2.3   Balanced-Specificity and Net Appropriation Regions

When will the economy exhibit balanced specificity as a result of technological choice? When will factors of production be segmented or appropriated? The answer to these questions depends on several elasticities. The general principle is that for an equilibrium to be in the balanced-specificity region, the following properties must hold: (1) there must be sufficient substitution possibilities between factors of production; (2) evaluated at the efficient technology, specificity cannot be too unbalanced; and (3) net factor specificity has to be sufficiently responsive to changes in technology. If these conditions are met, then technology selection can be used to reduced appropriation without inducing too much technological inefficiency.

More formally, note that

$$\lambda > 0 \Leftrightarrow 1 > \frac{\tilde{y}' - r}{\frac{d\Delta^{(k)}}{d\kappa}}.$$

Thus, as long as the numerator (the efficiency cost of departing from κ^*) is small and the denominator (the net specificity gain from departing from κ^*) is large, the economy is in the balanced-specificity region ($\lambda > 0$).

Figure 8.1 illustrates the balanced-specificity and segmented regions. The dashed line represents the efficient outcome. Between the two solid lines is a region where specificity is balanced (although the factor propor-

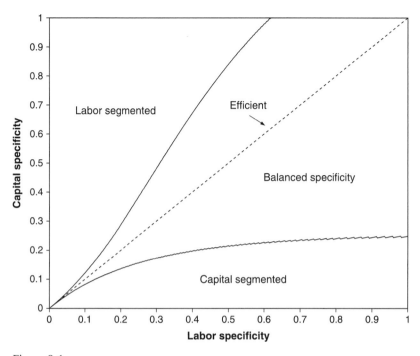

Figure 8.1
Balanced specificity and segmented regions

tion is not optimal). In the top left region capital is being appropriated, and in the bottom right region labor is being appropriated.

Let us now analyze technology selection inside each of these regions, starting with the balanced-specificity region. Segmentation is reintroduced in section 8.2.5.

8.2.4 Distorted Capital-Labor Ratio

By definition of the balanced-specificity region we have that $\Delta^{(k)} = \Delta^{(l)} = 0$. Thus, in equilibrium, κ and E are determined from

$$\tilde{y}(\kappa) = r\kappa + v(E) \tag{8.15}$$

and

$$\phi_k f_k(\kappa) r\kappa = \phi_l f_l(\kappa) v(E). \tag{8.16}$$

Recall that, with balanced specificity, the first-order condition to problem (8.13) simply provides the shadow value of a constraint. This is also

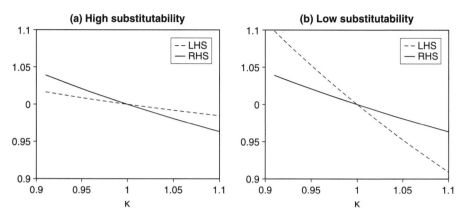

Figure 8.2
Exclusion and withdrawal effects

true for labor's optimization problem. Equilibrium is determined by the income-sharing rule and by the balanced-specificity condition.

Replacing the balanced-specificity condition in equation (8.15) allows us to characterize the equilibrium capital-labor ratio in Joint Production by studying the two sides of the expression

$$\frac{\tilde{y}(\kappa)}{\kappa} = r\left(1 + \frac{\phi_k f_k(\kappa)}{\phi_l f_l(\kappa)}\right). \tag{8.17}$$

What is the impact of an increase in the degree of appropriability of capital—modeled as an increase in ϕ_k—on equilibrium technology κ and employment E? To analyze this question, figure 8.2 plots the left-hand side (LHS) and the right-hand side (RHS) of equation (8.17). The LHS measures the average productivity of capital and is downward-sloping because of the diminishing marginal product of capital. The RHS is also downward-sloping because f_k is decreasing and f_l is increasing in κ. It is apparent from the figure that the key factor in answering the question is whether the RHS crosses the LHS from above or from below. For given specificity functions, the nature of the crossing is determined by the elasticity of the technological menu, which translates into how flat the LHS curve is.

The figures are drawn so that the efficient economy with substitution has $\kappa^* = 1$. This calibration ensures that the capital-labor ratio in the efficient economy with substitution coincides with the efficient economy without substitution (one unit of capital per one unit of labor), a version of which was analyzed in chapter 3.

The Exclusion Effect Panel (a) of figure 8.2 illustrates the case where capital and labor are highly substitutable in the long-run technological menu. In this case, the LHS (the average product of capital) is nearly flat at $\kappa = \kappa^*$. An appropriability push caused by a rise in ϕ_k shifts the RHS upward, resulting in a new technology with a higher capital-labor ratio. What causes this partial technological "exclusion" of labor in response to an appropriability push? An increase in the appropriability of capital increases the rent component of wages. Given the initial level of κ, the upward shift in the RHS curve causes a gap between capital's outside opportunity cost and its (low) return in Joint Production. To restore equilibrium, a new technology is selected with higher κ that reduces the appropriability of each unit of capital by reducing $f_k(\kappa)$ and increasing $f_l(\kappa)$. The new technology partially excludes labor from Joint Production in order to reduce the degree of net specificity. Since substitution is high, the reduction in net specificity obtained from exclusion does not have high productivity costs.

What happens to E in this case? Differentiating equation (8.15) with respect to κ yields

$$\frac{dE}{d\kappa} = \frac{\tilde{y}' - r}{v'}. \tag{8.18}$$

Close to the efficient equilibrium, $\tilde{y}' \approx r$ from equation (8.8), so there is no effect on aggregate employment. Away from it, as capital has already excluded labor, we have that $\tilde{y}' < r$, and employment falls as capital intensity rises. Again, in equilibrium labor ends up paying for the appropriation push as it absorbs the technological inefficiency introduced by capital's adaptation to the new institutional environment.

By homogeneity of degree one in production, we have that if $\tilde{y}' < r$, the marginal product of labor must be greater than the wage. Moreover, the wage falls since under balanced specificity the wage equation reduces to

$$w(\kappa, E) = v(E),$$

and employment falls. The counterpart of these two statements is that in equilibrium both κ and r/w rise. This *excess substitution* away from labor is a fundamental departure from standard classical explanations of unemployment that see the impact of labor market regulation as operating entirely through a rise in the wage rate. As we will see in the next chapter, a theory of excess substitution is needed to explain the Western European experience during the last three decades. Over the long run, the puzzle is not to explain why unemployment rose in continental Europe, but why it did despite the fact that the early wage gains from the institutional push were more than given up over the course of the next two decades (see Blanchard 2005 for a similar view on the nature of the puzzle).

The Withdrawal Effect   Panel (b) of figure 8.2 presents the withdrawal effect. Suppose that, even in the long run, technological substitution possibilities are limited. In this case, the LHS curve is steep at $\kappa = \kappa^*$, reflecting the fact that the average productivity of capital declines sharply as less labor is used with it. An increase in the appropriability of capital causes the RHS curve to shift upward and the rent component of wages to rise. If the capital-labor ratio is increased, the average productivity of capital falls sharply, and this makes it even more difficult to cover the increase in wage rents. On the contrary, the equilibrium response is to reduce the capital-labor ratio and increase the specificity of capital but, in so doing, simultaneously increase the productivity of capital and its ability to compensate labor. This "withdrawal" of capital is reminiscent of the market response of capital absent any technological choices.

Having determined that κ falls, one can use equation (8.18) again to find the effect of technological substitution on aggregate employment:

$$\frac{dE}{d\kappa} = \frac{\tilde{y}' - r}{v'}.$$

Close to the efficient equilibrium, $\tilde{y}' \approx r$, and there is no effect on employment. Away from it, as capital has already withdrawn, we have that $\tilde{y}' > r$, and employment falls together with the withdrawal of capital.

Moreover, since there is no segmentation in the balanced-specificity region, it must again be that $w(\kappa, E) = v(E)$. That is, as E falls, the wage rate also falls despite the appropriability push by labor. What has happened? As capital withdraws from Joint Production, the push backfires, and labor also ends up paying for the distorted technological choice.

Box 8.2
Directed technical change

The idea that the prevailing productive technology adapts to the institutional environment is important. Kennedy's (1964) *directed technical change* analysis characterized technological choice as the optimal outcome given a menu of possible innovations (i.e., the innovation possibilities frontier). More recently, Acemoglu (1998, 2005) formalizes this idea and shows that the degree of factor bias in technological choice depends on the interplay of two forces: (1) the price effect, which encourages innovation toward scarce factors (which produce goods with a higher relative price); and (2) the market size effect, which encourages innovation toward abundant factors (which have a lower relative return). In his setting, the elasticity of substitution between factors determines which force prevails, and hence the factor bias of technological progress. If the elasticity of substitution between factors of production is sufficiently high, the market size effect dominates.

Acemoglu (2002) also shows that this theory may explain the evolution of the wage skill premium in the United States over the last fifty years. As the relative supply of skilled (college-educated) labor grew in the 1960s, the wage premium declined as would be expected from standard economic reasoning. The following decades, however, are suggestive of a dominant market size effect, as technological progress became more biased to take advantage of the growing relative supply of skilled workers. Skill-biased technological progress, as it is popularly known, may therefore have been an endogenous response to changes in relative factor supply. Concomitant with such technological developments, the wage premium increased. Moreover, the observation that there has been an acceleration in the degree of skill bias in the 1980s accounts for the sharper increase in the wage premium over the same period and during the 1990s. The key ingredient for the analysis is that the elasticity of substitution between skilled and unskilled labor has to be sufficiently high (close to two, which is not far from empirical estimates).

In the context of continental Europe, Acemoglu again applies the idea of directed technical change to the behavior of the wage premium. The wage premium in continental Europe has not increased substantially in the last fifty years, due in part to labor market institutions that are biased toward wage compression. For illustration of this idea consider, for example, a binding minimum wage. The existence of a minimum wage creates an incentive for firms to adopt or create technologies that are biased toward unskilled workers. Why? Because, applying the concepts discussed in this book in a context of a binding minimum wage, the firm is the full residual claimant of the productivity of unskilled workers. Such technological considerations inhibit a large rise in the wage premium endogenously, which compound the effects of explicit wage compression.

8.2.5   Market Segmentation Reemerges

At some point, the productivity loss brought about by substitution (either through exclusion or withdrawal) becomes too burdensome, and the adjustment margin shifts more directly to the number of production units, as in the case without substitution. The emergence of segmented labor markets means that the economy is in the top left region of figure 8.1. This occurs when the marginal effect of changing firm κ on profits

$$\tilde{y}(\kappa) - r\kappa - w(\kappa, E)$$

equals zero; that is,

$$\tilde{y}' = r + w_\kappa. \tag{8.19}$$

Since technology selection no longer fully offsets the appropriation push, labor segmentation reemerges and only the free-entry condition of capital holds in equilibrium:

$$\tilde{y}(\kappa) = r\kappa + w(\kappa, E) = r\kappa + v(E) + \Delta^{(k)}(\kappa, E) > r\kappa + v(E), \tag{8.20}$$

with strict inequality because the economy is no longer in the balanced-specificity region.

Differentiating equation (8.20) and substituting equation (8.19) into it yields an expression for the decline in employment resulting from the institutional push in the segmented region:

$$\frac{dE}{d\Delta^{(k)}} = -\frac{1}{v'} < 0.$$

A similar expression holds for the effect of an increase in $\Delta^{(k)}$ on employment E for the model in chapter 3 (in the absence of factor substitution).

Let us take stock at this point. When κ is fixed, an institutional push against capital results in an equilibrium fall in $v(E)$ through a decline in E. When κ can react, the fall in E depends upon technological substitution, but either way the inefficiencies introduced by the technological distortion are still borne by labor, since this is the relatively inelastic factor of production in the long run.

8.2.6   More Excess Substitution: Capital Supply and Sclerosis Channels

I already showed that one can arrive at a situation where the marginal product of labor exceeds the equilibrium wage rate (the exclusion effect).

In response to an appropriation push, capital excludes labor from Joint Production beyond what is implied by the standard neoclassical first-order condition. In fact, in equilibrium both employment and wages fall. Here I argue that there are realistic considerations that exacerbate this excess substitution outcome.

Capital Supply   I have assumed up to now that the supply of uncommitted capital is infinitely elastic. Suppose instead that this supply is upward-sloping, so that $r = r(\kappa E)$ with $r' > 0$. It is easy to see in this case that as κ rises with an appropriation push by labor, the opportunity cost of capital rises for any given E. This means that the production unit has less surplus left to pay workers and hence that the wage rate needs to fall further than when capital was infinitely elastic. In equilibrium, this is achieved by reducing the opportunity cost of labor, v, which in turn requires a larger fall in employment.

To see this, differentiate equation (8.20) to get

$$\frac{dE}{d\kappa} = \frac{\tilde{y}' - r'\kappa - r - \Delta_\kappa^{(k)}}{v' + \Delta_E^{(k)}} < \frac{\tilde{y}' - r - \Delta_\kappa^{(k)}}{v' + \Delta_E^{(k)}},$$

where the inequality holds if the two expressions are evaluated at the same equilibrium interest rate.

Sclerosis Channel   Let us momentarily remove the microeconomic excess substitution channel, so that $w_\kappa = 0$, and $\tilde{y}' = r$. This is precisely the case studied in Caballero and Hammour (1998a), where excess substitution results from a pure equilibrium channel. I develop that model in greater detail in the next chapter.

For now, let us sketch the argument and introduce an infinitesimal unit that lives through many repeated periods. Its (relative) productivity falls over time at the rate δ, so it is eventually scrapped when it can no longer cover the opportunity cost of labor. Denote this scrapping time by T. Assume further that capital is fully sunk in this unit, and that technology cannot be changed after it is chosen at date $t = 0$. The entry condition for this firm is

$$\kappa = \int_0^T (e^{-\delta t}\tilde{y}(\kappa) - w(\kappa, E_t))e^{-rt}\, dt,$$

and the corresponding first-order condition with respect to technology choice is

$$\tilde{y}'(\kappa) = \frac{r + \delta}{1 - e^{-(r+\delta)T}}.\tag{8.21}$$

The scrapping time occurs when the marginal product of the unit is exactly equal to the opportunity cost of labor:

$$T = \frac{1}{\delta} \ln\left(\frac{\tilde{y}(\kappa)}{v(E_T)}\right).\tag{8.22}$$

But since an institutional push by labor lowers v in equilibrium, T must rise. By equation (8.21), this means that κ rises, yielding the excess substitution result through a sclerosis channel. The reduced opportunity cost of labor means that existing Joint Production units can generate surplus at lower levels of productivity. This lengthening of the time horizon restores the return to capital, but it comes at the cost of sclerosis, which is ultimately completely paid by labor through reduced employment and wages.

8.2.7 Deregulation and Globalization

The argument concerning the interaction of appropriability and technology is quite general, and it can also be applied to *demand* factors that determine the menu of opportunities available to capital. In economies with heavily regulated labor markets, the current process of globalization has effects similar to an increase in the technological substitutability of capital and labor, as it offers further chances for capital to specialize and exclude labor. Aggregate substitution possibilities depend not only on available technologies, but also on the characteristics of demand for the range of producible goods. Globalization increases the potential for specialization—and, hence, factor substitution—by giving firms access to new markets; it also broadens the technological menu by facilitating international technology transfers. The result can be an improvement in investment and growth; but labor may not share in the benefits if its market is heavily regulated (see box 8.3). In such an environment, greater substitution possibilities can lead to lower earnings for workers and a stagnant or deteriorating employment outlook. Thus, an even distribution of the benefits of globalization probably requires a simultaneous process of labor market deregulation.

Box 8.3
"Globalization" and labor market rigidities in Europe

> The progressive liberalization of goods and financial markets is an additional development that may have played a role in undermining the position of labor since the 1980s. Globalization offers an international menu of labor market institutions for capital to choose from and increases the flexibility of its outside options. For economies that suffer from a heavy institutional burden, the result may be higher unemployment and weaker labor. The notion that globalization is incompatible with maintaining the stability of existing labor market structures has been strongly voiced by Nobel Prize laureate economist Maurice Allais (1994, 194): "It is in the explosive cocktail of those two factors, the liberalization of international trade and the legislation or agreements on minimum wages, that one must see the essential cause of the core trend that inevitably leads all developed countries of the European Community toward increasingly massive unemployment."
>
> Some recent evidence suggests that all developed countries will not suffer the same fate. In fact, labor market institutions, such as wage-setting institutions (measured by the percentage of workers covered by collective bargaining), have become more diverse in advanced economies over the last two decades (Freeman 2000). Brügemann (2003) presents a theoretical model to explain this development. Using a Ricardian model, he argues that trade openness enables a country with rigid institutions to specialize in activities less dependent on flexibility, mitigating the cost of rigidity. Conversely, it makes a country with flexible institutions less willing to become rigid as well. He also shows that labor market rigidities may slow down the reallocation needed to realize the potential gains from trade created by openness.

8.3   Conclusion

The long-run consequences of excessive institutional buildup in favor of a factor of production can have large costs for the appropriating factor of production once technology adapts. Typically, a phenomenon of excess substitution will develop whereby that factor may end up suffering from both less employment and a lower factor return.

In addition, the "adequate" or "bearable" level of institutional buildup depends on aggregate economic conditions and competition. A change in these conditions, such as that brought about by the process of globalization or by major recessionary shocks, can also break the balance and trigger these undesirable trends.

An efficient political process would keep institutions and the economic context aligned. Failure to sustain this balance can have dire consequences, as I further describe in the next chapter.

8.4   Appendix: Simulation Parameters

Figure 8.1 was generated using the following functional forms and parameters: $\tilde{y}(\kappa) = \kappa^{0.5}$, $f_k(\kappa) = 1/\kappa$, $f_l(\kappa) = \kappa$, and $r = 0.5$.

The functional forms and parameters for figure 8.2 are $\phi_k = \phi_l$, $f_k(\kappa) = 1/\kappa^{0.4}$, $f_l(\kappa) = \kappa^{0.4}$, and $r = 0.5$. On the left panel output is given by $\tilde{y}(\kappa) = \frac{a+bk}{a+b}$, whereas on the right panel it is given by $\tilde{y}(\kappa) = c$. Parameter values are $a = 1$, $b = 0.2$, $c = 1$.

Note

1. This chapter is based on Caballero and Hammour (1998b).

References and Suggested Readings

Acemoglu, Daron. 1998. "Why Do New Technologies Complement Skills? Directed Technical Change and Wage Inequality." *Quarterly Journal of Economics* 113(4): 1055–1089.

Acemoglu, Daron. 2002. "Technical Change, Inequality and the Labor Market." *Journal of Economic Literature* 40(1): 7–72.

Acemoglu, Daron. 2005. "Equilibrium Bias of Technology." Mimeo., Massachusetts Institute of Technology.

Algan, Yann, and Pierre Cahuc. 2006. "Civic Attitudes and the Design of Labor Market Institutions: Which Countries Can Implement the Danish Flexicurity Model?" IZA Discussion Paper No. 1928.

Allais, Maurice. 1994. *Combats pour l'Europe, 1992–1994*. Paris: Clément Juglar.

Ball, Laurence. 1996. "Disinflation and the NAIRU." In Christina D. Romer and David H. Romer, eds., *Reducing Inflation: Motivation and Strategy*, 167–185. Chicago, Ill.: University of Chicago Press.

Becker, Gary. 1964. *Human Capital*. New York: Columbia University Press.

Becker, Gary. 1983. "A Theory of Competition among Pressure Groups for Political Influence." *Quarterly Journal of Economics* 98(3): 371–400.

Binmore, Kenneth, Ariel Rubinstein, and Asher Wolinsky. 1986. "The Nash Bargaining Solution in Economic Modeling." *Rand Journal of Economics* 17(2): 176–188.

Blanchard, Olivier J. 2005. "European Unemployment: The Evolution of Facts and Ideas." MIT Working Paper 05-24.

Blanchard, Olivier J., and Juan F. Jimeno. 1995. "Structural Unemployment: Spain Versus Portugal." *American Economic Review* 85(2): 212–218.

Blanchard, Olivier J., and Justin Wolfers. 1999. "The Role of Shocks and Institutions in the Rise of European Unemployment: The Aggregate Evidence." Harry Johnson Lecture, March 1999.

Boone, Jan, and J. C. van Ours. 2004. "Effective Active Labor Market Policies." Mimeo., Tilburg University.

Brügemann, Bjorn. 2003. "Trade Integration and the Political Support for Labor Market Rigidity." Mimeo., Yale University.

Bulow, Jeremy I., and Lawrence H. Summers. 1986. "A Theory of Dual Labor Markets with Application to Industrial Policy, Discrimination, and Keynesian Unemployment." *Journal of Labor Economics* 4(3): 376–414.

Caballero, Ricardo J., and Mohamad L. Hammour. 1994. "The Cleansing Effect of Recessions." *American Economic Review* 84(5): 1350–1368.

Caballero, Ricardo J., and Mohamad L. Hammour. 1996a. "On the Timing and Efficiency of Creative Destruction." *Quarterly Journal of Economics* 111(3): 805–852.

Caballero, Ricardo J., and Mohamad L. Hammour. 1996b. "On the Ills of Adjustment." *Journal of Development Economics* 51(1): 161–192.

Caballero, Ricardo J., and Mohamad L. Hammour. 1997. "Improper Churn: Social Costs and Macroeconomic Consequences." Mimeo., Massachusetts Institute of Technology.

Caballero, Ricardo J., and Mohamad L. Hammour. 1998a. "Jobless Growth: Appropriability, Factor Substitution and Unemployment." *Carnegie-Rochester Conference Series on Public Policy* 48: 51–94.

Caballero, Ricardo J., and Mohamad L. Hammour. 1998b. "The Macroeconomics of Specificity." *Journal of Political Economy* 106(4): 724–767.

Cahuc, Pierre, and André Zylberberg. 2004. *Labor Economics.* Cambridge, Mass.: The MIT Press.

Danish Economic Council. 2002. *Danish Economy, Autumn 2002.* Copenhagen: Danish Economic Council.

De Long, J. Bradford. 1990. "Liquidation Cycles: Old-Fashioned Real Business Cycle Theory and the Great Depression." NBER Working Paper No. 3546.

De Long, J. Bradford, and Lawrence H. Summers. 1988. "How does Macroeconomic Policy Affect Output?" *Brookings Papers on Economic Activity*, no. 2: 433–495.

Dow, Gregory K. 1993. "Why Capital Hires Labor: A Bargaining Perspective." *American Economic Review* 83(1): 118–134.

Freeman, Richard. 2000. "Single Peaked vs. Diversified Capitalism: The Relation Between Economic Institutions and Outcomes." NBER Working Paper No. 7556.

Grossman, Gene, and Elhanan Helpman. 2001. *Special Interest Politics*. Cambridge, Mass.: The MIT Press.

Grossman, Sanford J., and Oliver D. Hart. 1986. "The Costs and Benefits of Ownership: A Theory of Vertical and Lateral Integration." *Journal of Political Economy* 94(4): 691–719.

Grout, Paul A. 1984. "Investment and Wages in the Absence of Binding Contracts: A Nash Bargaining Approach." *Econometrica* 52(2): 449–460.

Hart, Oliver. 1995. *Firms, Contracts and Financial Structure: Clarendon Lectures in Economics*. Oxford: Oxford University Press.

Hart, Oliver, and John Moore. 1990. "Property Rights and the Nature of the Firm." *Journal of Political Economy* 98(6): 1119–1158.

Hart, Oliver, and John Moore. 1994. "A Theory of Debt Based on the Inalienability of Human Capital." *Quarterly Journal of Economics* 109(4): 841–880.

Heckman, James J., and Pedro Carneiro. 2003. "Human Capital Policy." NBER Working Paper No. 9495.

Jespersen, Svend, Jakob Munch, and Lars Skipper. 2004. "Costs and Benefits of Danish Active Labor Market Programs." Mimeo., University of Aarhus.

Katz, Lawrence F., and Lawrence H. Summers. 1989. "Industry Rents: Evidence and Implications." *Brookings Papers on Economic Activity: Microeconomics* 1989: 209–275.

Kennedy, Charles. 1964. "Induced Bias in Innovation and the Theory of Distribution." *Economic Journal* 74(3): 541–547.

Klein, Benjamin, Robert G. Crawford, and Armen A. Alchian. 1978. "Vertical Integration, Appropriable Rents, and the Competitive Contracting Process." *Journal of Law and Economics* 21(2): 297–326.

Kluve, J., and C. M. Schmidt. 2002. "Can Training and Employment Subsidies Combat European Unemployment?" *Economic Policy* 35: 411–448.

Krueger, Alan B., and Lawrence H. Summers. 1988. "Efficiency Wages and the Inter-Industry Wage Structure." *Econometrica* 56(2): 259–293.

Lindbeck, Assar, and Dennis Snower. 1986. "Wage Setting, Unemployment and Insider-Outsider Relations." *American Economic Review* 76(2): 235–239.

MacLeod, W. Bentley, and James M. Malcomson. 1993. "Investments, Holdup, and the Form of Market Contracts." *American Economic Review* 83(4): 811–837.

Makowski, Louis, and Joseph M. Ostroy. 1995. "Appropriation and Efficiency: A Revision of the First Theorem of Welfare Economics." *American Economic Review* 85(4): 808–827.

Myerson, Roger B., and Mark A. Satterthwaite. 1983. "Efficient Mechanisms for Bilateral Trading." *Journal of Economic Theory* 29(2): 265–281.

North, Douglass C., and Barry R. Weingast. 1989. "Constitutions and Commitment: The Evolution of Institutions Governing Public Choice in Seventeenth-Century England." *Journal of Economic History* 49(4): 254–283.

Organization for Economic Cooperation and Development (OECD). 1996. *Employment Outlook*. Paris: OECD.

Phelps, Edmund S., and Sidney G. Winter, Jr. 1970. "Optimal Price Policy under Atomistic Competition." In Edmund S. Phelps et al., eds., *Microeconomic Foundations of Employment and Inflation Theory*, 309–337. New York: W. W. Norton.

Ramey, Garey, and Joel Watson. 1996. "Bilateral Trade and Opportunism in a Matching Market." Economics Department Discussion Paper No. 96-08, University of California, San Diego.

Ramey, Garey, and Joel Watson. 1997. "Contractual Fragility, Job Destruction and Business Cycles." *Quarterly Journal of Economics* 112(3): 873–911.

Robinson, James A. 1995. "Incomplete Contracting, Capital Accumulation, and Labor Market Institutions." Mimeo., University of Southern California.

Robinson, James A. 1996. "The Dynamics of Labor Market Institutions." Mimeo., University of Southern California.

Roe, M. J. 1994. *Strong Managers, Weak Owners: The Political Roots of American Corporate Finance*. Princeton, N.J.: Princeton University Press.

Shaked, A., and John Sutton. 1984. "Involuntary Unemployment as a Perfect Equilibrium in a Bargaining Model." *Econometrica* 52(6): 1351–1364.

Shleifer, Andrei, and Robert W. Vishny. 1996. "A Survey of Corporate Governance." NBER Working Paper No. 5554.

Sichel, Daniel E. 1992. "Inventories and the Three Phases of the Business Cycle." Economic Activity Working Paper No. 128, Board of Governors of the Federal Reserve System.

Simons, Henry C. 1944. "Some Reflections on Syndicalism." *Journal of Political Economy* 52(1): 1–25.

Thomas, Jonathan, and Tim Worrall. 1994. "Foreign Direct Investment and the Risk of Expropriation." *Review of Economic Studies* 61(1): 81–108.

Topel, Robert. 1990. "Specific Capital and Unemployment: Measuring the Costs and Consequences of Job Loss." *Carnegie-Rochester Conference Series on Public Policy* 33: 181–214.

Williamson, Oliver E. 1979. "Transaction-Cost Economics: The Governance of Contractual Relations." *Journal of Law and Economics* 22(2): 233–261.

Williamson, Oliver E. 1985. *The Economic Institutions of Capitalism*. New York: Free Press.

Williamson, Oliver E. 1988. "Corporate Finance and Corporate Governance." *Journal of Finance* 43(3): 567–591.

9
Application: Three Decades of Unemployment in Western Europe

This chapter applies the ideas of chapter 8, and more generally of this book, to analyze the changing face of European unemployment in the last three decades of the twentieth century. The European experience offers a good laboratory. Western European economies experienced a substantial institutional buildup in favor of labor, which allows us to examine the macroeconomic consequences of an increase in capital appropriability at different frequencies.[1]

As I have argued before, the general-equilibrium outcome of increased appropriability depends crucially on individual factors' supply elasticities, and on the degree to which labor and capital need each other in production. This observation highlights two basic characteristics of technology that are the principal focus of this chapter's analysis: the embodiment of technology in capital, and capital-labor substitutability in the available technological menu. Technological embodiment means that capital is effectively much less elastic in the short than in the long run, and is therefore more exposed to appropriation. Substitutability implies that an attempt at appropriating capital will induce a substitution of capital for labor in the long run, an additional instrument to thwart appropriation.

This chapter explores observable aspects of the dynamic mechanism that governs the interplay of appropriability and the previously mentioned technological features. The chapter traces the general-equilibrium implications of appropriability over time—in particular, the technological dimension. Appropriation operates at various levels of interaction between capital and labor that range from individual transactions up to the political economy of labor market regulation. The empirical focus

here is on the higher, political levels of interaction, because they are easier to identify and track over time.

The deep transformations experienced by Western European capital-
labor relations during the last three decades are well documented. The
1950s and 1960s saw the development of basic institutions that were to
become a platform for political intervention in capital-labor relations.
This period culminated in the intensification of the labor movement and
the wage pressures of the late 1960s and early 1970s—May 1968 in
France, the "hot Italian autumn" of 1969, and movements elsewhere.
These developments, while arguably warranted as a way for labor to
share more evenly in the rapid European expansion since the end of
World War II, had the misfortune to clash directly with the oil shocks
of the 1970s. From a pure efficiency point of view, an appropriate response to the depressed conditions of the 1970s would have been an
institutional shift and wage adjustments in favor of capital. The actual
outcome, on the contrary, was characterized by a sustained political momentum for further institutional gains by labor. Faced with deteriorating
aggregate conditions, labor insiders attempted to build fences around
themselves through a combination of job protection regulations, early retirement compensation, hikes in social charges on payrolls, and political
resistance to large-scale industrial labor shedding and increases in unemployment. Lazear (1990), for example, estimates that the costs of severance payments and advance notification for job termination rose by an
average of 60 percent in OECD countries from the late 1960s to the late
1970s, with the rise substantially more marked in the large European
economies.

With the aforementioned developments in capital-labor relations came
the well-known buildup in unemployment, from levels below 3 percent
during the 1960s to levels above 10 percent by the 1990s. The rise in European unemployment was slow during the first half of the 1970s and
only gradually reached its peak levels, with a short pause during the economic expansion of the late 1980s. During the 1970s, the trade-off did
not seem unfavorable to labor: unemployment increased, but so did
wages and the labor share. Moreover, the protective measures taken appear to have softened the impact of aggregate shocks on employment.
Analysts of that period saw in the widening "wage gap"—apparent in
the growth of wages and of the labor share—evidence pointing to classi-

cal unemployment (e.g., Sachs 1979; Bruno and Sachs 1985; Krugman 1985; Kouri, de Macedo, and Viscio 1985).

While unemployment kept rising in the 1980s, wage growth slowed down below productivity growth, the labor share plummeted, and the deal turned sour for labor (see Blanchard 1997, who documents the large decline of the labor share during the 1980s and 1990s for France, Italy, and Germany; this decline was not observed in countries with more "flexible" labor markets, such as the United States or the United Kingdom). Unemployment had turned nonclassical. The OECD (1986) study on labor market flexibility, for example, while agreeing with the view that a wage gap was responsible for high unemployment in the 1970s, pointed out that this gap had been declining while unemployment kept rising. Moreover, what appears as a virtual "depression" from the point of view of employment appears much less so from the point of view of capital. Although capital and aggregate output never resumed the "catching-up" growth rates of the 1950s and 1960s, both exhibited sustained growth—especially once one controls for the productivity slowdown and for the high interest rates of the 1980s and early 1990s. During this period, capital and labor parted company in Europe, with capital growing by the 1990s at sustained rates and yielding returns comparable to those of the 1960s, while labor followed a much gloomier path.

The Western European economies' rich dynamic response is consistent with the interaction of appropriation and technology at different frequencies. Put succinctly, the joint increase in unemployment and in the labor share during the 1970s is consistent with the short-run response of existing capital that faces an appropriation push. Given the irreversibility of investment and technology choice, the response of capital already in place is highly inelastic—with limited possibilities to withdraw or substitute labor away. Increased appropriation can therefore be effective in the short run, and shift part of the quasi-rents in favor of labor. Over the longer run, however, capital is much more flexible. In response to an appropriation attempt, it will select and develop technologies that are much less labor intensive, and capital will reach an equilibrium investment level that will guarantee itself returns equivalent to what it can get elsewhere in the world. The first result indicates that capital investment may continue at a sustained rate, despite further increases in

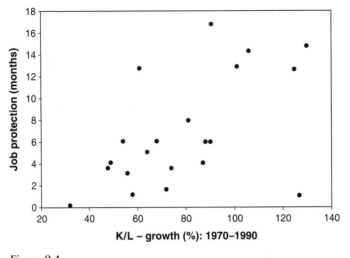

Figure 9.1
Capital-labor substitution and job protection
Source: Caballero and Hammour (1998a).

unemployment; and the second that capital investment will recover its profitability, at the expense of the short-run gains made by labor. This implies a rise in the capital-labor ratio and a recovery in the capital share—which has not only recovered in Europe, but clearly overshot its initial level.

In fact, there is clear evidence of a correlation between capital-labor substitution and indicators of appropriability. Figure 9.1 plots the change in the capital-labor ratio between 1970 and 1990 against an index of job protection (the sum of maximum mandatory severance payments, in months of wages, and of the advance notification period, also in months) for the OECD countries. The relationship is clearly positive (the only exception corresponds to Japan, in the lower right corner, which has entirely different labor market traditions and institutions).

It is important to highlight the fact that the marked differences in the economy's short- and long-run response to an appropriation push are not driven by a reversal in the shock itself. The common presumption at the time, that European labor markets had regained substantial flexibility in the 1980s, was based on the observation that wages had grown slower than productivity—in addition to clear specific cases where extensive reforms had been implemented (e.g., in Britain). However, even in the absence of any institutional reversal, the observed decline in wage growth and in the labor share are a natural outcome of the general-equilibrium mechanisms outlined earlier. Paradoxically, as described in chapter 8, once dynamics have worked their way through the system, detrended wages may fall *below* their level prior to the appropriation push, as capital-labor substitution takes place over the long-run.

To further explore the role of specificity and appropriability in the European unemployment problem, the rest of this chapter is divided into four sections. Section 9.1 describes the specific case of France in more detail, as representative of the European experience. Section 9.2 outlines a dynamic model of the interaction between appropriation and technology, while section 9.3 calibrates the model based on French data and examines its ability to track the dynamics of basic macroeconomic variables—unemployment, the capital-output ratio, the labor share, the profit rate, and so forth—based on the major institutional and aggregate shocks experienced by the French economy. Section 9.4 concludes.

9.1   The French Experience

In order to analyze the European experience, let us pick France as a prototypical case. Many of the phenomena that characterize French macroeconomic performance find a ready counterpart in the other Western European economies, although often with important differences in timing and magnitude.

9.1.1   French Macroeconomic Performance

Figure 9.2 presents the time path over the 1967–1995 period of a number of French macroeconomic variables that play a central role in the argument developed in this chapter. In the top two panels, the unemployment rate and the capital-output ratio characterize the fortunes of labor and capital during this period. Having remained below 2 percent until around 1967, unemployment climbed to 3 percent in 1968 and hovered around that level until 1974. At that point it began rising sharply for more than a decade, a surge that was only interrupted temporarily by the economic expansion of the late 1980s. What appears as a depression from the perspective of employment looks much less so from the point of view of capital—which grew at a generally sustained rate despite the high real interest rates prevailing in France during the 1980s and early 1990s (see panel [f]). A marked substitution phenomenon seems to have dominated this period, taking the capital-output ratio in the business sector from around 2.5 in the early 1970s to around 2.8 in the early 1990s. In comparison, the same ratio in the United States remained essentially flat throughout this period. The pattern is particularly pronounced in manufacturing. Looking at the capital-labor ratio over the period 1970–1990, we find that it increased by 122 percent in French manufacturing versus 88 percent in the United States. Normalized by the capital-labor ratio in the traded sector, the increase was 25 percent in France versus 8 percent in the United States.

Panels (c) and (d) document the evolution of wages and profits. The period can be divided into three distinct episodes. The first episode, which ended around 1974, was characterized by fast growth in wages and healthy profit rates. It appeared to be the continuation of the expansionary 1950s and 1960s, but with worker compensation making more rapid progress. A break occurred in 1974, starting an episode that lasted until the early 1980s, where wages continued growing at a brisk rate while the profit rate plummeted. Wage progression was all the more striking considering the oil shocks of the 1970s, and seems to have taken place at the expense of existing capital. This is a strong indication of progress in labor's position in the sharing of quasi-rents. The last episode, from the mid-1980s to 1995, was characterized by a significant slowdown in wage progression coupled with a strong recovery in profits. The effect of appropriability on the profitability of capital does not seem to have persisted over the longer term. Another way to characterize these three phases is to look at the share of value added that went to each factor, as depicted in panel (e). The labor share was around 0.67 in the first phase, peaked at about 0.72 in the second phase, and then experienced a sharp decline down to 0.60 in the third phase.

The period was characterized by a number of major aggregate shocks. After the three decades of brisk economic growth in the postwar era, France (like other countries) experienced the two oil shocks of the 1970s, followed by general monetary and fiscal restraint throughout the rest of the period. Panel (f) of figure 9.2 depicts the path of real interest rates. Both short and long rates were very low in the inflationary 1970s,

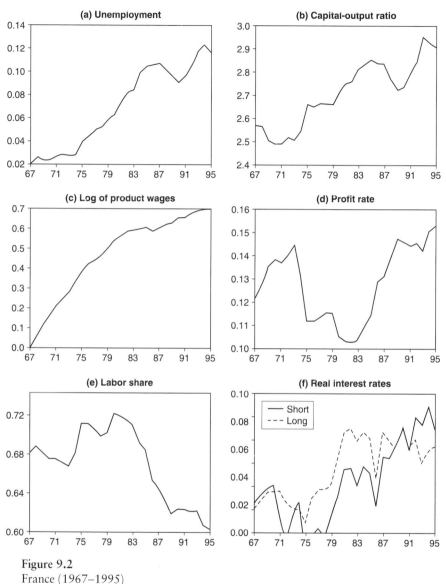

Figure 9.2
France (1967–1995)
Source: Caballero and Hammour (1998a).

and very high following the monetary tightening of the early 1980s—
peaking near the period's end during a phase of currency turbulence
and the determined policy to defend the franc.

9.1.2   The Evolution of Capital-Labor Relations

A detailed chronology of postwar institutional developments in French
capital-labor relations is given in box 9.1. In essence, one can break
the postwar period into five policy phases. Phase I covered the period
1945–1968, characterized by rapid economic growth and labor shortages
—which necessitated a steady flow of immigrant labor. That period saw
the creation of a number of institutions that were to become the basis for
political intervention in capital-labor relations: the generalized social
security system, the unemployment insurance system (UNEDIC, and the
ANPE), the minimum wage (the SMIG, later to become the SMIC),
and new representative bodies for centralized bargaining (the CNPF for
firms, and the CGT-FO and CFDT labor unions).

The institutional push in favor of labor unfolded during phases II to
IV. Phase II started with the student revolts and general strike in May
1968 and ended with the first oil shock in 1973. It was characterized by
rapid wage growth and institutional gains by labor, as epitomized by the
Grenelle accords of May 27, 1968. Given that wage growth had been
slower than productivity, this phase can be seen as a step toward a
more even participation of labor in the fruits of economic growth. Phase
III started with the first oil shock in 1973 and ended with the left coming
to power in 1981. This period was characterized by a sustained political momentum for institutional gains by labor in an environment of
depressed aggregate conditions. Given the rise in unemployment, the political focus turned to protection of existing jobs: the 1975 introduction
of an administrative authorization requirement for economically motivated dismissals; more protective unemployment benefits; and early retirement compensation (which exerts an effect on wage determination
similar to unemployment benefits). Phase IV started with the 1981 elec-
tion of François Mitterrand and his socialist-communist coalition and
ended with the socialists' defeat in the 1986 legislative elections. The
new government introduced an array of "prolabor" measures: a rapid
increase in the minimum wage, a reduction in the work week and the
adoption of a fifth week of paid vacation, restrictions on determined-

Box 9.1
A chronology of postwar French labor market developments

1945   The *comité d'entreprise* is instituted in firms with more than one hundred employees, a consultative body that groups management and employee representatives (February 22). The generalized social security system is instituted. It applies to all wage earners and covers health, retirement, maternity, workplace accidents, and invalidity (October 4).

1946   The forty-hour work week is reestablished, with the possibility of overtime work (February 25). Because of labor shortages, the average work week remains near forty-five hours until the mid-1960s. The CNPF is created to represent corporate interests.

1948   The CGT-FO labor union, whose members separated from the CGT, is created, the latter organization being perceived as excessively close to the Communist Party (April). Later in the year, a wave of strikes takes place (October 1).

1950   Minimum wage legislation is introduced in the form of the SMIG (February). The right to strike is extended to public servants.

1952   A "mobile wage scale" is adopted, with automatic indexation to the SMIG as a way to introduce price discipline (July 18).

1953   A 1 percent payroll tax is introduced for private firms with more than ten employees, to finance housing construction.

1958   The UNEDIC, a privately financed unemployment insurance system, is created (December 31). Unemployment insurance had previously been limited to unsystematic and scant public assistance.

1964   The CFDT labor union is created as a nonreligious offshoot of the CFTC (November).

1967   The ANPE, a national employment agency, is created (July 13). The unemployment insurance system is reformed, with municipal funds being replaced by state benefits.

1968   Student revolts are followed by a general strike of 9 million employees, which paralyzes the economy (May 22). The Grenelle accords (May 27) bring about large wage increases (the SMIG is increased by 35 percent), and ultimately lead to agreements on the reduction of the work week and the creation of union representation at the firm level. The National Assembly is dissolved (May 30). Work resumes in many sectors; attempts at restarting strikes lead to violence at the Renault factory in Flins (June 3–6).

1969   A fourth week of paid vacation is introduced.

1970   The SMIG turns into the SMIC, which is indexed to the price level and, partly, to average real wages. Renault, promptly followed by many sectors of the economy, changes manufacturing employment contracts from an hourly to a monthly wage system.

Box 9.1
(continued)

1973   The law of July 13 regulates employee dismissals and requires "real and serious" motives. The first oil shock causes the value of oil imports to rise from 1.5 percent to 4.5 percent of GDP (October).
1974   Valéry Giscard d'Estaing is elected president (May 19). The country's borders are officially closed to foreign immigration (July).
1975   The law of January 3 imposes an administrative authorization requirement for economically motivated dismissals.
1977   The distinction between hourly and monthly employment is fully eliminated.
1981   François Mitterrand is elected president (May 10). The stock market falls by 20 percent within a few days. Exchange controls are introduced. Mitterrand dissolves the National Assembly, and brings about a socialist-communist coalition government. Between June 1981 and March 1983, the SMIC is increased several times, by a total of about 40 percent. In two years, 110,000 public-sector jobs are created. The work week is reduced to thirty-nine hours, and a fifth week of paid vacation is adopted (July).
1982   Restrictions are imposed on temporary work and determined-duration contracts (February). A program is adopted to nationalize major industrial groups and banks (February). The Auroux labor laws are adopted. The first Auroux law institutes the employee's right of expression within the firm concerning work conditions and organization (August 4). The second law introduces new representative institutions for employees and reinforces the role of the *comité d'entreprise* (October 28). The third law broadens the scope of collective agreements and makes annual wage negotiations mandatory (November 13). The fourth law institutes hygiene and security committees in all firms with more than fifty employees (December 23).
1983   The retirement age is reduced from 65 to 60 years, and the possibility for early retirement at age 55 is extended (April).
1984   An industrial restructuring plan is adopted that involves job losses in the steel, coal, and naval construction industries (March).
1986   Legislative elections bring right-wing parties to power (March). The removal of exchange controls begins. The administrative authorization requirement for dismissals is eliminated (July 3). A privatization program is started with the sale of Saint-Gobain (December).
1987   Growth resumes, with GDP growing briskly for the next three years. Corporate taxes are reduced from 50 percent to 42 percent.
1988   François Mitterrand is reelected president, and the socialists return to power (May). The RMI is instituted.
1990   Exchange controls are eliminated (January 1).

Box 9.1
(continued)

> **1991** Introduction of the CSG, which partly shifts the financing of the social security system to nonwage income.
> **1993** The corporate tax rate is reduced to 33.33 percent. Parliamentary elections bring right-wing parties back to power (May). Currency crises involving the French franc are followed by a widening of the European Monetary System (EMS) currency bands from ±2.25 percent to ±15 percent (August).
> **1994** Two decrees institute the CIP, which involves paying young workers 80 percent of the SMIC (February). After a wave of protests by students and by labor unions, the CIP is replaced by subsidies for the hiring of young workers (March).
> **1995** Jacques Chirac is elected president (May). Economics minister Alain Madelin resigns, in disagreement with the limited scope of the government's economic reform program (September).

Sources: Teulon (1996); Rivero and Savatier (1993).

Key to French labor market terms

ANPE	Agence Nationale pour l'Emploi (National Employment Agency)
CFDT	Confédération Française Démocratique du Travail (French Democratic Confederation of Labor)
CFTC	Confédération Française des Travailleurs Chrétiens (French Christian Workers' Confederation)
CGT	Confédération Générale du Travail (General Confederation of Labor)
CGT-FO	Confédération Générale du Travail–Force Ouvrière (General Confederation of Labor–"Force Ouvrière")
CIP	Contrat d'Insertion Professionnelle (Youth Employment Contract)
CNPF	Conseil National du Patronat Français (National Council of French Employers)
CSG	Contribution Sociale Généralisée (Universal Social Security Contribution)
RMI	Revenu Minimum d'Insertion (Guaranteed Minimum Income)
SMIC	Salaire Minimum Interprofessionnel de Croissance (National Minimum Wage, 1970–)
SMIG	Salaire Minimum Interprofessionnel Garanti (National Minimum Wage, 1950–1970)
UNEDIC	Union Nationale pour l'Emploi dans l'Industrie et le Commerce (National Union for Employment in Industry and Commerce)

duration and temporary work contracts, the Auroux labor laws of 1982, and a nationalization program for banks and major industrial groups.

Importantly, laws and regulations do not capture the full determinants of capital-labor relations. In particular, the severity with which an existing labor code is applied is highly responsive to contingent political pressures. The administrative authorization for dismissals, for example, involved a visit by a "labor inspector" who at that point had the discretion to apply the full rigor of the labor code to the totality of the firm's practices, and not simply to the case in question. Based on interviews with inspectors, Berger and Piore (1980) report that their actions were highly responsive to the government's political objectives.

Finally, phase V spanned the period from the return of right-wing parties to power in 1986 until the mid-1990s. Although consecutive governments did introduce limited reforms, this phase is primarily characterized by a relative status quo in capital-labor relations. Government alternated several times between left- and right-wing coalitions, but the differences between the two had narrowed substantially. Moreover, it had become clear that any reforms that undermined the special interests of a major group would be difficult to pass.

9.2   Appropriability, Putty-Clay Technology, and Factor Substitution

In order to capture the dynamic interactions between appropriation and technology, let us modify the dynamic model in chapters 4 and 5 to incorporate: (1) a putty-clay technology that is characterized by capital-labor substitution in the ex ante technological menu, and ex post fixed proportions after investment takes place; and (2) specific variables that reflect regulatory features of the European labor market.

The model economy is set in continuous time, with an infinite horizon. Since aggregate uncertainty is not essential for studying the medium-run response to infrequent institutional shocks, the model is solved under perfect foresight, starting from completely unexpected structural changes. There are two factors of production, capital and labor, and a single consumption good, chosen as the numeraire. Aggregate capital and employment at time t are $K(t)$ and $N(t)$; aggregate output is $Y(t)$. As we have seen in previous chapters, the relative supply elasticities of the two factors are central determinants of the general-equilibrium implications of

Box 9.2
The constituency effect

Saint-Paul (1993, 2000) captures the essence of the political economy of European labor market reforms. He highlights the tension between the unemployed who would normally support a decrease in firing costs (or other labor protection measures) and the employed who would oppose it. The reason for each group's position is directly linked to the impact of reducing firing costs on the increase in the probability of finding and losing a job, respectively. However, since the employed are always more numerous than the unemployed, labor market reforms are essentially stalled. Saint-Paul refers to this mechanism as the "constituency effect."

Saint-Paul (1993) also analyzes the political economy of a two-tier system, where labor flexibility (i.e., low or no firing costs) for new jobs coexists with labor protection for old jobs. This system would be supported by both groups in a static setting. However, in a dynamic setting with a reformist government (i.e., a government that always wants to decrease firing costs), the employed would not support even moderate reductions in firing costs, fearing that the constituency effect may eventually turn against them. This result accounts well for the Spanish reform of the mid-1980s creating fixed-term contracts and the strong union opposition to the reform (and to subsequent reforms). This result also helps to understand the status quo observed in most European countries. Temporary contracts in some countries are extremely flexible and require lower social security contributions than is the case for permanent contracts. Furthermore, it is difficult to roll over temporary contracts for sustained periods. The result is that employment flows into and out of jobs offering temporary contracts is substantial.

Brügemann (2004) examines the constituency effect within a version of the Mortensen-Pissarides model of job creation and destruction. His analysis is motivated by the proposition that job duration is valuable to workers not due to rents per se but because of its delaying effect upon bilaterally inefficient separation. Consider a setting with ex post heterogeneity in match productivity but no bilaterally inefficient separations. Under Nash bargaining, the principal beneficiaries of employment protection are the high-productivity workers, but employment protection shifts the composition of matches toward the low-productivity workers. Therefore the "constituency effect" diminishes. On the other hand, if there is a possibility of bilaterally inefficient separations, and employment protection reduces the probability of occurrence of such separations, then low productivity workers will benefit most from protection policies. Furthermore, the policies shift the distribution of matches toward the low productivity matches, who support the protection. Employment protection can generate its own support.

Another interesting conclusion of this literature is the possibility of multiple equilibria. Countries having relatively high levels of employment protection tend to maintain the status quo when faced with shocks, while countries with relatively low levels of protection tend to decrease labor market protection when facing shocks.

Box 9.3
Product and labor market regulation in Europe

Labor market reform is fundamentally interlinked with reform of product markets, and both have been important in the European context. Blanchard and Giavazzi (2001) pursue a different approach to this chapter and locate the origins of wage bargaining in uncompetitive product markets, which generate large rents and therefore the incentive to bargain over the distribution of such rents. In their setup, monopolistic competition in the goods market determines the size of rents while bargaining in the labor market determines wages. These in turn fix unemployment and the labor share.

The authors examine the experience of Germany, France, Italy, and Spain since 1970. In all of these countries, unemployment rose in the 1980s and persisted throughout the 1990s. Recently unemployment has begun to decrease. In addition, these countries have experienced sharp decreases in labor shares starting in the early to mid-1980s. In France, for example, the labor share fell dramatically from 74 percent in the early 1980s to 60 percent in 2001. The decline of the labor share is the short-run response one would have expected from the authors' model if the bargaining power of workers had been reduced through labor market reform. On the other hand, product market deregulation would have been expected to raise real wages by lowering product prices. The implication is that widespread European-level product market deregulation has been offset by labor market reforms which on the surface appear to have been of a more piecemeal nature. The authors contend that this result is not completely surprising; rather, product market reforms have themselves weakened the bargaining power of workers.

In terms of the political economy of reform programs, product market deregulation may help implement labor market deregulation. If product market deregulation reduces total rents, then workers will have less incentive to appropriate a share of these rents. Therefore, the final bargained labor share will be lower when product market rents decline. The intensity of union wage bargaining will decrease, or the coverage by unions of the working population will diminish. Ultimately, labor market deregulation is the de facto result of the product market reform, even if the structure of employment legislation has not explicitly changed.

appropriability. Labor supply is assumed to be fully inelastic, equal to the infinitely lived labor force $\overline{N} = 1$. With a caveat explained in what follows, the supply of uncommitted capital is assumed fully elastic and must yield an interest rate $r > 0$. The underlying assumption is that all agents maximize linear utility discounted at rate r.

Technology   Investment is putty-clay. The ex ante technological menu at time t is characterized by a CES production function for output with elasticity of factor substitution σ:

$$F(k, A(t)n) = z[\alpha k^{(\sigma-1)/\sigma} + (1 - \alpha)(A(t)n)^{(\sigma-1)/\sigma}]^{\sigma/(\sigma-1)}$$

$$z, \sigma, \alpha > 0, \ \alpha < 1, \tag{9.1}$$

where k and n represent capital and labor inputs. Labor-augmenting technical progress takes place at rate $\gamma > 0$:

$A(t) = A(0)e^{\gamma t}$.

   If investment is sunk at time t_0 into a chosen technology, the ex post production function has the *fixed* productivity $A(t_0)$ and the fixed capital intensity $\kappa(t_0) \equiv \frac{k}{A(t_0)n}$ of the technology chosen at t_0. $F(k, A(t)n)$ is interpreted as a *technological menu*, which can be thought of as an envelope of the possible Leontief production functions whose technologies could be developed. In order to capture the notion that new technologies very different from those currently in use take time to be developed, the simulations that follow introduce an ad hoc constraint on the speed at which technologies with new capital intensities $\kappa(t)$ can be developed:

$$\left| \frac{d\kappa(t)/dt}{\kappa(t)} \right| \leq \hat{\kappa}^{\max}, \qquad \hat{\kappa}^{\max} > 0. \tag{9.2}$$

Thus, the technological menu that is immediately available depends upon the technologies that have been recently implemented. Note that a technology is determined by $A(t)$ as well as κ, which means that technologies developed in the past with the same κ can be very different if they correspond to a much lower value of $A(t)$.

Productive Structure   In order to characterize the productive structure in place, let us define a *production unit* created at time t_0 as the combination of one unit of labor and $\kappa(t_0)A(t_0)$ units of capital, which generates a revenue of $A(t_0)F(\kappa(t_0), 1)$. Because they face the same conditions, all production units of a given vintage are identical. At any time t, the economy's productive structure is characterized by a pair of age distributions $\{n(a,t), \kappa(t-a)\}_{a \in [0, \bar{a}(t)]}$, which respectively denote the number (i.e., density) and capital-intensity of units of age a, and where $\bar{a}(t)$ denotes the age of the oldest unit in operation at time t. These distributions fully determine the aggregate stock of capital, employment, and output:

$$K(t) = \int_0^{\bar{a}(t)} \kappa(t-a)A(t-a)n(a,t)\,da, \tag{9.3}$$

$$N(t) = \int_0^{\bar{a}(t)} n(a,t)\,da, \tag{9.4}$$

$$Y(t) = \int_0^{\bar{a}(t)} A(t-a)F(\kappa(t-a),1)n(a,t)\,da. \tag{9.5}$$

Creative Destruction   In the presence of technical progress, the putty-clay nature of technology implies that new units need to be continuously created to replace outdated units based on obsolete technology. Denoting aggregate capital investment by $I(t) = i(t)A(t)$, the unit cost of investment is given by

$$c(i) = c_0 + c_1 i, \qquad c_0, c_1 \geq 0. \tag{9.6}$$

As in previous chapters, let $T(t)$ be the planned lifetime of a unit created at time t. This function is related to the scrapping age $\bar{a}(t)$ through the perfect foresight assumption, so

$$\bar{a}(t + T(t)) = T(t). \tag{9.7}$$

There is also a rate $\delta \geq 0$ at which a production unit fails exogenously, before its planned liquidation, and must be scrapped.

Appropriability   As we discussed in chapter 3, there are both technological and institutional factors that affect the degree to which invested capital is appropriable. At the microeconomic level, this phenomenon is again captured by assuming that part of capital invested becomes relationship-specific, in the sense that it is lost if capital separates from labor.

If a production unit is created at t, let $\bar{\phi}(t)$ denote that part of invested capital $\kappa(t)$ that is relationship-specific and cannot be precontracted upon. At the political level, there are various ways in which labor, as an interest group, can attempt to appropriate capital. Let us introduce three devices that seem of particular practical relevance, and let us assume that these institutional restrictions cannot be contracted away:

• Firing costs can be instituted which effectively increase capital specificity. Let us assume that a production unit incurs a loss of $x^f(t)A(t)$ at the time of a separation decision, but not in case of exogenous failure. Note that firing restrictions give rise to complex regulatory and bargaining considerations. One can distinguish between a pure severance *transfer* component, that does not constitute a loss for the production unit as a whole, and a pure *deadweight loss* component. A severance payment typically takes the form of a transfer from capital to labor that increases with the length of the employment relationship being severed. The deadweight loss results from inefficient bargaining (due to asymmetric information), as well as from a multitude of regulatory restrictions (notification periods, proof of cause of dismissal, administrative authorizations for dismissals, etc.). Emerson (1988, 791–792) reports that according to a 1985 European Commission survey, "the financial cost of redundancy payments was in all countries considered to be a less important problem than the length of notice periods and the difficulty of legal procedures. This is particularly so the case of France." In the model, firing costs are of the deadweight loss kind. A key modelling advantage of this type of firing cost is that it captures the delaying effect of firing restrictions on separation decisions. Under efficient bargaining with pure severance transfers, this effect does not arise.

• The *effective* appropriability of capital is also increased by the presence of unemployment benefits, which improve workers' bargaining position by raising the value of their outside option (of becoming unemployed)— at least in partial equilibrium. Let us assume that these benefits are determined as a fraction $x^b(t)$ of the shadow wage $v(t)A(t)$ defined later.

• Finally, the appropriation of capital can come through the levying of social charges on firm employment that are then redistributed to workers. Let us assume that employment taxes are levied as a given fraction $x^\tau(t)$ of the shadow wage (this is mechanically simpler than as a proportion of the actual wage and has no substantive cost): $\tau(t)A(t) = x^\tau(t)v(t)A(t)$.

Quasi-Rents and Equilibrium   Specific quasi-rents arise as the difference between the value of a production unit and the ex post outside opportunity costs of capital and labor. From the firm's viewpoint, a firing cost $x^f(t)A(t)$ must be incurred if it separates from the worker. The firm may decide either to scrap existing capital or to utilize it with a new worker—in which case it would have to employ the same embodied technology chosen at the original time of creation. To replace the worker, let us assume that the firm must reinvest the relationship-specific component $\bar{\phi}(t)$ of capital. On the worker's side, separation means joining the unemployment pool to receive the expected "shadow" wage $v(t)A(t)$, which includes unemployment benefits $x^b(t)$.

Therefore, the specific quasi-rents in a production unit that has just been created are equal to

$$
S(t) = \int_t^{t+T(t)} [F(\kappa(t), 1)A(t) - \tau(s)A(s)]e^{-(r+\delta)(s-t)}\, ds
$$
$$
- x^f(t + T(t))A(t + T(t))e^{-(r+\delta)T(t)}
$$
$$
- [(\kappa(t) - \bar{\phi}(t))c(i(t)) - x^f(t)]A(t)
$$
$$
- \int_t^{t+T(t)} v(s)A(s)e^{-(r+\delta)(s-t)}\, ds. \tag{9.8}
$$

The first two terms of the expression capture the value added in the production unit; the two expressions at the bottom subtract the outside opportunities of capital and labor, respectively. Assuming no precontracting possibilities and generalized Nash bargaining, each factor gets the value of its outside opportunity cost plus a share of the quasi-rents. As before, let us denote the share of labor by β, and that of capital by $(1 - \beta)$.

As in section 4.2.6, this present-value split yields a path of *actual* wage payments $w(t; t_0)A(t)$ over the period $t \in [t_0, t_0 + T(t_0)]$ for a unit created at time t_0, consistent with continuous-time bargaining. Section 9.5 describes the nature of this solution. As usual, wage payments $w(t; t_0)A(t)$ are equal to the worker's outside opportunity cost (or shadow wage) $v(t)A(t)$ plus a quasi-rent premium. The shadow wage itself is equal to the flow rate of finding a job (in the model all gross hiring $H(t)$ takes place from unemployment $U(t)$) times the resulting increase in human wealth plus unemployment benefits:

$$
v(t)A(t) = \frac{H(t)}{U(t)}\beta S(t) + x^b(t)v(t)A(t)
$$
$$
= \left(\frac{1}{1 - x^b(t)}\right)\frac{H(t)}{U(t)}\beta S(t).
$$

Aggregate investment, scrapping, and the capital intensities are the result of free entry and optimization on the part of firms. Assuming *free entry* in the creation of production units implies that the firm's share of quasi-rents should compensate it for the specific investment it is sinking into the production unit:

$$\bar{\phi}(t)c(i(t))A(t) + x^f(t)A(t) = (1 - \beta)S(t). \tag{9.9}$$

Value maximization by the firm implies that separation takes place when the unit reaches the scrapping age $\bar{a}(t)$ that satisfies the following *exit condition*:

$$F(\kappa(t - \bar{a}(t)), 1)A(t - \bar{a}(t)) = (v(t) + \tau(t))A(t)$$
$$- \left[(r + \delta - \gamma)x^f(t) - \frac{dx^f(t)}{dt}\right]A(t). \tag{9.10}$$

The revenues of a production unit at the destruction margin should equal the (after-tax) shadow wage of the worker minus a term that measures the benefit of delaying the deadweight firing cost. Value maximization also implies that, as long as constraint (9.2) is not binding, capital intensity $\kappa(t)$ is determined by the following *first-order condition*:

$$\int_t^{t+T(t)} F_n(\kappa(t), 1)A(t)e^{-(r+\delta)(s-t)}\, ds$$
$$= \int_t^{t+T(t)} [w(s, t) + \tau(s)]A(s)e^{-(r+\delta)(s-t)}\, ds$$
$$+ x^f(t + T(t))A(t + T(t))e^{-(r+\delta)T(t)}. \tag{9.11}$$

In present-value terms, the marginal revenue product of labor is set at the marginal labor cost—including actual wage payments, social security charges, as well as future firing costs. The notion that factor proportions are determined by capital rather than labor is because labor is the appropriating factor and therefore exhibits market segmentation (see chapter 8).

9.3   Technological Dimensions of Appropriability

9.3.1   Calibration
The parameter values for the simulation are set to match the French situation, assuming that France was roughly in steady-state equilibrium around 1967.

Table 9.1
Basic parameters

Parameter	Value
Interest rate (r)	0.06
Growth rate (γ)	0.04
Failure rate (δ)	0.08
Technological substitution (σ)	6.00
Capital share	0.34
Maximum technical change $(\hat{\kappa}^{\max})$	0.05
Capital-output ratio	2.60
Slope of investment cost (c_1)	2.00

Source: Caballero and Hammour (1998a).

Basic Parameters   Table 9.1 summarizes the basic parameters selected to fit the initial steady state. Let us set the real interest rate $r = 0.06$, the rate of labor-augmenting technical progress $\gamma = 0.04$, and the exogenous failure rate at $\delta = 0.08$ (which lies between the standard depreciation rates used for structures and equipment). Together with the active scrapping rate that results from other parameter choices, the effective depreciation rate adds up closer to the standard rate for equipment—which better fits the model's concept of capital.

The technological menu (9.1) is determined by three parameters: σ, α and z. Because the argument depends on a significant degree of technological substitution, let us set $\sigma = 6.0$. Naturally, this value is empirically consistent with much lower short-run substitutability in the "aggregate production function." This is all the more apparent if one recognizes that it takes time to develop new technologies, with the speed of technical change capped by the upper bound given in expression (9.2).

Setting $\alpha = 0.210$ yields a steady-state capital share of 0.34, consistent with that observed for France in the late 1960s. Note that, even in the Cobb-Douglas case $(\sigma = 1)$, the vintage structure means that α is not equal to the capital share. There are two reasons for this. Recall that first-order condition (9.11) sets the present value of the marginal product of labor equal to the present value of employee compensation plus separation costs. First, the measured share of labor aggregates over wages paid to *existing* cohorts, rather than over the discounted flows of future payments to a *given* cohort. Second, the cost of labor includes a waste term (firing costs) that is not part of employee compensation.

Aggregate output is set to one in the initial steady state by normalizing $A(0) = 1$ and setting the aggregate productivity term $z = 1.088$. The upper bound (9.2) on the speed of technical change avoids high-frequency jumps to entirely new technologies in the simulations, and slows down the speed of technological adaptation to shocks. The maximum annual rate for $\hat{\kappa}^{\max}$ is set to 5 percent, which is never binding for actual data over the period of interest.

The capital series reported in national accounts do not take into account time variations in the scrapping rate. For comparability, the simulations report a "constructed" capital counterpart defined as cumulative investment depreciated at an exponential rate of 5.2 percent. Of course, exponential depreciation is clearly only an approximation to the richer depreciation schedules used to construct capital series. For French data in the 1970s, the implicit average service life of capital is 33 years for structures and 12 years for plant and equipment (Keese, Salou, and Richardson 1991, table 2, 14). The average service life for the depreciation rate used in the simulations is 19 years, and lies somewhere in between these two estimates.

In the initial steady state the unit cost of investment $c(i) = c_0 + c_1 i$ is set to 1.357, which yields a constructed capital-output ratio equal to the 2.6 ratio reported for France in the late 1960s. In terms of the argument presented in this chapter, the importance of the specific decomposition between the c_0 and $c_1 i$ components lies in determining the effective elasticity of capital supply in the long run. This, in turn, determines possibilities for long-term appropriation. Choosing a value $c_1 = 2.0$ implies a capital supply elasticity of 2.9 in the initial steady state.

Labor Market Institutions   The highly stylized path depicted in figure 9.3 for the model's institutional parameters is intended to capture the French situation, as described in section 9.1.2. Breaks in the path of these variables in 1968, 1975, 1981, and 1986 are taken as surprises in the simulation. For example, until 1975 agents forecast the equilibrium path of the economy with the expectation that x^f will permanently remain at 0.11. In 1975, they revise their forecasts, with the expectation that x^f will permanently remain at 0.25.

In order to limit the number of surprises in the simulations, events are shifted by a year or two to make different shocks coincide, then the

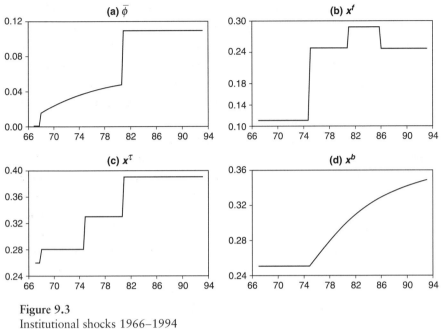

Figure 9.3
Institutional shocks 1966–1994
Source: Caballero and Hammour (1998a).

simulations plot the response of the economy to the combination of shocks. Table 9.2 summarizes the initial and final values for these institutional parameters.

The Nash bargaining parameter is set to $\beta = 1/2$ throughout the period. The path of unemployment benefits, $x^b(t)$, and social security contributions, $x^\tau(t)$, were set to match the data in a stylized manner (*Source:* CEP-OECD dataset for the period 1950–1992). Measures of the unemployment benefit replacement ratio in France increased gradually from 0.25 to 0.37 between 1975 and 1987. The employment tax rate also increased, from approximately 0.26 in 1967 to 0.39 in 1990 (where the employment tax rate is defined as the total amount of employer social security, private pension and welfare plan contributions, divided by the difference between employee compensation and the previously mentioned employer contributions). This increase is captured in three unanticipated steps in the path of $x^\tau(t)$.

Given the above variables, the remaining institutional parameters— specificity $\bar{\phi}$ and firing costs x^f—determine the creation and sharing of

Table 9.2
Institutional parameters

Parameter	Initial value	Final value
Bargaining share (β)	0.50	0.50
Specificity ($\bar{\phi}$)	0.00	0.11
Firing cost (x^f)	0.11	0.25
Unemployment benefits (x^b)	0.25	0.37
Social security contributions (x^τ)	0.26	0.39

Source: Caballero and Hammour (1998a).

specific quasi-rents, and, therefore, equilibrium hiring and unemployment. For the initial steady state, those variables are set to yield an unemployment rate $U = 0.028$ (around the level of French unemployment in the late 1960s) and a gross job creation rate $H/N = 0.11$ (roughly consistent with the churn rate for developed economies reported in chapter 2).

The jumps in $\bar{\phi}$ and x^f in the years 1968, 1975, 1981, and 1986 are designed to capture events during phases II to IV described in section 9.1.2. Those two variables have similar long-term effects, and are not easily disentangled. The total increase in these variables is fixed such that—combined with the increases in x^b and x^τ—it yields a final steady-state unemployment rate around 12 percent, with each of $\bar{\phi}$ and x^f contributing roughly equally to this increase. Specificity increases from $\bar{\phi} = 0.00$ to a final value of 0.11, which amounts in the final steady-state equilibrium to about 3 percent of investment. Firing costs increase from $x^f = 0.11$, the equivalent of 1.9 months of a worker's compensation in the initial steady state in 1968, to a final value of 0.25, equivalent to 4.4 months of compensation in the final steady state.

9.3.2   Appropriation in the Long Run

Let us start with a *long-run* analysis of the interactions between appropriability and technology in general equilibrium, comparing steady states with different degrees of appropriability. Table 9.3 presents the value of a number of aggregates for an "initial" steady state that corresponds to the institutional parameters calibrated for France in the late 1960s, and a "final" steady state with the institutional parameters calibrated for the

Table 9.3
Long-run effects of appropriation

	Initial	Final Technology fixed	Technology adjusts
Unemployment (U)	0.027	0.120	0.119
Hiring (H)	0.106	0.093	0.086
Shadow wage (v)	0.548	0.481	0.464
Compensation per worker	0.703	0.714	0.689
Labor share	0.692	0.712	0.639
Scrapping age ($\bar{a}$)	16.260	17.530	20.810
Capital intensity (κ)	2.180	2.180	2.870
Capital-output ratio	2.540	2.500	2.850
Investment (i)	0.231	0.202	0.247
Output (Y)	0.987	0.882	0.949

Source: Caballero and Hammour (1998a).

early 1990s. Note that variables in the initial steady state take slightly different values from those used to calibrate the model. The reason is that the calibration was based on an exact continuous-time solution for the steady state; while table 9.3 reports computations based on a time discretization intended to be fully comparable with the dynamic simulations presented in the next section.

In order to highlight the effects of technology choice, let us present results for an economy where technology remains unchanged (κ fixed) and for the economy with adapting technology (κ varies). From here on, variables with a γ-trend (wages, output, investment, etc.) are reported and discussed in detrended terms.

It is clear that the appropriation shocks worsen the functioning of the labor market, causing higher unemployment and lower hiring. Because of the increase in unemployment duration, the opportunity cost of labor v falls, which reduces pressure to scrap obsolete units and causes an increase in technological sclerosis (i.e., a higher scrapping age $\bar{a}$). With technology choice, firms choose to reduce their exposure to appropriation by decreasing the labor intensity of production units, causing an increase in the capital-output ratio. The long-term effect is to limit appropriation possibilities, making it difficult for average employee compensation to rise (actually causing it to fall with our parameter values) and resulting in a fall rather than an increase in the labor share. The rest of this section analyzes the precise mechanisms behind these effects.

Wages, Unemployment and Productivity Let us first consider the effect of appropriability with a *fixed technology*. The long-run equilibrium outcome is determined by free-entry condition (9.9), which can be rewritten as

$$c(i(t))\kappa(t)A(t) = \int_t^{t+T(t)} F(\kappa(t), 1)A(t)e^{-(r+\delta)(s-t)}\,ds$$

$$- \int_t^{t+T(t)} [w(s,t) + \tau(s)]A(s)e^{-(r+\delta)(s-t)}\,ds$$

$$- x^f(t + T(t))A(t + T(t))e^{-(r+\delta)T(t)}. \tag{9.12}$$

This condition equates the creation cost of a production unit to the present value of output minus labor costs (equal to wages, social security contributions and firing costs).

What is the effect of an increase in the appropriability parameters in table 9.2? Suppose first that both the price of capital, c, and the lifetime of a production unit, T, remain constant. It is then clear from equation (9.12) that with fixed technology (i.e., constant κ), labor costs cannot rise in equilibrium. The increase in the appropriability of capital is offset, in general equilibrium, by a fall in hiring and a rise in unemployment that reduce the outside opportunity cost of labor, v. The equilibrium level of unemployment is needed to guarantee capital its market return, which undermines whatever advantage labor was able to obtain through political intervention in labor market institutions.

The reason appropriation attempts are entirely unsuccessful in the above argument is the perfectly elastic long-run response of the supply of capital. The notion of a capital supply that is less than perfectly elastic can be roughly captured with an increasing $c(i)$ function. In that case, as investment falls, the price of capital falls, and the part of value added in equation (9.12) that must go to capital also falls. Some increase in labor costs is possible in general equilibrium, and appropriation attempts can be partly successful. As can be seen in the table, compensation per employee and the labor share can rise. Nevertheless, because capital remains highly elastic, the institutional shocks in the table will generate a significant long-run increase in unemployment.

Appropriability does not simply affect the sharing of value added in the productive sector, it also affects the productivity of the sector through resource misallocation. In the model, resource misallocation takes the form of a higher production unit lifetime T. Since the equilibrium shadow wage v must decline in response to the appropriability push, there will be lower pressure on less productive units to shut down and, by exit condition (9.10), the scrapping age $\bar{a}$ (equal to T in steady state) will rise. As explained in chapter 8, this "sclerosis" effect of appropriability has a negative effect on average compensation per employee: in the cross-section, the higher age of production units necessarily means lower wages than in the initial steady state, since units were unable to survive that long at initial wages. The reduced-efficiency effect of appropriability is quite general, and could also arise through sectoral misallocation in a multisector model. In the same way that elastic capital thwarts appropriation in the long term, preventing wage increases through higher unemployment, it also causes labor to bear most of the cost of reduced productivity. However, with the parameters used to generate the fixed-technology column of table 9.3, this negative effect on wages does not fully offset the wage gains from increased capital appropriation.

Labor Exclusion   Let us now allow for technology choice, and focus on the last column of table 9.3. In this case, capital intensity is determined by the first-order condition (9.11), which sets the present value of the marginal product of labor equal to the present value of labor costs. As described in chapter 8, in response to an appropriation shock the partial-equilibrium response is to increase the capital intensity κ of units. This puts the free-entry condition (9.12) in disequilibrium. This condition can be rewritten as

$$c(i(t))A(t) = \int_{t}^{t+T(t)} F_k(\kappa(t), 1)A(t)e^{-(r+\delta)(s-t)}\,ds, \qquad (9.13)$$

taking account of equation (9.11) and the constant-returns nature of technology (equation [9.1]). In order to make it worthwhile again for capital to enter, either the expected lifetime T must rise (allowing capital to recoup its investment over a longer period) or investment i must fall (reducing the cost c of investment). In the latter case, it is easy to see that T must rise as well, because lower i requires even lower hiring (given that κ rises); this, in turn, implies a lower opportunity cost v for labor and reduced pressure on obsolete units to exit. In any case, the appropriation shock leads to a misallocation of resources, which has a negative effect on the average cross-sectional wage rate.

Looking at the last column of table 9.3, capital intensity and the capital-output ratio rise in response to appropriation. In this particular calibration, the free-entry condition is reequilibrated exclusively through an increase in the scrapping age (equal to T in steady state), which comes through a reduction in hiring and the shadow wage rate. Investment actually rises, as increased capital intensity more than offsets the effect of lower hiring. Because of this, technological substitution per se does not cause a rise in unemployment beyond the fixed-technology level. This conclusion is not robust, and would be overturned with different parameters or model specifications that cause investment to fall and put less weight on the endogenous rise in T (as in chapter 8). To give another example, a minimum wage would make the scrapping of low productivity units less endogenous, and effectively cause the economy to behave as if T were constant.

Technological substitution limits appropriation possibilities by causing the opportunity cost v of labor to fall. Combined with the effect of misallocating resources in low productivity (high T) units, this causes average compensation per employee to fall compared to the initial steady state. This appears paradoxical, given the rise in capital intensity whose raison d'être is an increase in labor costs. The explanation is, first, that capital intensity is a function of the discounted value of future labor costs for a *given* vintage of capital, while compensation per employee averages payments for a cross-section of *existing* vintages.

Second, the firing-cost component of labor costs is a deadweight loss that is not part of employee compensation. To see this, set $r = \delta = 0$ for simplicity and normalize $A(0) = 1$. In steady state, the labor cost that is set equal to F_n in equation (9.11) for a unit created at time zero can be written as

$$\frac{1}{T}\left[\int_0^T (w(t,0) + \tau)e^{\gamma t}\, dt + x^f e^{\gamma T}\right]. \tag{9.14}$$

On the other hand, average employee compensation at time zero is

$$\frac{1}{T}\int_{-T}^{0}(w(0,t)+\tau)A(0)\,dt.$$

Since $w(0,-t)=w(t,0)$ in steady state, and using the normalization above, this expression may be rewritten as

$$\frac{1}{T}\int_{0}^{T}(w(t,0)+\tau)\,dt. \tag{9.15}$$

An increase in x^f drives a wedge between the marginal product of labor and average employee compensation, through a direct and indirect effect. Since x^f does not explicitly appear in equation (9.15), an increase in firing costs directly raises the marginal product of labor (implying a higher capital-labor ratio) but not average employee compensation. This increases the divergence between the two terms. From the previous reasoning, there is also an indirect effect of the rise in firing costs and other appropriability parameters that operates through the increase in the scrapping age T. To see this, let us differentiate expression (9.15) with respect to T:

$$\frac{T((w(T,0)+\tau)-\int_{0}^{T}(w(t,0)+\tau)\,dt}{T^2}<0.$$

The expression is negative because the detrended wage $w(t,0)$ decreases with time (it is a function of the present value of the unit-specific quasi-rent, which diminishes as the age of the unit approaches the scrapping age). On the other hand, the expression for the derivative of the marginal product of labor with respect to the scrapping age T is ambiguous. It is therefore possible for the indirect effect to exacerbate the divergence between the marginal product of labor and the average employee compensation terms.

Note that this argument is reminiscent of the excess substitution argument presented in section 8.2.6 in the "sclerosis channel" model. Labor market policies that raise firing costs correspond to an appropriation push by labor, which generates sclerosis and a concomitant rise in the scrapping age. Average employee compensation can therefore fall even as the capital-labor ratio rises.

Institutional Interactions   How much does each of the stylized institutional shocks calibrated above affect the long-term increase in unemploy-

Table 9.4
Institutional interactions

	Effect on U
Initial U	0.027
$\Delta\bar{\phi}$	0.036
Δx^f	0.032
Δx^τ	0.003
Δx^b	0.005
Interaction	0.016
Final U	0.119

Source: Caballero and Hammour (1998a).

ment? Table 9.4 decomposes the difference between the initial and final steady-state unemployment rates into the differences due to the change in each institutional parameter added separately, and that are due to the interaction between the parameters. The table is constructed for the case *with* technological adjustment.

Increases in specificity $\bar{\phi}$ and firing costs x^f have the largest effects on unemployment. As explained in section 9.3.1, those two shocks have similar effects and are difficult to disentangle. The relative magnitudes were chosen so that they end up making a similar contribution to the increase in unemployment. The effect of firing costs on unemployment are consistent with the panel data evidence in Lazear (1990) documenting the potentially high impact of severance restrictions on the unemployment rate. Other models in the literature conclude that firing costs have an ambiguous effect on unemployment, and most often reduce it. One such line of research removes firing costs from bargaining and wage considerations, emphasizing only the tax aspect of these costs (see, e.g., Bentolila and Bertola 1990; Bertola 1990). Another line emphasizes the protective effect of firing costs in response to *transitory* adverse shocks, preventing a type of temporary unemployment which is less relevant to the medium- to long-term analysis conducted here.

According to the table, the next most important source of unemployment is the interaction term. One can divide institutional variables into two groups: those that directly increase the specificity of investment (namely, $\bar{\phi}$ and x^f); and those that indirectly "leverage" off of existing specificity to strengthen the bargaining position of labor (x^b and x^τ). In the model, the latter variables would create no unemployment if the former institutional factors were nonexistent. The interaction term is precisely due to this leveraging off of increased specificity. This interaction is crucial to the design of labor market reforms, which ought to give priority to the primitive sources of specificity ($\bar{\phi}$ and x^f) and treat other institutional reforms as complementary policies.

9.3.3   Putty-Clay Technology and Factor Substitution: Dynamic Response

The Wage Push and Dynamic Factor Substitution   Let us now turn to the *dynamic* effect of appropriation shocks. Figure 9.4 illustrates the path of different aggregates following an unanticipated permanent jump in $\bar{\phi}$, of the same magnitude as that in the preceding steady-state experiments. The other institutional variables are fixed at the final values they took in those experiments. Dashed lines correspond to the case where technology is kept fixed, while solid lines correspond to the case where technology adjusts. All series are presented in deviation from their preshock values.

Briefly, the method for arriving at the equilibrium solution is as follows. Given a history $\{n(a,0), \kappa(a,0)\}_{a \geq 0}$ at $t = 0$, an equilibrium is essentially a path $\mathscr{E} = \{i(t), v(t), \kappa(t)\}_{t \geq 0}$ that satisfies equilibrium conditions (9.9)–(9.11) with compatible rational expectations $\{T^E(t), v^E(t)\}_{t \geq 0}$. The iterative method starts with arbitrary expectations, solves for the path $\mathscr{E}$, updates expectations based on $\mathscr{E}$, solves again for $\mathscr{E}$, and so on until convergence.

In both fixed- and flexible-technology cases unemployment jumps after the shock, and keeps climbing for a while thereafter. Compensation per worker rises rapidly and substantially upon the shock's initial impact. The counterpart for firms is a drop in the profit rate. Because of putty-clay technology, capital in place is highly vulnerable to appropriability. However, as new capital is invested, in equilibrium it obtains a return commensurate with the cost of capital, and the profit rate recovers to its initial level. The mechanism by which this happens is a fall in hiring and rise in unemployment, both of which depress labor's employment opportunities and cause a long-term reduction in wages.

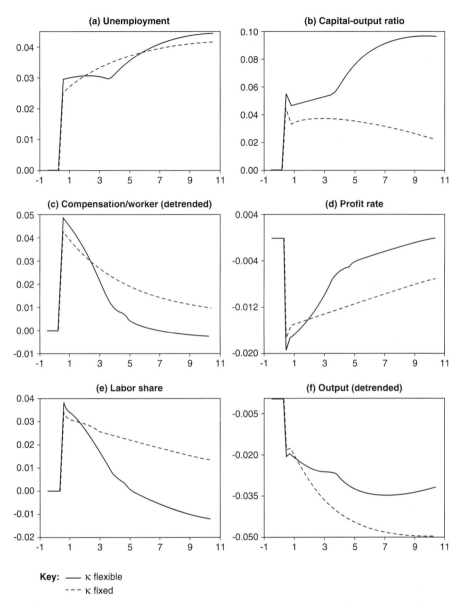

Key: —— κ flexible
--- κ fixed

Figure 9.4
Response to an appropriation shock
Source: Caballero and Hammour (1998a).
Note: Years on horizontal axis.

Unlike the fixed-technology case, the economy with technological substitution is characterized by progressive capital deepening, as manifested in the rising K/Y ratio. The short-run impact of both scenarios on wages and profits is similar; but substantial differences arise in the long run, when technological substitution possibilities can be fully exploited. With technological substitution, wages fall faster and lower and profits recover more rapidly. In fact, capital deepening causes compensation per employee to return near its original level, while unemployment keeps climbing—causing the trade-off between wage levels and unemployment to disappear. Both the lower wages and higher capital intensity associated with technological substitution affect the labor share. After increasing with higher wages in the short run, the labor share drops by much more than in the fixed-technology case, and ultimately falls below its original level. Finally, substitution causes output to benefit from more sustained investment levels, and to fall by less than in the fixed-technology case.

Experiment Based on the French Experience   Let us now put together the combined appropriability shocks designed to capture the French experience, as depicted by figure 9.3. The main macroeconomic effects are presented in figure 9.5, which provides a model counterpart to the French data series presented in panels (a)–(e) of figure 9.2. Results correspond to the case with technological substitution. Of course it must be expected that the abruptness and unanticipated nature of the stylized shocks would generate predicted time series that exhibit step changes.

The patterns that emerge from the model are certainly reminiscent of the French experience, and, with different speeds and magnitudes, resemble that of other major European economies. Unemployment rises following each appropriability shock, then keeps climbing afterward. Progressive capital deepening takes place along the path. Compensation per employee (detrended by the growth rate γ in figure 9.5, but not in figure 9.2) and the labor share rise after each shock, but decrease thereafter and ultimately fall below their initial levels. The profit rate declines after the shocks, then recovers over time.

Changing Aggregate Conditions   This account of the European experience has, so far, ignored the role of changes in aggregate conditions—

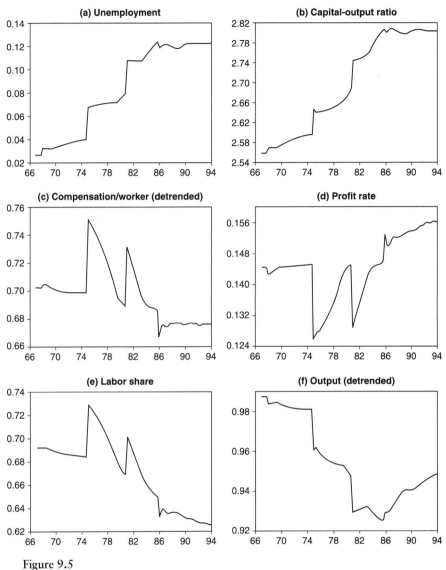

Figure 9.5
Simulation based on France
Source: Caballero and Hammour (1998a).

Box 9.4
Turbulence and European unemployment

Ljungqvist and Sargent (1998, 2005) propose a complementary, but not unrelated, view of European unemployment. They explain the different patterns of unemployment in the United States and Europe since the 1950s in terms of the interactions between microeconomic shocks and labor market institutions. They argue that the main force behind these shifts has been an increase in the turbulence (defined as the variance of skill losses at layoff), which when interacted with different unemployment benefit arrangements has generated different paths for the unemployment rate in the two areas. Their 1998 paper provides an explanation for the rise in Europe's unemployment rate relative to the United States during the 1980s. They model the process for accumulation of human capital, which increases during employment but is greatly depreciated after an involuntary layoff. They show that an increase in the volatility of this loss leads to higher unemployment in a welfare state economy with high unemployment benefits (like Europe), but not in a laissez-faire economy (such as the United States). Their 2005 paper has an even more ambitious goal, which is to explain not only the divergence of unemployment rates in the 1980s but also why unemployment was actually lower in Europe than in the United States in the 1950s and 1960s despite Europe's generous unemployment benefits. To do this, they introduce a cost of firing workers, as well as a Markov process for wages per unit of human capital. With a low level of turbulence, high firing costs push unemployment down by reducing frictional unemployment, capturing the facts of the 1950s and 1960s. However, when the volatility of human capital loss upon unemployment is high, this effect is reversed, since in turbulent times unemployment has both frictional and structural components. This explains the more recent facts. Ljungqvist and Sargent's papers are important contributions to the understanding of the comparative evolution of European and U.S. unemployment. It would be interesting to see whether they can also capture the rich evolution of capital deepening and labor shares observed in the data over the period of their study.

oil shocks, monetary and fiscal policy shocks, and so on. The effect of these shocks may be to complement the preceding story for an economy like France, but they hardly constitute an *alternative* explanation for the dynamic features of wages, profits, factor intensities, and unemployment highlighted earlier.

The French economy clearly went through cyclical fluctuations during the period of study, associated with the oil shocks of the 1970s, the high interest rates of the 1980s and 1990s, and the expansion of the late 1980s. Although much of the secular increase in unemployment took place during recessions, this does not obviously constitute evidence of causality—one would expect precisely that pattern from an independent combination of trend and cycles. If one is to construct an argument that more or less standard aggregate shocks are responsible for the buildup of unemployment, one would have to rely either upon the effect of transitory shocks becoming permanent through "hysteresis" mechanisms, or upon the idea that Europe has suffered a permanent economic depression.

Given the two recessionary oil shocks, it is difficult to explain the continued high growth of real wages through the 1970s without an appropriation push in mind. This logic is what led that period's contemporary analysts to infer that the rise in unemployment was of the classical type. The slowdown of wage growth in the 1980s makes a Keynesian account of unemployment changes more sustainable. However, such an account would be unable to explain why the full recovery of the profit rate during that period was accompanied by an increase—rather than a decrease—in unemployment. Moreover, one would expect the depressed conditions of the 1980s, along with the associated high interest rates and slowdown in wages, to cause a substitution away from capital. However, despite these conditions and despite the resulting episodes of low investment, the capital-output ratio increased and indicated a substitution trend away from labor.

9.4   Conclusion

The institutional buildup in France makes it possible to trace the macroeconomic response to an appropriability push at different frequencies. As

Box 9.5
The German "Agenda 2010"

The Social Democrat-led government of Chancellor Gerhard Schröder proposed a package of structural reforms in March 2003. One of the principal and most opposed components of this package was labor market reforms. The main reason for these reforms was to decrease unemployment and recover economic growth. Germany had the lowest rate of GDP growth among the core members of the European Union (the so-called EU-15) during the 1991–2004 period. Unemployment figures have risen to historical highs (almost two million workers in western Germany and more than four million workers in eastern Germany in the 2000s). Most analysts suggest that labor market regulations have been an important causal factor behind these ills. Collier (2004) documents that hourly real labor costs in manufacturing have increased by more than 140 percent since 1970 (while they have increased by 25 percent in the United States), and aggregate hours in manufacturing have decreased by more than 40 percent in the same period (in contrast with a decrease of less than 10 percent in the United States).

The labor market reform package included the following:

• *Easing employment protection rules*   The provisions of the old Employment Protection Act no longer applied for firms with ten or fewer employees from January 2004 on (before the reform, only firms with five or fewer employees had been excluded from the provisions of the act). Moreover, the reform allowed temporary employment contracts to be concluded for up to four years after the foundation of a new business without the firm having to give concrete reasons for the use of such contracts.

• *New regulations for the unemployed*   Since February 2006, entitlement to unemployment benefit has been limited to twelve months. Employees who have reached the age of 55 are now able to claim unemployment benefit for a period of up to eighteen months (down from a maximum of thirty-two months before the reform).

• *Restructuring of the employment office*   This reform basically modernized the management of the employment office in 2003.

• *Minijobs and "Me plcs"*   Starting in 2003, job seekers who set up their own business as an "Ich-AG" (Me plc.) became eligible for stepped subsidies (tax-free and nonrepayable) from their local employment office for a period of three years. A "minijob" involves part-time employment with gross pay of up to 400 euros a month. These jobs became tax- and deduction-free—even as secondary employment alongside a taxable main job.

• *New craft regulations*   The reform of craft regulations included the end of the need for a master craftsman's diploma in fifty-three of the ninety-four skilled trades starting in 2003. Previous craft regulations made this qualification the precondition for founding or taking over a craft business.

Box 9.5
(continued)

Clearly these changes were probably only moderate steps toward increasing labor market flexibility in Germany. Still, they have raised plenty of opposition among Germans—in fact, Chancellor Gerhard Schröder lost support in several state elections and then was defeated in federal elections in September 2005. Interestingly, most of the elements of the reform program, and the opposition that has emerged, fit the political economy models of Saint-Paul (1993, 2000). The government has only proposed moderate reform aimed at creating a two-tier market. There has been strong opposition from insiders. In this case the political economy of reform has been more complicated because of the notion that labor market reforms would create job destruction for jobs within Germany and benefit workers of the (poorer) new members of the European Union (see box 8.3 on globalization and labor market institutions). In addition, as suggested by Saint-Paul, a period of slow growth and slack in the labor market amplified the opposition of insiders to the reform.

Nevertheless, in recent years Germany has been an outlier—at least in Europe—in terms of the behavior of real wages and labor costs. During the period 2000–2005, while European real wages increased, the pressure of around six million true outsiders contributed to a decline in German real compensation per employee.

an explanation of the French experience over the last thirty years, the appropriation push scenario provides a highly parsimonious account. One can offer a unified explanation for the path of a number of key aggregates that, far from having moved in tandem, experienced dramatic changes in their comovements. More traditional accounts of European unemployment based on "aggregate shocks" or purely classical mechanisms are unable to offer such a unified explanation.

In recent years, and with the added competitive pressures of globalization, many Western European economies have begun reversing and replacing some of the most damaging labor market institutions. For them, the message of this chapter is that the payoff from such actions are likely to be large, especially in the medium to long run as technology reacts to new conditions, but it may take a period of time before the full benefits are realized. In the meantime the transition costs for some workers may be large. This is just the flipside of much of what we have seen during the last three decades.

9.5   Appendix: Wage Payments

At any time t, there is an age threshold $a^*(t) \in (0, \bar{a}(t))$ for production units such that all units younger than $a^*(t)$ would find it profitable to rehire a new worker if they separate from their current worker, while more obsolete units would not.

For units younger than $a^*(t)$, the maximum loss a worker can cause is limited to his or her replacement cost. As a consequence, the quasi-rent premium in $w(t; t_0)A(t)$ is proportional to an "annuity" value of this replacement cost.

For units older than $a^*(t)$, all capital is effectively specific to the relationship, since the unit's value would drop to zero if the worker leaves. The wage premium in this case is essentially a fraction of the flow quasi-rents.

It is interesting to note the "profit-sharing" implications of this rule. In young units $(a(t) < a^*(t))$, capital is the "residual claimant" of all shocks that do not directly affect $v(t)$ or the worker's replacement cost. In older units $(a(t) > a^*(t))$, part of those shocks is absorbed by wages.

Note

1. This chapter is based on Caballero and Hammour (1998a). Tables 9.1–9.4 are reprinted from *Carnegie-Rochester Conference Series on Public Policy* 48, Ricardo J. Caballero and Mohamad L. Hammour, "Jobless Growth: Appropriability, Factor Substitution and Unemployment," 51–94, Copyright (1998), with permission from Elsevier.

References and Suggested Readings

Blanchard, Olivier J. 1997. "The Medium Run." *Brookings Papers on Economic Activity*, no. 2: 89–158.

Blanchard, Olivier J., and Francesco Giavazzi. 2001. "Macroeconomic Effects of Regulation and Deregulation in Goods and Labor Markets." Massachusetts Institute of Technology, Working Paper 01-02.

Bentolila, Samuel, and Giuseppe Bertola. 1990. "Firing Costs and Labor Demand: How Bad is Eurosclerosis?" *Review of Economic Studies* 57(3): 381–402.

Berger, Suzanne, and Michael J. Piore. 1980. *Dualism and Discontinuity in Industrial Societies*. New York: Cambridge University Press.

Bertola, Giuseppe. 1990. "Job Security, Employment and Wages." *European Economic Review* 34(4): 851–886.

Brügemann, Bjorn. 2004. "Does Employment Protection Create Its Own Political Support? The Role of Wage Determination." Mimeo., Massachusetts Institute of Technology.

Bruno, Michael, and Jeffrey Sachs. 1985. *Economics of Worldwide Stagflation.* Cambridge, Mass.: Harvard University Press.

Caballero, Ricardo J., and Mohamad L. Hammour. 1994. "The Cleansing Effect of Recessions." *American Economic Review* 84(5): 1350–1368.

Caballero, Ricardo J., and Mohamad L. Hammour. 1996a. "On the Timing and Efficiency of Creative Destruction." *Quarterly Journal of Economics* 111(3): 805–852.

Caballero, Ricardo J., and Mohamad L. Hammour. 1996b. "On the Ills of Adjustment." *Journal of Development Economics* 51(1): 161–192.

Caballero, Ricardo J., and Mohamad L. Hammour. 1997. "Improper Churn: Social Costs and Macroeconomic Consequences." Mimeo., Massachusetts Institute of Technology.

Caballero, Ricardo J., and Mohamad L. Hammour. 1998a. "Jobless Growth: Appropriability, Factor Substitution and Unemployment." *Carnegie-Rochester Conference Series on Public Policy* 48: 51–94.

Caballero, Ricardo J., and Mohamad L. Hammour. 1998b. "The Macroeconomics of Specificity." *Journal of Political Economy* 106(4): 724–767.

Coe, D. T., and D. J. Snower. 1996. "Policy Complementarities: The Case for Fundamental Labor Market Reform." International Monetary Fund Working Paper No. 96/93.

Collier, I. 2004. "Can Gerhard Schröder Do It? Prospects for Fundamental Reform of the German Economy and a Return to High Employment." IZA Discussion Paper No. 1059.

Emerson, M. 1988. "Regulation and Deregulation of the Labour Market: Policy Regimes for the Recruitment and Dismissal of Employees in the Industrialized Countries." *European Economic Review* 32(4): 775–817.

Keese, M., G. Salou, and P. Richardson. 1991. "The Measurement of Output and Factors of Production for the Business Sector in OECD Countries" (The OECD Business Sector Data Base). OECD Economics and Statistics Working Paper No. 99.

Kouri, P., J. de Macedo, and A. Viscio. 1985. "Profitability, Employment and Structural Adjustment in France." In J. Melitz and C. Wyplosz eds., *The French Economy*, 85–112. London: Westview Press.

Krugman, Paul. 1985. "The Real Wage Gap and Employment." In J. Melitz and C. Wyplosz, eds., *The French Economy*, 51–69. London: Westview Press.

Lazear, Edward P. 1990. "Job Security Provisions and Employment." *Quarterly Journal of Economics* 105(3): 699–726.

Ljungqvist, Lars, and Thomas J. Sargent. 1998. "The European Unemployment Dilemma." *Journal of Political Economy* 106(3): 514–550.

Ljungqvist, Lars, and Thomas J. Sargent. 2005. "The European Unemployment Experience: Uncertainty and Heterogeneity." Mimeo., Stockholm School of Economics.

Melitz, J., and C. Wyplosz. 1985. *The French Economy*. London: Westview Press.

Mortensen, Dale T. 1978. "Specific Capital and Labor Turnover." *Bell Journal of Economics* 9(2): 572–586.

Organization for Economic Cooperation and Development (OECD). 1986. *Flexibility in the Labour Market: The Current Debate*. Technical report. Paris: OECD.

Organization for Economic Cooperation and Development (OECD). 1993. *Employment Outlook*. Paris: OECD.

Rivero, J., and J. Savatier. 1993. *Droit du Travail*. Paris: Presses Universitaires de France.

Sachs, Jeffrey. 1979. "Wages, Profits, and Macroeconomic Adjustment: A Comparative Study." *Brookings Papers on Economic Activity*, no. 2: 269–319.

Saint-Paul, Gilles. 1993. "On the Political Economy of Labor Market Flexibility." In Olivier J. Blanchard and Stanley Fischer, eds., *NBER Macroeconomics Annual 1993*, vol. 8, 151–187. Cambridge, Mass.: The MIT Press.

Saint-Paul, Gilles. 2000. *The Political Economy of Labour Market Institutions*. Oxford: Oxford University Press.

Teulon, F. 1996. *Chronologie de l'Economie Française*. Paris: Le Seuil.

Wolff, Edward N. 1996. "The Productivity Slowdown: The Culprit at Last? Follow-Up on Hulten and Wolff." *American Economic Review* 86(5): 1239–1252.

V

Conclusion

10
Final Remarks

Heraclitus' observation at the outset of chapter 1—"Nothing endures but change. There is nothing permanent except change. All is flux, nothing stays still"—captures the coming to realization by the pre-Socratics of the dynamic nature of things. Economic analysis, and macroeconomics in particular, cannot escape this truism. One of the central tenets of the work described in this book is that many of the symptoms of institutional and policy weaknesses manifest themselves through a variety of ills in the process of *creative destruction* (the economist's concept of flux). Studying this process gives us useful hints on what the main frictions in an economy are, and in which areas policy reforms may have the highest payoffs. This book presents models that help us understand what to expect from this process, what can go wrong with it, and what the costs of these malfunctions are.

The key organizing concept in the view presented in this book is that of *specificity*. Its technological dimension is the main source of restructuring. Considerations of specificity in factor relationships, which are continually formed and destroyed via the massive restructuring process, give rise to opportunism—and a concomitant role for sound institutions that curb opportunistic behavior. In practice, these institutions alleviate microeconomic transactional problems but do not eliminate them. The unresolved opportunism permeates the macroeconomy through multiple channels.

There is an Occam's razor aspect to the concept of specificity, as it offers a minimalist explanation to a wide variety of phenomena in macroeconomics, development economics, and restructuring. In moderate amounts, unresolved microeconomic opportunism gives rise to business-cycle patterns such as those observed in the most developed and flexible economies. This ingredient can help explain perennial macroeconomic issues such as the cyclical behavior of unemployment, investment, and wages, as well as the decoupled comovement of gross job flows. In higher doses, by limiting the economy's ability to harness new technological opportunities and adapt to a changing environment, widespread opportunism results in dysfunctional factor markets, resource misallocation, economic stagnation, and exposure to deep crises.

In this book, I have exploited the rich implications of specificity to explore economic problems at different frequencies, in different industries, in different markets, and in different regions of the world. Along the way, I have tried to illustrate the relevance of the analysis using a wide range of episodes and phenomena, including the cyclical features of job creation and destruction in the United States and around the world, the obstacles faced by transition economies and the impact of trade liberalization, the costs of supporting zombie firms in Japan, the productivity costs of crises damaging the financial sector, and the burden of excessive labor market regulation in continental Europe.

Looking toward the future, many of the issues highlighted in this book are likely to become an increasingly central component in understanding a variety of developments. Globalization and the associated increase in competitive pressures from every corner of the world are likely both to accelerate the process of creative destruction and to raise the costs for economies that fail to remove artificial impediments to this process.

Index

static-multiple-margin model and,
154–162
static-single-margin model and, 62–
70, 81–82
Tobin's q and, 73–74
unemployment and, 70–72
Makowski, Louis, 62
Malcomson, James M., 62
Manufacturing sector, 199–200
Annual Survey of Manufactures
(ASM) and, 41
creative destruction in, 19, 22–27
good faith exceptions and, 41–42
recessions and, 33
Markets, 271
appropriability and, 256–257, 291–
305
bargaining and, 98–101, 103
capital supply and, 262–263
contract failure and, 167–169
core mechanism of, 3
cost of entry and, 91–92
creative destruction and, 15 (*see also*
Creative destruction)
Danish model and, 251–252
deregulation and, 249, 264–265
distortions in, 217–218
dynamic restructuring model and,
87–97, 162–176 (*see also* Dynamic
restructuring model)
excess substitution and, 259–260,
262–264
exit conditions and, 92, 95
factor rents and, 198–199
financial frictions and, 154–162
France and, 275–282
free entry and, 69–70, 74, 121, 136–
137, 210, 247, 254, 289, 295
globalization and, 264–265
gross flows and, 15–38
impediments and, 38–46
institutional rigidity and, 249–250
labor and, 38–42 (*see also* Labor)
manufacturing sector and, 19, 22–
27, 33, 41–42, 199–200
recessions and, 26–38
sclerosis and, 50, 263–264

segmentation and, 62, 70–72, 159–
160, 254, 262
specificity and, 4–8 (*see also*
Specificity)
tariffs and, 47
technology response and, 253–
265
trade restrictions and, 46–49
two-tier system and, 283
welfare and, 247–249
zombie firms and, 42–45
Markov processes, 304
Marquez, J., 42
Marshall, Isabel, 220
Marx, Karl, 67
Maskin, Eric, 65
Mazumdar, Dipak, 216
Merger and acquisition (M&A)
activity, 34–38
Mexico, 27
Meyer, Bruce D., 199
Microeconomics, 3
contracting problems and, 60
flexibility and, 38–42
fundamental transformation and,
59–83
labor regulation and, 38–42
specificity and, 4–6
Migration, 17, 40, 161
Minijobs, 306
Mitterand, François, 278, 280
Moldova, 214
Moore, John, 60–61, 65, 157, 175,
188
Mortensen, Dale T., 97–98, 121
Motor vehicle industry, 96
Multiple shooting method, 94
Munch, Jakob, 251
Munshi, Kaivan, 161
Myerson, Roger B., 79–80

Nagypal, E., 98
Nash equilibrium, 69, 168, 195–196,
283, 292
Neary, J. Peter, 215
Netherlands, 250
Nickell, Stephen, 130